Tax Havens and
International Human Rights

This book sails in uncharted waters. It takes a human rights-based approach to tax havens, and is a detailed analysis of structures and the laws that generate and support these. It makes plain the unscrupulous or merely indifferent ways in which, using tax havens, businesses and individuals systematically undermine and for all practical purposes eliminate access to remedies under international human rights law. It exposes as abusive of human rights a complex structural web of trusts, companies, partnerships, foundations, nominees and fiduciaries; secrecy, immunity and smoke screens. It also lays bare the cynical manipulation by tax havens of traditional legal forms and conventions, and the creation of entities so bizarre and chimeric that they defy classification. Yet from the perspective of the tax havens themselves, these are entirely legitimate: the product of duly enacted domestic laws.

This book is not a work of investigative journalism in the style of the Pulitzer Prize-winning authors of *The Panama Papers*, exposing political or financial corruption, money laundering or the financing of terrorism. All those elements are present of course, but the focus is on international human rights and how tax havens do not merely facilitate but actively connive at their breach. The tax havens are compromising the international human rights legal continuum.

Paul Beckett currently practises as an Isle of Man advocate and English solicitor at MannBenham Advocates, Isle of Man. He has over thirty-five years' experience as a lawyer, both within the international private banking and fiduciary services industries and in private practice. He is a member of the Solicitor Judges Division, Law Society of England and Wales; a member of the Chartered Institute of Arbitrators; and a member of the Society of Trust and Estate Practitioners. He is a Fellow of the Royal Society for the encouragement of Arts, Manufactures and Commerce. His academic work extends over five decades. He graduated from Worcester College, Oxford in 1978 with first class honours in jurisprudence, being awarded his Master of Arts in 1982. He is also a member of New College, Oxford and was awarded his Master of Studies in International Human Rights Law in 2014.

Human Rights and International Law
Series editor: Professor Surya P. Subedi, OBE, QC (Hon)

About the series editor

Professor Surya P. Subedi, OBE, QC (Hon) is Professor of International Law, University of Leeds, member of the Institut de Droit International and former UN Special Rapporteur for human rights in Cambodia.

This series will explore human right law's place within the international legal order, offering much-needed interdisciplinary and global perspectives on human rights' increasingly central role in the development and implementation of international law and policy.

Human Rights and International Law is committed to providing critical and contextual accounts of human rights' relationship with international law theory and practice. To achieve this, volumes in the series will take a thematic approach that focuses on major debates in the field, looking at how human rights impacts on areas as diverse and divisive as security, terrorism, climate change, refugee law, migration, bioethics, natural resources and international trade.

Exploring the interaction, interrelationship and potential conflicts between human rights and other branches of international law, books in the series will address both historical development and contemporary contexts, before outlining the most urgent questions facing scholars and policy makers today.

A full list of titles in this series is available at: www.routledge.com/ Human-Rights-and-International-Law/book-series/HRIL

Business and Human Rights
History, Law and Policy: Bridging the Accountability Gap
Nadia Bernaz

The Emerging Law of Forced Displacement in Africa
Development and Implementation of the Kampala Convention on Internal Displacement
Allehone M. Abebe

Human Rights and Development in International Law
Tahmina Karimova

Human Rights and Charity Law
International Perspectives
Kerry O'Halloran

Tax Havens and International Human Rights

Paul Beckett

Routledge
Taylor & Francis Group

LONDON AND NEW YORK

First published 2018 by Routledge

2 Park Square, Milton Park, Abingdon, Oxfordshire OX14 4RN
52 Vanderbilt Avenue, New York, NY 10017

Routledge is an imprint of the Taylor & Francis Group, an informa business

First issued in paperback 2019

British Library Cataloguing in Publication Data
A catalogue record for this book is available from the British Library

Library of Congress Cataloging in Publication Data
Names: Beckett, Paul, 1956-, author.
Title: Tax havens and international human rights / Paul Beckett.
Description: New York : Routledge, 2017. | Series: Human rights and
international law | Includes bibliographical references and index.
Identifiers: LCCN 2017025609 | ISBN 978-1-138-66887-4 (hardback)
Subjects: LCSH: Tax havens. | Human rights.
Classification: LCC K4464.5 .B43 2017 | DDC 343.05/23—dc23
LC record available at https://lccn.loc.gov/2017025609

ISBN: 978-1-138-66887-4 (hbk)
ISBN: 978-0-367-87776-7 (pbk)

Typeset in Galliard
by Fish Books Ltd, Enfield

This book is dedicated to my wife, Dr Lesley M. Stone

Contents

Acknowledgements

In 2014 an essay which I had written about the Isle of Man, my home jurisdiction, and its relationship to the international human rights continuum was
published as part of a collection of essays dedicated to the memory of the late
Polish Statesman Dr Janusz Kochanowski. The editor of that work, Professor
Jo Carby-Hall, encouraged me to write more, and Taylor & Francis gave me
the opportunity to do so. I have written this book under the editorship of
Professor Surya Subedi QC, whom I met when he too was a contributor to
the memorial series of essays. Without their active encouragement and guidance, this book would not have been written.

It was at Worcester College, Oxford in the mid-1970s that I had first stud
ied jurisprudence. Encouraged by my friend Julian Knowles QC,
inspirational human rights lawyer and the leading light of his generation, in
2012 I applied to return to study at Oxford. In 2015 I was awarded a Master
of Studies in international human rights law as a member of New College.
Professor Margaret Bedggood and Dr Elizabeth Umlas tutored me in business and human rights, and Professor Fareda Banda and Dr Nazila
Ghanea-Hancock in minority and women's rights. Dr Andrew Shacknove
not only doubled up his duties by heading up the course administration, but
saw it as his mission to bind us all together into an enduring international
community of friends and colleagues. These brilliant, dedicated, selfless
academics have made a huge difference not only in my life but in the lives of
all who have taken part in the Oxford programme of continuing education.
If there is any original thought in this book, they gave me the means to set
it free.

My school and Oxford contemporary (the first time round) Professor
Peter Rutland impressed upon me that this was a book which had to be
written.

Here in the Isle of Man, over the past two years of research and drafting,
I have been urged on by my younger colleague at the Manx Bar, Advocate
Andrew Newton, who has sent me articles and leads which set many trains
of thought in motion, not the least of which became Chapter 6. Mark Solly,
former Isle of Man assessor of income tax (the head of the island's revenue
service) and himself an author of a seminal work on tax havens over forty

years ago, spent hours with me debating the origins and evolution of the tax haven phenomenon.

My friend and former Oxford fellow-graduate student Cynthia Orchard tirelessly converted my manuscript into the required OSCOLA editing standard (only those who have had to work with the arcane OSCOLA rules know just how mind-meltingly awful a job that can be).

My wife Dr Lesley Stone has accommodated my passion for human rights for decades. It is to her that this book is dedicated.

Paul Beckett
Union Mills, Isle of Man
7 May 2017

Introduction

This book sails in uncharted waters. It takes a human rights-based approach to tax havens, and is a detailed analysis of structures and the laws that generate and support these. It makes plain the unscrupulous or merely indifferent ways in which, using tax havens, businesses and individuals systematically undermine and for all practical purposes eliminate access to remedies under international human rights law. It exposes as abusive of human rights a complex structural web of trusts, companies, partnerships, foundations, nominees and fiduciaries; secrecy, immunity and smoke screens. It also lays bare the cynical manipulation by tax havens of traditional legal forms and conventions, and the creation of entities so bizarre and chimeric that they defy classification. Yet from the perspective of the tax havens themselves, these are entirely legitimate; the product of duly enacted domestic laws.

This book is not a work of investigative journalism in the style of the Pulitzer Prize-winning authors who reported on the Panama Papers,[1] exposing political or financial corruption, money laundering or the financing of terrorism. All those elements are present of course, but the focus is on international human rights and how tax havens do not merely facilitate but actively connive at their breach. The tax havens are compromising the international human rights legal continuum.

How has this come about? It is the result of simple market forces, where greed and self-interest are commonplace.[2] A traditional, almost clichéd, perspective for any book on international or domestic human rights is to focus on the victims of abuse and to identify which of their rights have been infringed or denied. While it is strongly arguable that '[E]conomic globalization is serving to alienate rather than incorporate human rights for much of the world's population'[3] it is equally arguable that economic globalisation

---

1   Bastian Obermayer and Frederik Obermaier, *The Panama Papers: Breaking the Story of How the Rich and Powerful Hide their Money* (Oneworld, 2016).

2   Human rights erect a 'barrier to a worldwide, voracious, and highly divisive brand of supranational capitalism.' C A Gearty *Human Rights* in A Kuper and J Kuper (Eds) *The Social Science Encyclopaedia* (3rd edition, Routledge, 2004) Vol 1, 468, at 470–1.

3   Margot Salomon *Global Responsibility for Human Rights* (OUP, 2007) 5.

is bringing a host of benefits to entities which profit hugely from their use of tax havens and in the process ride roughshod over international human rights without any realistic prospect of being held accountable for their actions.[4] This book explains how those who benefit from such abuse are able to remain immune and hidden from view.

The abusive effect of aggressive tax evasion and avoidance on human rights was for decades just the elephant in the room; and all attention was focused on the merely fiscal implications and a calculation of lost revenues. Now there is a vast literature of how aggressive tax planning has adverse consequences for the enforcement and application of international human rights. By comparison, the structural analysis and definition of tax havens from a human rights based perspective is in its infancy.

What is a tax haven? There are many competing and usually conflicting definitions. The concept can be applied not only to the palm fringed offshore isles of popular imagination but also to mainstream jurisdictions such as Switzerland and the USA. A key human rights indicator is the extra-territorial impact of their laws and incentives, to which tax havens turn a blind eye. What in human rights debating circles has been a concentration on the protection of individuals from abuses inflicted on them by the state in which they live, is supplanted by an examination of the abuse of developing states themselves at the hands of those exploiting the many and varied possibilities on offer in the tax havens.

This book assumes a general familiarity on the part of the reader with international human rights norms (but contains extensive illustrations, footnotes and bibliographies to enable the reader to pursue further research on all of the topics with which the book deals). As such, it is not about international human rights law, but about tax havens and their relationship with international human rights law.

The book is structured as six self-contained chapters, which can be read in any order, and a seventh chapter setting out the author's suggestions for future directions of study and for steps which governments and non-governmental organisations may wish to consider taking to curb the abuses which the book has identified. Read in the order in which they appear, the chapters define tax havens, review the strategies and structures which tax havens employ, focus first on the avoidance of beneficial ownership and then on tax avoidance and evasion, and conclude somewhat counter-intuitively with detailed examinations of the Isle of Man (which is found not to be a tax haven) and Switzerland (which is the grandfather of tax havens).

---

4   'The human rights movement is structurally predisposed to focus on victims – they are the ones to whom the rights violated belong. In recent decades, with the development and institutionalisation of international criminal law, there has also been scrutiny of perpetrators, at least in the case of abuses that constitute international crimes. But very little mention is ever made of beneficiaries. Those who (directly or indirectly) live off the practices and processes that victimise others have been allowed to remain comfortably out of sight.' Susan Marks 'Human Rights and Root Causes' 74(1) *MLR* 57–78, at 76 (2011).

Chapter 1 looks at the defining characteristics of tax havens and the uses to which they are being put. It looks at the evolution of tax havens and their morphing into international finance centres; and examines the statistics. The USA is used as a case study of a state which on the one hand itself has many of the elements of a tax haven and which on the other is one whose residents and institutions make use of tax havens to the USA's detriment. The conundrum of how to define tax havens is examined by looking at the classical, macroeconomic, value added, blacklisting and intuitive methods, and is resolved by the proposal of a human rights based definition. The chapter shows how the Faustian pact of tax havens with their own finance sectors renders them politically and economically incapable of reform: once a tax haven, always a tax haven. The chapter concludes with a review of tax havens and humanitarian abuse, and by way of examples examines the relationship with tax havens of Australia, Africa (with specific references to the Democratic Republic of Congo, Kenya and Uganda), Bangladesh and China.

Chapter 2 looks at how common structures such as companies and trusts have been adapted by tax havens, often as the result of artificial design which results in the creation of chimera – structures which are classified as companies or trusts, but whose nomenclature hides the fact that, morphed to meet market driven customer expectations, these have little or no legal DNA in common with the entities whose names they bear. They are designed to conceal their true ownership, the extent of their wealth and their purpose. In terms of human rights accountability, they are the brick wall against which human rights enforcers bang their heads to no avail. Without a reasonably detailed knowledge of these, any human rights tax haven abuse assessment would be incomplete. Specifically, the chapter explains the use of generic corporations, and in the context of corporations, looks at the use of nominee directors and nominee shareholders, the absence of information on public record (using the Seychelles IBC as an example) and an 'orphan' structure, The Bahamas Executive Entities. Trust structures are examined, with specific reference to charitable trusts, non-charitable purpose trusts (using Isle of Man Purpose Trusts as an example), Cayman STAR Trusts and BVI VISTA Trusts. Foundations, which are a hybrid of corporations and trusts, are reviewed using as examples the Liechtenstein Private Benefit Foundation, the Panama Private Foundation and the Nevis Multiform Foundation. Not simply how the structures themselves, but how these structures benefit from secrecy and immunity is examined.

Chapter 3 analyses the current global phenomenon of creating 'orphaned' structures, owned by no one and accountable to no one. From an international human rights perspective the trend towards accountability avoidance is hugely magnified by their creation and exploitation. The current international trend is for the registration of beneficial owners, as a means of ensuring accountability on the part of ultimate beneficial owners: but orphaned structures have no beneficial owner and there is no one to register. The chapter looks at beneficial ownership avoidance counter-initiatives on the part of the Financial Action Task Force, and the initiatives of the G20 in Brisbane 2014, Washington DC in April 2016 and Hangzhou in September 2016. It examines whether the 2014 G20 High Level Principles on Beneficial Ownership Transparency are effective, and concludes that they are not fit for purpose. The chapter concentrates on the use of non-charitable purpose trusts, which have become a world-wide phenomenon. These are trusts without beneficiaries: any assets held in such a trust fund are owned legally by the trustees, but beneficially by no one. By the use of this simple, albeit counter-intuitive, trust without beneficiaries, the G20 High Level Principles are sidelined and defeated. Case studies of the Isle of Man (the home jurisdiction of the author) deal with the use of purpose trusts and provide an assessment of the efficacy of beneficial ownership registration regulation, and also include details of the commitment by the Isle of Man to share beneficial ownership information with the United Kingdom (April 2016) and the MONEYVAL Mutual Evaluation Report on the Isle of Man (December 2016).

Chapter 4 explains the terminology. To evaluate the threat posed in monetary terms to human rights implementation globally by the tax havens, an outline understanding of tax avoidance and tax evasion, which for many tax havens has been their *raison d'être*, is essential. The chapter focuses primarily on the twenty year programme of the OECD from the 1990s onwards which has attempted to curb both avoidance and evasion, a programme which has seen only limited success. Attempting first to apply indicators of harmful tax regimes (which fell foul of political opposition, principally from the USA), the OECD then championed a system of white, grey and black lists. This was defeated by tokenism and mock compliance. In 2014 the Common Reporting Standard was introduced, predicated on automatic information exchange, but is immensely time-consuming, resource hungry and has a complexity which may prove its undoing. The chapter looks at how human rights norms could be integrated into the anti-avoidance, anti-evasion strategies to strengthen them. Though 'human rights impact' often implies that human rights are being abused, the reverse may also be true, and human rights may themselves impact other situations. Adding human rights indicators to the OECD reporting process, using the existing matrix to carry that information to where it is most needed, turns the victim into the foe. The chapter then assesses the United Nations Global Compact (2000) and the United Nations Guiding Principles on Business and Human Rights (2011, also known as the Ruggie Principles), neither of which initiatives has met with marked success, but which are fully compatible one with the other. It proposes that the Global Compact and the Ruggie Principles be combined with the Common Reporting Standard. Reporting entities under the Common Reporting Standard would be guided by International Organi-zation for Standardization abuse indicators drafted for this purpose, drawn from the Ruggie Principles. Any enterprise otherwise reportable under the Common Reporting Standard which became a compliant member of Global

Compact would be exempted from the Common Reporting Standard procedure.

Chapter 5 takes as its premise that although it is possible to consider tax havens as a generic form, specificity can illuminate the analysis, examines the Isle of Man and the extent to which it has the characteristics of a tax haven. This is a companion chapter to Chapter 6, which looks at Switzerland. At first glance, the Isle of Man would appear to have tax haven characteristics by virtue of its geography and the predominance in the local economy of its finance and services sectors; Switzerland would appear to have nothing more sinister than a long-established private banking sector. Yet on closer analysis, and perhaps counter-intuitively, it is the Isle of Man that does not meet tax haven criteria, and Switzerland that does. Chapter 5 looks at the constitutional position of the Isle of Man and identifies the international human rights instruments which bind it. Tax haven indicators (based on express avoidance strategies found in tax havens, as discussed in Chapter 2) are then weighed against the Isle of Man's regulatory and general legislative provisions: taxation, concealment of funds and of beneficial ownership, banking secrecy, reciprocal enforcement of judgments, limitation periods, forced heirship, fraudulent transfers, asset protection, orphan structures, public registration, non-disclosure of business objects, perpetual existence, fiduciary responsibilities and shape shifting forms. These are then reviewed in light of the Maastricht Principles (2011), the Ruggie Principles and the 2030 Agenda for Sustainable Development. The chapter concludes that the Isle of Man is not among the most aggressive or secretive of the low tax areas, and is well advanced on the tax haven-international finance centre spectrum towards the latter status.

Chapter 6 describes how Switzerland, presenting itself as a beacon of democracy and host of the United Nations, is the world's leading tax haven, now under pressure from the United Nations to reform its taxation and financial secrecy policies which are seen as abusive of international human rights. The chapter focuses on one of the consequences, the deleterious effect on women's rights and gender equality worldwide. In light of what are now widely acknowledged to be the extraterritorial obligations of States in matters of economic, social and cultural rights, it looks at the criticisms of Switzerland which have been made in November 2016 by the Committee on the Elimination of Discrimination Against Women. Various definitions of what constitutes illicit financial flows are reviewed, and the chapter is written on the understanding that such flows are those which have no social or economic justification, and are intended to benefit no one save the entity or individual initiating the transfer – in short, driven by financial operations rather than real activities. Switzerland's obligations under the Convention on the Elimination of All Forms of Discrimination against Women 1979 (CEDAW), and General Recommendations No 25 (2004) and No 28 (2010) of the CEDAW Committee, and concludes that Switzerland's status as a tax haven is therefore, in terms of CEDAW as developed and re-interpreted by the CEDAW

Committee, incompatible with its State obligations under CEDAW. The chapter also assesses Switzerland's tax haven strategies in light of the Maastricht Principles on Extraterritorial Obligations in the area of Economic, Social and Cultural Rights (2011), concluding that from the human rights perspective of the Maastricht Principles, Switzerland's banking and investment sector coupled with a high degree of secrecy amounts to nothing less than State-sanctioned plunder and hoarding. The report of the Swiss Federal Council approved on 12 October 2016 'Flux financiers déloyaux et illicites en provenance des pays en développement' and the opposing joint submission to the CEDAW Committee entitled 'State Responsibility for the Impacts of Cross-border Tax Abuse on Women's Rights and Gender Equality' from the Center for Economic and Social Rights, Global Justice Clinic at NYU School of Law, Public Eye (formerly Bern Declaration), the Tax Justice Network and Alliance Sud (2 November 2016) are contrasted. The chapter closes with the concluding observations of the CEDAW Committee in November 2016, following the publication in June 2015 of the CEDAW Committee's initial consideration of the fourth and fifth reports submitted to it by Switzerland are set out, showing that Switzerland is in the opinion of the CEDAW Committee having a negative impact on the ability of other states to fund the fulfilment of women's rights.

Chapter 7 briefly highlights the areas of concern which have emerged from the previous six chapters, and suggests an agenda for change aimed at non-governmental organisations and governments alike, together with areas of further study and research which the academic community could undertake in what is a wholly new field of study.

This book has been written for human rights defenders, for students, and for those for whom tax havens hold an interest but who may never have realised just how complex and deleterious an effect on the enforcement of international human rights these money-orientated jurisdictions create. Written by a middle-aged lawyer, it has the faults of all legal writings (and of middle-aged lawyers), and may at times lapse into the arcane. For this, the author apologises.

1 Overview of tax havens and international finance centres

Introduction

It is a question of perspective, and of synonyms. What is meant when writing about 'tax havens' or 'low tax areas' or 'secrecy jurisdictions' or 'international finance centres' depends largely on the political, economic or human rights agenda of the author. In truth, there is no generally accepted definition.

Are they jurisdictions in which taxation is anathema, government revenues seemingly generated out of thin air? To define tax havens purely in fiscal terms would be misleading. There are issues of secrecy and accountability, and in the context of human rights these hugely compound the abuse that stems from illicit fund flows. Just as much as the attractions of low or no taxation, it is the structuring possibilities that sets these jurisdictions apart, often using artificially engineered, chimeric entities,[1] which target (as a matter of government policy and not merely as an unintended side-effect) those individuals and corporations outside the tax haven who may, up to the point where they engage, have no connection with that tax haven.

We have the researchers behind the Panama Papers[2] to thank for bringing to world attention the massive scale on which tax havens are used: whether revelations or mere allegations, this data, drawn from only one law firm in a single tax haven, and though the analysis concentrates on tax evasion, money laundering and crime, is the silent witness of systematic, targeted human rights abuse.

This chapter pulls the camera back and explores the defining characteristics of tax havens as the landscapes in which the human rights abusive structures are located, providing examples of humanitarian abuse linked to tax havens. Chapter 2 then focuses in on the structures themselves.

---

1 See Chapter 2.
2 International Consortium of Investigative Journalism, 'The Panama Papers: Politicians, Criminals and the Rogue Industry that Hides their Cash' (*International Consortium of Investigative Journalism*, 2016) <https://panamapapers.icij.org> accessed 10 April 2017.

Historical perspective[3]

While they are not necessarily mere palm-fringed sand spits called into international existence at the whim of taxation-averse plutocrats, kleptocrats and amoral corporations, in many cases tax havens have indeed been created of necessity from failing marginal or subsistence economies:

> Regardless of the motivations for non-residential financial dealings with OFCs [offshore financial centres] (local *savoir faire*, zero taxation, lax regulations, etc.) and the nature of the activities undertaken (banking, insurance, special purpose vehicles, or otherwise), the setting up of an OFC usually results from a conscious effort to specialize the economy in the export of financial services, in order to generate revenues that often constitute a critical proportion of the national income.[4]

Building on the concepts of non-resident entities and of strict banking and fiduciary secrecy – pioneered in the commercial Courts in London and in the banking halls of Zurich – jurisdictions which had previously serviced their subsistence economies with straightforward, inward looking legislation regulating day-to-day affairs of local commerce turned their gaze outwards.

In the United States of America, as early as 1899 the State of Delaware was pioneering the use of non-resident, low tax corporations.[5] In Europe, the Principality of Liechtenstein led the field: impoverished after the First World War, it looked to well-established domestic structures in other European countries (principally Austria and Switzerland) and both pioneered and, in the process, re-imagined the foundation (*stiftung*), the *anstalt,* and a civil law equivalent of trusts in 1926 with the enactment of the Law of Persons and Institutions.[6] In Switzerland, the 1920s saw the development of non-resident holding structures and favourable tax deals for foreigners in the previously destitute cantons of Glarus and Zug. Luxembourg, by its Law of 31 July

---

3   For a concise overview see Ronen Palan, 'History of Tax Havens' (*History and Policy*, 1 October 2009) <www.historyandpolicy.org/policy-papers/papers/history-of-tax-havens> accessed 10 April 2017. For an in depth statistical and historical analysis, see Ronen Palan, *The Offshore World: Sovereign Markets, Virtual Places and Nomad Millionaires* (Cornell University Press, 2003); Gabriel Zucman, *The Hidden Wealth of Nations: The Scourge of Tax Havens* (Teresa Lavender Fagan tr, University of Chicago Press, 2013), ch 1, 'A Century of Offshore Finance' ('The Offshore World').

4   Ahmed Zoromé, 'Concept of Offshore Financial Centers: In Search of an Operational Definition' (April 2007) IMF Working Paper WP/07/87 <www.imf.org/external/pubs/ft/wp/2007/wp0787.pdf> accessed 10 April 2017.

5   General Corporation Act 1899. See Joel Seligman, 'A Brief History of Delaware's General Corporation Law of 1899' [1976] 1 Del J Corp L 2.

6   Landesverwaltung Fürstentum Liechtenstein <www.gesetze.li> accessed 10 April 2017. For a current statistical analysis of the economy, see 'Liechtenstein in Zahlen 2017' (Amt für Statistik Fürstentum Liechtenstein, November 2016) (in German) <www.llv.li/files/as/fl-in-zahlen-deutsch-2017.pdf> accessed 10 April 2017.

1929, introduced the concept of the holding company, exempt from income taxes.[7] Following the Second World War and with the encouragement of the City of London, the Crown Dependencies of Jersey, Guernsey, and the Isle of Man began to fill out their body of domestic legislation with fiscal, banking and insurance laws which in the main appeared to have no compelling domestic requirement to exist. In the Pacific Rim,[8] first Norfolk Island (1966) then Vanuatu (1970–71), Nauru (1972), the Cook Islands (1981), Tonga (1984), Samoa (1988), the Marshall Islands (1990) and Nauru (1994) threw their hats into the ring and copied legislation from established tax havens. In South America, Panama has become the world's iconic secrecy jurisdiction.

The list of jurisdictions designated as tax havens (though any form of agreed international classification has proved elusive) is not closed. It expands to meet the needs of globalisation:[9]

> [T]ax havens do not just happen. These are creations of the wealthiest and most powerful in our society. Advanced countries' governments are now dominated by giant multinational oligopolies, and bringing to an end this abusive global system is by no means an easy task.[10]

Tax havens have become 'a set of unique juridical enclaves operating in a number of economic sectors and perfectly suited to the needs of global capitalism'.[11]

The sequence of imported legislation[12] has included provision for low or zero taxation for companies deemed exempt or actually non-resident,

---

7 The Law of 31 July 1929. The 1929 holding companies regime proved extremely successful and lasted until 2010 when it fell foul of European Union legislation. In 2006, following a four-year review between Luxembourg and the EU, the European Commission declared the 1929 law to be in violation of EU state treaty aid rules. The 1929 law was abolished on 22 December 2006, with a transition period phasing it out by 31 December 2010. See Allen & Overy, 'The Transitory Period for 1929 Holding Companies Ending on 31 December 2010' (30 September 2010) <www.allenovery.com/publications/en-gb/Pages/The-transitory-period-for-1929-holding-companies-ending-on-31-December-2010.aspx> accessed 10 April 2017.

8 Jason C Sharman, 'South Pacific Tax Havens: Leaders in the Race to the Bottom or Laggards in the Race to the Top?' [2005] 29 Accounting Forum 311-23, quoted in Ronen Palan, 'History of Tax Havens' (n 3).

9 Eg The Seychelles. Matthew Shaer, Michael Hudson and Margot Williams, 'Sun and Shadows: How an Island Paradise Became a Haven for Dirty Money' (*ICIJ*, 9 June 2014) <www.icij.org/offshore/sun-and-shadows-how-island-paradise-became-haven-dirty-money> accessed 10 April 2017.

10 Geoff Harcourt, quoted in Muheed Jamaldeen, 'The Hidden Billions: How Tax Havens Impact Lives of at Home and Abroad' (Oxfam Australia, June 2016) 5 <www.oxfam.org.au/wp-content/uploads/2016/06/OXF003-Tax-Havens-Report-FA2-WEB.pdf> accessed 10 April 2017 ('Hidden Billions').

11 Palan, 'The Offshore World' (n 3) 6.

12 Based on Palan's analysis in 'History of Tax Havens' (n 3).

banking secrecy laws going beyond simple banking confidentiality, trust and foundation laws of increasing complexity and artificiality, asset and forced heirship protection, collective investment schemes, captive insurance regimes, shipping and aircraft registries offering flags of convenience, and over the past decade favourable treatment of e-commerce, online gambling and crypto-currencies.

A key marker is the motivation for the introduction of such legislation. Nicholas Shaxson highlights the importance of recognising an imbalance, where the finance sector in a jurisdiction is disproportionately large in relation to the size and non-finance sector occupations of its inhabitants: 'But the most important feature of a secrecy jurisdiction – and it is a defining one – is that local politics is captured by financial services interests (or sometimes criminals, and sometimes both), and meaningful opposition to the offshore business model has been eliminated.'[13]

The counter-intuitive must not be discounted. Tax havens may spontaneously generate in jurisdictions which according to received wisdom are nothing of the kind. New Zealand has been identified in the Panama Papers as a case in point. In a recent study, Michael Littlewood of the University of Auckland Faculty of Law has put forward the proposition that the New Zealand tax system is so structured as to allow the country to be used as a tax haven. Specifically, it allows non-residents to use trusts established in New Zealand to avoid the tax they would otherwise have to pay in their home country.[14] Accusations have been made of the likelihood of a similar trend in a future post-Brexit United Kingdom.[15] The US is also in the frame (see the case study later in this chapter).

The scale of the problem: statistics

Current thinking is that the principal area of concern in relation to 'tax havens' is, as the sobriquet suggests, the illegal evasion or (increasingly) legal-but-immoral avoidance of taxation. In the lead up to the G8 Summit of June 2013, Professor Paul Collier wrote:

---

13 Nicholas Shaxson, 'What is a Tax Haven?' *The Guardian* (London, 9 January 2011). <www.theguardian.com/business/2011/jan/09/explainer-what-is-tax-haven> accessed 11 April 2017.

14 Michael Littlewood, 'Using New Zealand as a Tax Haven: How is it done? Could it be stopped? Should it be stopped?' (11 April 2016) <https://ssrn.com/abstract=2761993> accessed 11 April 2017. And see Gyles Beckford and others, 'NZ at Heart of Panama Money-go-round' (*Radio New Zealand*, 9 May 2016) <www.radionz.co.nz/news/panama-papers/303356/nz-at-heart-of-panama-money-go-round> accessed 11 April 2017.

15 Kirsty Major, 'George Osborne Is Trying to Turn Post-Brexit Britain into a Tax Haven – and It Won't Benefit Anyone except the Elite' *The Independent* (London, 4 July 2016) <www.independent.co.uk/voices/george-osborne-is-trying-to-turn-post-brexit-britain-into-a-tax-haven-and-it-wont-benefit-anyone-a7119211.html> accessed 11 April 2017.

Private financial wealth sitting in tax havens seems to be of the order of $21 trillion, of which around $9 trillion is from developing countries. Some miniscule jurisdictions … have become the legal home of trillions of dollars of corporate assets through offering the unbeatable attractions of zero taxation plus secrecy. Some industries are dominated by tax havens: half the world's shipping is registered in them.[16]

The key here is 'legal home'. There is no suggestion that from the perspective of the 'tax havens' themselves that which is on offer is anything other than legal. *But is that offer real?*

[T]here are over 700 independent tax jurisdictions, most fundamentally ill-suited to real economic activity. Since each of them can be the location for ownership of a company, competition between them has been so intense that it has remorselessly driven their corporate tax rates to zero: hence the tax havens.[17]

Many tax havens have morphed or are in the process of morphing into substantial international finance centres:

Financial and non-financial corporations from emerging market economies (EMEs) have increasingly turned to offshore financial centres (OFCs) to issue debt securities. At the end of June 2013, 25% of all international debt securities outstanding of EME corporates had been issued in OFCs, compared with 22% in the advanced economies. In the 12 months up to mid-2013, EME corporates raised $95 billion in OFCs, around one quarter of their overall issuance during that period. As a consequence, they have overtaken corporations headquartered in advanced economies ($32 billion) as the largest group of issuers in OFCs.[18]

Further statistics have been gathered by the Tax Justice Network in its Financial Secrecy Index (FSI), launched on 2 November 2015.[19] According to the FSI, an estimated US$21 trillion to US$32 trillion of private wealth is located in secrecy jurisdictions (the FSI's preferred term for tax havens). The FSI estimates what it sees as illicit financial flows at US$1 trillion to US$1.6 trillion per year, in stark contrast to the approximately US$135 billion in

---

16 Paul Collier, 'In Pursuit of the $21 Trillion' (*Prospect Magazine*, 27 March 2013) <www.prospectmagazine.co.uk> (article no longer available online).

17 Collier (n 16).

18 Adrian van Rixtel, 'Highlights of the BIS International Statistics' (2013) Bank Intl Settlements QR <www.bis.org/publ/qtrpdf/r_qt1309b.pdf> accessed 11 April 2017.

19 Tax Justice Network, 'Financial Secrecy Index' <www.financialsecrecyindex.com> accessed 11 April 2017.

global foreign aid. Significantly, from a human rights perspective, the FSI, in ranking the top fifteen secrecy jurisdictions in 2015, includes fewer traditional tax havens than could have been expected, given the extensive literature on what the FSI refers to as 'small, palm-fringed islands'.[20] This raises the spectre of *onshore* illicit funds flows blessed by mainstream jurisdictions complementing and being complemented by the tax haven structuring possibilities which augment these and at the very least calls into question the conformity of those onshore jurisdictions with the international human rights obligations which apply to them.[21]

Case study: the United States of America[22]

The 2016 report 'Offshore Shell Games 2016: The Use of Offshore Tax Havens by Fortune 500 Companies'[23] explores what is described as the standard use by Fortune 500 companies of tax havens to avoid US taxation. US-based multinational corporations have successfully lobbied to be able to set their own rules of the game under the US Tax Code:

> The most transparent and galling aspect of this is that often a company's operational presence in a tax haven may be nothing more than a mailbox. Overall, multinational corporations use tax havens to avoid an estimated [US]$100 billion in federal income taxes each year.[24]

---

20 The top fifteen are: (1) Switzerland, (2) Hong Kong, (3) US, (4) Singapore, (5) Cayman Islands, (6) Luxembourg, (7) Lebanon, (8) Germany, (9) Bahrain, (10) United Arab Emirates (Dubai), (11) Macao, (12) Japan, (13) Panama, (14) Marshall Islands and (15) United Kingdom.

21 See Chapter 6 for a discussion of illicit fund flows, Switzerland, and the Convention on the Elimination of all Forms of Discrimination Against Women.

22 See Richard Phillips and others, 'Offshore Shell Games 2016: The Use of Offshore Tax Havens by Fortune 500 Companies' (*US Public Interest Research Group Education Fund, Citizens for Tax Justice, and the Institute on Taxation and Economic Policy*, 2016) <http://ctj.org/ctjreports/2016/10/offshore_shell_games_2016.php> accessed 11 April 2017 ('Offshore Shell Games 2016').

23 Phillips and others, 'Offshore Shell Games' (n 22).

24 But it must be borne in mind that:

> The combination of US reliance on a worldwide system of taxation (compared to a territorial system of taxation used by most other industrialized nations) and one of the highest corporate tax rates in the world undercuts the tax competitiveness of the US compared to the other G-20 and OECD nations. The competitive tax disadvantage has created an incentive for US multinationals to hold foreign earnings overseas (over $2 trillion to date). These foreign earnings are not reinvested in a company's domestic operations because of the high tax cost of bringing those profits home.

Karl Frieden and Ferdinand Hogroian, 'State Tax Haven Legislation: A Misguided Approach to a Global Issue' (*State Taxation Research Institute*, February 2016) <http://cost.org/WorkArea/DownloadAsset.aspx?id=92483> accessed 11 April 2017 ('State Tax Haven Legislation').

The taxation aspects of themselves raise serious concerns, but from a human rights perspective this reveals deliberate and systematic taxation avoidance on the part of US multinationals whose reach is far wider than the US itself and whose impact on the economies in which they operate – but to which economies their fiscal contribution is low to zero – cannot be overestimated. The mathematics is straightforward: to deprive a jurisdiction of tax revenue is proportionally to reduce its potential to fund human rights provisions within its borders.

According to the report, most of the largest corporations in the US maintain subsidiaries in tax havens – the most popular (counter-intuitively) being The Netherlands, followed by Bermuda and the Cayman Islands. At least 367 companies (73 per cent of the Fortune 500) operate one or more subsidiaries in tax havens, totalling 10,366. Setting this in context, the report states that the profits that all US multinationals (including but not limited to the Fortune 500) collectively claimed they earned in Bermuda and in the Cayman Islands totalled 1,884 per cent and 1,313 per cent of each country's entire yearly economic output, respectively.

Fortune 500 companies hold US$2.5 trillion in accumulated profits offshore, which if repatriated would collectively owe US$717.8 billion in additional federal taxes. The report is not reluctant to name what it describes as 'some of the worst offenders': Apple, Citigroup, Nike, Pfizer, PepsiCo, Goldman Sachs, Walmart and Google.[25]

In February 2016, the State Taxation Research Institute reported on the number of states within the US which have independently of the federal government introduced tax haven legislation which seeks to expand the scope of state taxation to encompass income earned by foreign subsidiaries in countries that a state defines as tax haven jurisdictions. The report's authors decry these states' categorisations as 'arbitrary and unmanageable', which given the absence of any generally accepted fiscal definition of a tax haven is hardly surprising:

> Without any US or international guidance, the states have struggled to determine which countries, if any, should be listed as tax haven jurisdictions. The blacklist process is undermined because states (as subnational units) generally do not have expertise in, nor responsibility for, international tax rules, tax treaties, or foreign affairs.[26]

---

25 Professed human rights observance and corporate responsibility programmes on the part of multinationals sit awkwardly with such systematic avoidance. Nike is an example of a company which has turned around its human rights image but which nevertheless according to this report remains implicated in tax haven abuse. See Max Nisen, 'How Nike Solved Its Sweatshop Problem' (*Business Insider*, 9 May 2013) <www.businessinsider.com/how-nike-solved-its-sweatshop-problem-2013-5> accessed 11 April 2017.

26 Frieden and Hogroian, 'State Tax Haven Legislation' (n 24).

In the field of human rights defence, a modicum of cynicism never goes amiss. Though a victim of the tax havens in fiscal terms, it is arguable that the US is a long way along the road to becoming the world's largest tax haven itself, profiting from enhanced banking secrecy laws and less stringent disclosure requirements under the Foreign Account Tax Compliance Act than under the Common Reporting Standard promoted by the Organisation for Economic Co-operation and Development (OECD):

> After years of lambasting other countries for helping rich Americans hide their money offshore, the US is emerging as a leading tax and secrecy haven for rich foreigners. By resisting new global disclosure standards, the US is creating a hot new market, becoming the go-to place to stash foreign wealth ... [and] helping the world's rich move accounts from places like the Bahamas and the British Virgin Islands to Nevada, Wyoming and South Dakota.[27]

The approach to corporate formations in Delaware and to banking facilities for non-residents in Florida appear little different to those of some of the bottom end tax havens.[28]

Competing and often conflicting definitions

Attempts to define a tax haven compete, and the process of determining what are the defining characteristics, and of determining whether those characteristics are harmful or beneficial, is not helped by the use of terms which themselves pre-determine the outcome: *tax havens, low tax areas, secrecy jurisdictions, offshore finance centre* and *international finance centre* conjure conflicting images. The jury is out. Some favour and would actively promote the existence of low tax areas.[29] The political stability and legal certainties of

---

27 Jesse Drucker, 'The World's Favorite New Tax Haven is the United States' *Bloomberg Businessweek* (New York City, 27 January 2016) <www.bloomberg.com/news/articles/2016-01-27/the-world-s-favorite-new-tax-haven-is-the-united-states> accessed 11 April 2017.

28 See The Economist, 'The Missing $20 Trillion' (*The Economist*, 16 February 2013) <www.economist.com/news/leaders/21571873-how-stop-companies-and-people-dodging-tax-delaware-well-grand-cayman-missing-20> accessed 11 April 2017:

> Not all these havens are in sunny climes; indeed not all are technically offshore. Mr Obama likes to cite Ugland House, a building in the Cayman Islands that is officially home to 18,000 companies, as the epitome of a rigged system. But Ugland House is not a patch on Delaware (population 917,092), which is home to 945,000 companies, many of which are dodgy shells. Miami is a massive offshore banking centre, offering depositors from emerging markets the sort of protection from prying eyes that their home countries can no longer get away with.

29 Jamie Collier, 'Turn Down the Heat, Switch on the Light: A Rational Analysis of Tax Havens, Tax Policy and Tax Politics' (2013) IEA Current Controversies Paper #44

tax havens may even be an improvement on one's home jurisdiction.[30] Others speak of piratical jurisdictions operating on a corrupt, ad hoc basis with no international legitimacy:

> Tax havens don't just offer an escape from tax. They also provide wealthy and powerful elites with secrecy and all manner of ways to shrug off the laws and duties that come along with living in and obtaining benefits from society – taxes, prudent financial regulation, criminal laws, inheritance rules, and many others. Offering these escape routes is the tax havens' core line of business. It is what they *do*. … It is a place that seeks to attract money by offering politically stable facilities to help people or entities get round the rules, laws and regulations of jurisdictions elsewhere.[31]

Others go even further: 'So-called tax havens and their service providers … are nothing short of enemies of humanity.'[32]

<www.iea.org.uk/sites/default/files/publications/files/Turn%20down%20the%20heat, %20switch%20on%20the%20light.pdf> accessed 11 April 2017. And see Dhammika Dharmapala, 'What Problems and Opportunities Are Created by Tax Havens?' who comments that 'the real puzzle is not why some countries become tax havens, but rather why so many small countries do not'. [Winter 2008] 24 *O Rev Econ Policy* 4 <https://academic.oup.com/oxrep/article-abstract/24/4/661/547359/What-problems-and-opportunities-are-created-by-tax> accessed 11 April 2017. Neil Mohindra further observes:

> [Tax havens] actually play a vital role in facilitating investment to higher-risk countries, helping economic growth. … Development agencies including the African Development Bank and the development arm of the World Bank use places like the Cayman Islands and Mauritius to help facilitate investment into developing countries. … But it's clear that tax-hungry governments will continue to use them as scapegoats.

Neil Mohindra, 'In Defence of 'Tax Havens' *Financial Post* (Toronto, 8 June 2016) <http://business.financialpost.com/fp-comment/in-defence-of-tax-havens> accessed 11 April 2017.

30 'The growth of China's economy has outpaced legal, regulatory and disclosure practices. Therefore OFCs [offshore finance centres] may provide Chinese firms with a more secure and predictable legal system. … Many of the recent US listings from China are incorporated in offshore financial centers, particularly the Cayman Islands.' Warren Bailey and Edith X. Liu, 'Incorporation in Offshore Financial Centers: Naughty or Nice?' (*Cornell University*, 15 April 2014) 8–9 <https://courses.cit.cornell.edu/wbb1/papers/ BL_OFC_15Apr2014.pdf> accessed 11 April 2017. Forty per cent of the British Virgin Islands' offshore business comes from China and other Asian nations. Alexa Olesen and Michael Hudson, 'China's Scandal-Torn Oil Industry Embraces Tax Havens' *ICIJ* (Washington DC, 22 January 2014) <www.icij.org/offshore/chinas-scandal-torn-oil-industry- embraces-tax-havens> accessed 11 April 2017.

31 Nicholas Shaxson, *Treasure Islands: Uncovering the Damage of Offshore Banking and Tax Havens* (Palgrave Macmillan, 2011) 11.

32 Jean Ziegler, quoted in Bastian Obermayer and Frederik Obermaier, *The Panama Papers: Breaking the Story of How the Rich and Powerful Hide their Money* (Oneworld, 2016) 200.

Methodologies range from the classic view of tax havens as a place to which personally to relocate in order to avoid or mitigate one's own tax liability, the rigidly objective macroeconomic, the market-inspired value-added approach, and the assemblage of blacklists, to the purely intuitive which eschews definitions altogether. Analysts focus on tax advantages, looser banking and financial services regulations, money laundering, bribery and criminal derring-do. Yet in all the literature, there has been no definition from a human rights-based perspective.

Classic

The classic definition of a tax haven as 'a place of retreat affording shelter from taxes' was formulated in the 1970s.[33] It was all so very simple then, and predicated on the belief that an individual would move to a tax haven or transfer funds to trusts or holding companies set up in a tax haven specifically for this purpose. Hence the principal requirements of a tax haven were three-fold: it should operate a system of low direct taxation; it should be politically stable and relatively, if not completely, free from damaging interference or pressure from neighbouring jurisdictions; and it should be geographically accessible with no immigration or residence restrictions.

The advantages of offshore banking in the 1970s were thought to be self-evident. Present day concerns with tax evasion, money laundering, bribery, corruption and crime – indeed, any moral component – were unknown:

> Offshore banking is financial intermediation performed (primarily) for non-resident borrowers and depositors. The principal attraction of an offshore banking center (for banks as well as participants) is simply the absence of intrusive and expensive official regulation, including taxation and controls over the portfolio decisions of the banking community.[34]

What in the popular imagination is the simplest way in which to benefit from a tax haven – taking up residence in one – is the least significant from a human rights perspective. Monaco, San Marino, Switzerland, the United Kingdom[35] and Dubai[36] are among those jurisdictions still operating at this

---

33 Mark Solly, *Anatomy of a Tax Haven: The Isle of Man* (Shearwater Press, 1975) 5–10.

34 G Duffy and I Giddy, *The International Money Market* (Prentice-Hall, 1978) 37 quoted in Zoromé (n 4).

35 Experts for Expats, 'Non-Dom (Non-domiciled) Tax for Residents in the UK' (Experts for Expats, last updated 27 October 2016) <www.expertsforexpats.com/expat-tax/non-dom-non-domiciled-tax-in-the-uk> accessed 11 April 2017.

36 Issuing a tax domicile certificate is surprisingly straightforward – see the United Arab Emirates Ministry of Finance, 'Issuing Tax Domicile Certificate' (United Arab Emirates) <www.mof.gov.ae/En/mservices/VTAX/Pages/ServiceCardTax.aspx> accessed 11 April 2017.

simple level. But this relates to taxation avoidance and mitigation, and is wholly neutral from a human rights perspective. It is not the fiscal advantages taken by corporations and individuals in such jurisdictions which is in point, but whether such jurisdictions provide the opacity which of itself undermines human rights accountability. Safe within one of these tax havens, thumbing one's nose at other tax authorities, may give those concerned a sense of fiscal superiority, but of itself provides them with no place to hide from their human rights responsibilities.

Macroeconomic

An operational definition of offshore finance centres is, however, something which a decade before the EU's current tentative efforts was a priority for the International Monetary Fund (IMF).[37] Seeking objectivity, and noting an absence of any consensus among scholars and practitioners on what constitutes an OFC, a 2007 study proposed a definition of OFCs using a statistical methodology which 'distinguishes OFCs based strictly on their macroeconomic features and avoids subjective presumptions on their activities or regulatory frameworks.'[38] On a conceptual level, the study found three recurrent characteristics of OFCs: '(i) the primary orientation of business towards non-residents; (ii) the favorable regulatory environment (low supervisory requirements and minimum information disclosure) and (iii) the low or zero taxation schemes' and rejected this equation of OFCs with 'a regulatory and taxation phenomenon' in favour of capturing 'the intrinsic feature of the OFC phenomenon, which is its raison d'etre – the provision of financial services to non-residents, namely the export of financial services ... on a scale far exceeding the needs and the size of their economies'.[39]

Value added

Such political, macroeconomic focus fails to question whether, apart from taxation mitigation or the consumption of financial services, there is any economic advantage in an enterprise incorporating in a tax haven. Why take the risk of being dubbed a rogue, insubstantial, sham structure? So what advantage is there? Bailey and Liu in their 2014 empirical analysis of tax haven incorporated entities seeking to list in the US conclude that there is no hard and fast answer. By their own account, their paper:

> ... examines a rarely-explored dimension of the choices corporations make concerning their legal, regulatory, and disclosure environment. Offshore financial centers present both the hope of a more efficient, low

37   Zoromé (n 4).
38   Zoromé (n 4) 1.
39   Zoromé (n 4) 6.

cost legal home and the fear of a poorly-regulated environment that benefits managers and other insiders at the expense of ordinary share-holders. Our results suggest that, while in general the impact of OFC incorporation on valuation appears to be negative, it is necessary to consider individual firm characteristics and the firm's home country regulatory environment to assess the marginal impact of OFC incorpo-ration. We find that OFC incorporation can destroy value for growing firms from a high quality home country environment or can add value for firms from some less-developed environments. Thus, it seems there is nothing inherently naughty or nice about the use of OFCs as legal domiciles by corporations.[40]

The study's concentration on added value is within the parameters it set itself, but takes no account in the case of 'firms from some less developed environments' of the unseen agenda, which may equally include the ability to avoid – or to continue to avoid, if the home jurisdiction is also human rights abusive – accountability in human rights terms by the use of offshore structures unique to tax havens (in general, or specific to one) intentionally designed to do so.[41]

Blacklists

Following the meeting of the G20 in Washington DC in April 2016, the G20 Finance Ministers issued a communiqué initiating the assemblage of another OECD list of non-co-operative jurisdictions in matters of tax trans-parency:

> The G20 strongly reaffirms the importance of effective and widespread implementation of the internationally agreed standards on transparency. Therefore we call on all relevant countries including all financial centers and jurisdictions, which have not committed to implement the standard on automatic exchange of information by 2017 or 2018 to do so with-out delay and to sign the Multilateral Convention. ... We mandate the OECD working with G20 countries to establish objective criteria by our July meeting to identify non-cooperative jurisdictions with respect to tax transparency.[42]

Hence, the blacklisted jurisdictions will be simply those which do not exchange taxation information. To avoid being blacklisted, a jurisdiction

---

40   Bailey and Liu (n 30) 44.
41   See Chapter 2.
42   Communiqué, G20 Finance Ministers and Central Bank Governors' Meeting Washington, April 15, 2016 (*University of Toronto G20 Information Centre*, 15 April 2016) <www.g20.utoronto.ca/2016/160415-finance.html> accessed 11 April 2017.

need fulfil two out of three requirements: obtain a 'largely compliant' or higher rating from the OECD's Global Forum as regards the Global Forum's exchange of information on requested standard of transparency;[43] adopt the Common Reporting Standard;[44] and/or sign the Multilateral Convention on Mutual Assistance in Tax Matters.[45]

No other criterion will be applied. Meet the transparency requirements in matters of tax information, and sail on regardless.[46]

Intuitive

The European Union Commission has announced that during 2017 it will publish a list of tax havens, more robust than that of the OECD,[47] the EU having first published such a list in 2015 which, omitting Switzerland and any part of the US, was withdrawn within six months. EU Commissioner Pierre Moscovic is, however, vague when it comes to the indicators which are to be employed and has stated that 'rigid definitions might not be the right weapon'.[48] A triumph of art over science.[49]

The human rights perspective

Therefore in the definitional battle, the current international political con - cern is entirely market driven and fiscal – the focus is not on what activities

---

43 OECD, 'Tax Transparency 2016: Report on Progress' (*OECD Global Forum on Transparency and Exchange of Information for Tax Purposes,* 2016) <www.oecd.org/tax/transparency/GF-annual-report-2016.pdf> accessed 11 April 2017.

44 OECD, 'Common Reporting Standards' (*OECD Global Forum on Transparency and Exchange of Information for Tax Purposes*) <www.oecd.org/tax/automatic-exchange/common-reporting-standard> accessed 11 April 2017.

45 OECD, 'Convention on Mutual Administrative Assistance in Tax Matters' (*OECD*, last updated March 2017) <www.oecd.org/tax/exchange-of-tax-information/convention-on-mutual-administrative-assistance-in-tax-matters.htm> accessed 11 April 2017.

46 For a fuller critical analysis of the OECD Blacklist proposals see Tax Justice Network, 'Will the OECD Tax Haven Blacklist Be Another Whitewash?' (*Tax Justice Network,* 20 July 2016) <www.taxjustice.net/2016/07/20/oecd-another-go-hopeless-politicised-tax-haven-blacklisting> accessed 11 April 2017.

47 See Chapter 4 for a discussion on anti-tax haven initiatives by the G20 and OECD.

48 European Parliament, 'EU List of Tax Havens Likely by End 2017, Says EU Commissioner, Pierre Moscovici' *European Parliament News* (Brussels, 7 December 2016) <www.europarl.europa.eu/news/en/news-room/20161205IPR54576/eu-list-of-tax-havens-likely-by-end-2017-says-eu-commissioner-pierre-moscovici> accessed 11 April 2017.

49 And not without a political undercurrent: Fabio De Masi MEP (Germany) has expressed fears that the list would fall prey to political capture, stating that it would be good to have Panama on the list but that it is pivotal that the US be included. Oxfam, through its spokesperson Aurore Chardonnet, has expressed the wish that the list not exclude 'close partners' of the EU Member States. Aleksandra Eriksson, 'EU Tax Haven List Could Name US' *EU Observer* (Brussels, 16 September 2016) <https://euobserver.com/economic/135109> accessed 11 April 2017.

the business enterprises are pursuing, or on what offshore structures they adopt, but on how much profit they are making and how governments can tax such profits.

But the true position is infinitely more nuanced and complex, as the Bank for International Settlements (BIS) and the FSI statistics illustrate, and for a state representative to intone: 'I do not think it is fair any longer to refer to any of the Overseas Territories or Crown Dependencies as tax havens. They have taken action to make sure that they have fair and open tax systems' is disingenuous.[50] From a human rights perspective, this completely misses the point. The point is funds flow, opacity, and an absence of accountability.

Yet even the human rights community buys into the fiscal-centric model. 'A human rights approach … requires States to take steps to eliminate the prevalence of tax evasion, a problem that reduces the resources available for measures to realize human rights.'[51] This is an important element, but merely regulating low tax areas solely in terms of taxation – being bound by the self-definition of such jurisdictions – will prove to be ineffective, given the chameleonic nature of international tax planning and the endless supply of camouflage cloth available to those who wish to wrap their dealings. An appeal to conscience and morality is unlikely to succeed in the context of taxation, but conscience and morality are the bedrock of international human rights norms. If therefore the war on tax evasion/avoidance is constantly evolving and seemingly endless – 'the battle against tax avoidance is like that against disease: the only viable approach is repeated changing of the locks'[52] – it must follow that *the wrong war is being fought.*

Tax collection apart, there is no accountability mechanism. The low tax area structures channel global economic power centres and serve to focus that power where it can least be resisted. As Margot Salomon has demonstrated, there exist legal obligations of developed states (and, by extension, of those channelling states) to people outside their territories:

> [T]he socio economic rights of people in developing countries are of particular concern in light of the fact that other states are often deeply implicated in their ability to exercise their rights. … [I]nequality is not the result of some accidental deviation from neo-liberal capitalism, but rather a deliberate product of the international political economy.[53]

---

50   Former UK Prime Minister David Cameron, 10 September 2013. Ellan Vannin, 'David Cameron: Crown Dependency Tax Haven Banner "Not Fair"' *BBC News* (Isle of Man, 10 September 2013) <www.bbc.co.uk/news/world-europe-isle-of-man-24034768> accessed 11 April 2017.

51   United Nations Human Rights Council, 'Report of the Independent Expert on the Question of Human Rights and Extreme Poverty, Magdalena Sepulveda Carmona' (17 March 2011) UN Doc A/HRC/17/34.

52   Collier (n 16).

53   Margot Salomon, 'Why Should it Matter that Others Have More? Poverty, Inequality and the Potential of International Human Rights Law' (2010) LSE Working Papers 15/2010, 7, 10.

Tax evasion/avoidance is merely a symptom of a deeper malaise, rooted in the breach of more fundamental rights: human rights.[54] Human rights are a 'barrier to a worldwide, voracious and highly divisive brand of supranational capitalism'.[55] The traditional international human rights orientation of the relationship between a state and its citizens is, in response to the excesses of the new supranational or neo-capitalism, morphing into one of the relationship between a state and any persons (whether citizens or not, and whether resident in its territories or not) on whom its activities have an impact. A solely domestic human rights assessment of the structures facilitated in low tax areas is therefore as inappropriate as it is incomplete.[56]

Aggressive tax planning, evasive or avoidance, undoubtedly distorts international capital flows, and this distortion may impede the implementation by a state of its human rights obligations by limiting the means available to it. Yet tax planning of any kind exists only to serve the structures which it is designed to benefit. Although low-to-zero taxation is the most apparent Achilles heel when formulating a political attack on the low tax areas, of equal if not greater importance from the international human rights perspective are the constantly evolving *structuring* opportunities facilitated by the low tax areas.[57]

There is no evidence of a general political will in the tax havens to engage with human rights at an international level, and, particularly in the case of tax

---

54 The express connection between non-payment of tax and a breach of the duties which accompany human rights is not new: 'The individual shall have the duty ... [t]o work to the best of his abilities and competence, and to pay taxes imposed by law in the interest of the society.' African Charter on Human and Peoples' Rights 1981, Article 29.6.

55 Conor Gearty, 'Human Rights' in Adam Kuper and Jessica Kuper (eds), *The Social Science Encyclopaedia* (3rd edn, Routledge, 2004) vol I, 468, 470–71.

56 According to the analysis of Nicholas Shaxson and John Christensen in 'The Finance Curse: How Oversized Financial Centres Attack Democracy and Corrupt Economies' ('The Finance Curse') (*Tax Justice Network*, May 2013) 67<www.taxjustice.net/cms/upload/pdf/Finance_Curse_Final.pdf> accessed 11 April 2017: 'this 'offshore' model holds that *domestic* laws and rules are to be scrupulously applied, to reassure foreign capital owners that their money is safe – but that *foreign* laws are to be disregarded'. Though their analysis stops short of exploring the relationship between tax havens and international human rights, the pattern which the authors see in the context of criminality and fraud is indistinguishable from that evidenced in many of the more inventive tax havens in their attitude towards those rights.

57 Eg the developing international offshore bonds market:

> Many institutional investors do not have the mandates or the technical capacity to invest in EME domestic bond markets. And even if they do, purchasing bonds issued in OFCs lessens their administrative burden as a more homogeneous regime across investments helps to reduce the hazards of dealing with dozens of tax and legal frameworks. Bonds and other debt securities issued in OFCs are also attractive to some investors for tax-reasons.

> Robert N McCauley, Christian Upper and Agustín Villar, 'Highlights of the BIS International Statistics' (September 2013) Bank Int'l Settlements QR <www.bis.org/publ/qtrpdf/r_qt1309b.pdf> accessed 24 April 2017; and see Chapter 2.

havens subject to external oversight (such as the role played by the United Kingdom in relation to Crown Dependencies such as the Isle of Man, Jersey and Guernsey[58]) by constitutional convention the overseeing jurisdiction will not interfere in purely domestic affairs, trusting that a degree of natural synergy and mutual political expediency will suffice.[59]

In terms of human rights enforcement therefore, both internally and internationally, each tax haven is a law unto itself.[60]

58 Justice Committee, *Crown Dependencies: Developments since 2010* (HC Tenth Report of Session 2013–14).
59 The constitutional relationship between the United Kingdom and its Overseas Territories and Crown Dependencies was the subject of debate in the House of Commons on 21 February 2017 in the context of the Criminal Finances Bill. The government having argued that it could not impose its will on the Crown Dependencies and on the Overseas Territories to compel them to make public their proposed registers of corporate beneficial ownership [see Chapter 3], Diane Abbott MP for the Opposition sought to place the United Kingdom in context:

> I remind the House that the genesis of the Bill was the Panama Papers, which revealed extremely widespread and highly lucrative avoidance of tax on an industrial scale. There were 11 million leaked files, and Britain was the second most prominent country in which the law firm's middlemen operated. It was second only to Hong Kong. One British territory, the British Virgin Islands, was by far the most popular tax haven state used by the firms in the documents. The Minister has said that we are at the forefront of taking action on tax avoidance and money laundering, and so we should be. The UK has sovereignty over one third of tax havens internationally.

HC Deb 21 February 2017, vol 621, col 597–978.
60 By way of illustration, on 1 May 2007 the following framework for developing the international identity of the Isle of Man was signed:

> Following the statement of intent agreed on 11 January 2006, the Chief Minister of the Isle of Man and the UK Secretary of State for Constitutional Affairs have agreed the following principles. They establish a framework for the development of the international identity of the Isle of Man. The framework is intended to clarify the constitutional relationship between the UK and the Isle of Man, which works well and within which methods are evolving to help achieve the mutual interests of both the UK and the Isle of Man.
>
> 1   The UK has no democratic accountability in and for the Isle of Man which is governed by its own democratically elected assembly. In the context of the UK's responsibility for the Isle of Man's international relations it is understood that:
>   a   The UK will not act internationally on behalf of the Isle of Man without prior consultation.
>   b   The UK recognises that the interests of the Isle of Man may differ from those of the UK, and the UK will seek to represent any differing interests when acting in an international capacity. This is particularly evident in respect of the relationship with the European Union where the UK interests can be expected to be those of an EU member state and the interests of the Isle of Man can be expected to reflect the fact that the UK's membership of the EU only extends to the Isle of Man in certain circumstances as set out in Protocol 3 of the UK's Treaty of Accession.
> 2   The Isle of Man has an international identity which is different from that of the UK.

Paradoxically, however, no tax haven is master of its own economic destiny, and any strategy aimed at reforming the human rights profiles of tax havens by encouraging the tax havens themselves to curb their activities will not succeed. Once a jurisdiction has taken the decision to become a low or zero tax area, the die is cast. Once a tax haven, always a tax haven.[61]

It is a Faustian pact – or, as Adam Rosenzweig[62] puts it – tax haven states

3   The UK recognises that the Isle of Man is a long-standing, small democracy and supports the principle of the Isle of Man further developing its international identity.

4   The UK has a role to play in assisting the development of the Isle of Man's international identity. The role is one of support not interference.

5   The Isle of Man and the UK commit themselves to open, effective and meaningful dialogue with each other on any issue that may come to affect the constitutional relationship.

6   International identity is developed effectively through meeting international standards and obligations which are important components of the Isle of Man's international identity.

7   The UK will clearly identify its priorities for delivery of its international obligations and agreements so that these are understood, and can be taken into account, by the Isle of Man in developing its own position.

8   The activities of the UK in the international arena need to have regard to the Isle of Man's international relations, policies and responsibilities.

9   The UK and the Isle of Man will work together to resolve or clarify any differences which may arise between their respective interests.

10   The Isle of Man and the UK will work jointly to promote the legitimate status of the Isle of Man as a responsible, stable and mature democracy with its own broad policy interests and which is willing to engage positively with the international community across a wide range of issues.

61   The exception proves the rule. Vanuatu has declared itself no longer to be a tax haven and is proposing to abandon its zero corporation tax rate, recognising that reliance on passive foreign investment is a major exposure to the local economy. Vanuatu hopes that foreign direct investment will be forthcoming if the economy is sound, the legal system is effective, and if Vanuatu can provide a good environment for investment. Vanuatu Revenue Review, 'Tugeta Yumi Bildim Vanuatu: Overview of Consultation Paper: The case for Revenue Reform and Modernisation (*Revenue Review*, September 2016) <http://revenue review.gov.vu/images/Publications/Overview_Document_V5_-_final_20_sept_ 2016.pdf> accessed 11 April 2017. To what extent these positive characteristics will distinguish Vanuatu from its competitor jurisdictions in mainstream investment centres, and how eager investors are to invest in a burnt out tax haven economy, remains to be seen. The development since 2013 of the Vanuatu oil field may soften the blow, though the connection between the discovery of these exploitable reserves and the decision of Vanuatu to cease its tax haven status can be the subject merely of speculation. JX Nippon Oil & Gas Exploration Corporation, 'First Oil from Finucane South Field, North West Shelf, Australia' (*JX Nippon Oil & Gas Exploration Corporation*, 24 May 2013) <www.nex.jx-group.co.jp/english/newsrelease/2013/20130524_01.html> accessed 11 April 2017 and Oil & Gas Industry Today, 'Vanuatu Oil & Gas Companies News Topics' (Oil & Gas Industry Today) <http://oilandgas.einnews.com/category/oil-gas-companies/vanuatu> accessed 11 April 2017.

62   Adam H Rosenzweig, 'Why Are There Tax Havens?' (2010) 52 Wm & Mary L Rev 923, 962–63 <http://scholarship.law.wm.edu/wmlr/vol52/iss3/5> accessed 11 April 2017. The theory is not merely academic. See Oliver Bullough, 'The Fall of Jersey: How a Tax

are impaled on Morton's Fork.[63] Their dilemma is to face two choices both of which are equally unattractive. They are in a negative feedback loop, unable to raise sufficient revenue to spend on development beyond their minimum revenue needs:

> [I]f they increase domestic taxes to raise revenue, they lose the tax base they attracted with tax competition in the first place, while if they do not they cannot raise additional revenue to invest in those public goods necessary to spur development beyond their minimum revenue needs. Absent relieving the pressure to rely on such institutions by providing other ways to access capital, such countries may effectively be incapable of ceasing to act as tax havens even in the face of increasing punishment.[64]

The tax havens trade off political stability and a supportive local economy for the bright lights, and this can be self-defeating:

> [B]eing a tax haven has unexpected costs. Precipitous economic, political and social declines have occurred so often in such states that

Haven Goes Bust' *The Guardian* (London, 8 December 2015) <www.theguardian.com/uk-news/2015/dec/08/fall-of-jersey-how-tax-haven-goes-bust> accessed 11 April 2017. 'Jersey has appalling standards of wealth distribution, with large working and under-class populations who struggle to exist. ... Jersey is, undoubtedly, a good place to be if you are middle class or rich. For the rest of us, living here is a daily struggle.' Stuart Syvret, Former Jersey Health Minister, 'Why? Of Tax-Dodging, Child Abuse and the Oppression of an Honest Police Chief: Graham Power's Statement – Part 2' (Ex-Senator Stuart Syvret Blog, 27 June 2012) <http://freespeechoffshore.nl/stuartsyvretblog/2012/06> accessed 11 April 2017, quoted in Shaxson and Christensen, 'The Finance Curse' (n 56) 54. And see the concern expressed by the Ministry of Finance, Bermuda in its 2017/2018 Budget Statement (delivered on 24 February 2017) at massive public debt and a stagnating economy:

> Government's multi-dimensional, multi-year campaign to turn around the economy and restore confidence has been succeeding, yet we know that ending The Great Bermuda Recession did not end the recession for everyone. The recovery has been uneven and hardship continues for many, most keenly through the debilitating pressures to pay bills and put food on the table.

E T Richards, Minister of Finance, '2017-18 Budget Statement: In Support of the Estimates of Revenue and Expenditure' (Government of Bermuda, 24 February 2017) <www.gov.bm/sites/default/files/7333_2017%20Budget%20Statement_Final_Portal.pdf> accessed 11 April 2017.

63 See JA Simpson, ESC Weiner, *Oxford English Dictionary* (2nd edn, 1989) vol 9, 1106.
64 Oxfam tacitly acknowledges this in calling for support for those tax havens which are economically dependent on their tax haven status to build fairer, more sustainable and diversified economies. Esmé Berkhout, 'Tax Battles: The Dangerous Global Race to the Bottom on Corporate Tax' (Oxfam, 12 December 2016) <www.oxfam.org/sites/www.oxfam.org/files/bp-race-to-bottom-corporate-tax-121216-en.pdf> accessed 12 April 2017 ('Tax Battles').

observers have coined a new term for it: 'the finance curse'. When the finance curse strikes a country, there is a recurrent pattern. While its democracy, economy and culture remain formally intact, they are increasingly oriented to and co-opted by international elites. In other words such countries gradually become organized around the interests of people who don't live there, to the detriment of those who do. The services produced by these countries protect cosmopolitans' wealth, but the riches never flow to the local producers, undermining their capacity for self-governance and social cohesion, as well as the development of infrastructure and institutions.'[65]

With, it seems, no appreciation of irony, the tax havens whose existence and activities abuse the human rights of others, by encouraging their finance sectors aggressively to compete with and eventually to crowd out other areas of the local economy, undermine the prosperity and development potential, and thereby the human rights, of their own peoples. Their very sovereignty is hollowed out:

> Although they claim their sovereign rights, these states have an independence that is more apparent than real, for their developmental and social goals are subject to the whim of foreign capital. As a rule, tax havens do not lack transparency only in financial matters – opacity pervades the entire state. The majority are controlled by a small, often invisible, oligarchy.[66]

If there is to be reform, the focus must be on those who benefit from the tax havens, not merely fiscally (for this incentive can and will never be removed by the tax havens themselves, captured as they have been by their finance sectors), but structurally. The artificial, chimeric entities which have been introduced in many tax havens are at the heart of the problem. Their creation and promotion is born of marketing and mutual competition between the tax havens, but this aggressive self-promotion and distortion of legal norms is not a *sine qua non* of low or zero taxation regimes. Establishing accountability, not repatriating offshore funds for the purposes of onshore taxation, is the sole viable strategy. In human rights terms, taxation – though undoubtedly forming a substantial part of the problem of abuse in its own right, in the distortion of national revenues – is a sub-plot. The main focus of the action has to be upon the structures themselves.

---

65   Brooke Harrington, 'Why Tax Havens Are Political and Economic Disasters' *The Atlantic* (Washington DC, 28 July 2016) <www.theatlantic.com/business/archive/2016/07/tax-haven-curse/491411> accessed 12 April 2017. For a detailed analysis of the phenomenon, see Shaxson and Christensen, 'The Finance Curse' (n 56).

66   Ronen Palan, Richard Murphy and Christian Chavagneux, *Tax Havens: How Globalization Really Works* (Cornell University Press, 2010) 187.

This structural perspective leads to the *rights-based working definition of a tax haven*. Two elements suffice to construct such a working definition from a human rights-based perspective:

- legislation may or may not be regarded by the issuing state as being human rights compliant within its borders, but this domestic compliance does not extend to the effects of such legislation external to that state; and/or
- state legislation intentionally promotes, facilitates and ensures accountability avoidance.[67]

If either of these elements is present, then the jurisdiction is one of low or zero accountability and as such human rights abusive.

Tax havens and humanitarian abuse

Though the early part of the twenty-first century is witnessing a decline in the observation of international human rights standards,[68] the needs of those for the protection of whom those standards were principally intended grow more desperate:

> Dazu kommen in unserer Gesellschaft sozialdarwinistische Tendenzen; für sie gilt das Recht des Stärkeren und die rücksichtslose Durchsetzung eigener und eigennütziger Interessen. Diejenigen, die nicht mithalten können, geraten leicht unter die Räder und zwischen die Mühlsteine. Vor allem im Zug der Globalisierung der Wirtschaft und die Finanzmärkte sind unkontrollierte entfesselte neokapitalistische Kräfte mächtig geworden, für die Menschen und ganze Völker oft ebarmungslos zum Spielball der eigenen Gier nach Geld geworden sind.[69]

> *Author's translation:* In addition social Darwinist leanings are now appearing in our business community; for whom what counts is the right of the stronger and the unheeding implementation of one's own self-serving interests. Those who cannot keep up simply fall beneath the wheels and between the millstones. Above all, as a consequence of the globalisation of financial markets and of the economy, unregulated and unrestricted neo-capitalist powers have assumed control, for whom individuals and whole peoples are frequently and pitilessly reduced to the status of pawns in their lust for money.

67 See Chapter 2 for examples of artificially engineered legislation of this kind, and in particular the Bahamas Enterprise Entity and the Nevis Multiform Foundation.
68 Silvia Magnoni and Kira Youdina, '5 Things to Know about the Decline of Human Rights' (*World Economic Forum*, 9 December 2016) <www.weforum.org/agenda/2016/12/decline-of-human-rights-civic-spaces> accessed 12 April 2017.
69 Cardinal Kasper Walter, *Barmherzigkeit: Grundbegriff des Evangeliums – Schlüssel christlichen Lebens* (Verlag Herder GmbH, 2012) 24.

Giving a global update on human rights on 13 June 2016, the UN High Commissioner for Human Rights pointed to the absence of a human rights dialogue in matters of business:

> When human rights, the two words, are so rarely found in the world of finance and business, in its literature, in its lexicon – why? Because it is shameful to mention them? ... Then do we really still have an international community? When the threads forming it are being tugged away and the tapestry, our world, is unravelling? Or are there only fragmented communities of competing interests – strategic and commercial – operating behind a screen of feigned allegiance to laws and institutions?[70]

Yet the role in this decline played by the tax havens often goes unrecognised. They feature not at all in the catalogue of abusive regimes presented by the High Commissioner. In assessing the challenges facing the world economy in 2017 and analysing their origins, the World Economic Forum, while vigorously defending the role of civil society in the defence of human rights and decrying its suppression in certain countries, does not see the elephant in the room and makes no mention of tax havens or even of taxation mechanisms in general.[71]

Examples of the connections between the tax havens and humanitarian abuse are not in short supply nor, though their origins and cause are opaque, are the abuses themselves concealed:

> The abuses are not only shocking, but staring us directly in the face. We didn't need the Panama Papers to know that global tax corruption through the havens is rampant, but we can say that this abusive global system needs to be brought to a rapid end. That is what is meant by good governance under the global commitment to sustainable development.[72]

Nevertheless, there remains a concentration on fiscal and developmental issues, and the solutions which are proposed to remedy such abuse, while compatible with human rights norms and expectations, make no reference to

---

70   Zeid Ra'ad Al-Hussein, 'Hate is Being Mainstreamed – Global Update by the High Commissioner' (*United Nations Office of the High Commissioner for Human Rights*, 13 June 2016) <www.ohchr.org/EN/NewsEvents/Pages/Globalhumanrightsupdateby HC.aspx> accessed 12 April 2017.
71   World Economic Forum, 'The Global Risks Report 2017' (*World Economic Forum*, 11 January 2017) <www.weforum.org/reports/the-global-risks-report-2017> accessed 12 April 2017.
72   Jeffery Sachs, one of a number of leading economists quoted in Patrick Wintour, 'Tax Havens Have No Economic Justification Say Top Economists' *The Guardian* (London, 9 May 2016) <www.theguardian.com/world/2016/may/09/tax-havens-have-no-econ omic-justification-say-top-economists> accessed 12 April 2017.

those norms. A rights-based approach is not applied. A concentration on transparency and registration is wide of the mark: in the context of the Extractive Industries Transparency Initiative, Human Rights Watch is of the opinion that 'while *transparency* has improved, *accountability* does not appear to have changed much.'[73]

As the following examples illustrate, resonating most strongly in the opacity of the tax havens, and in the words of Human Rights Watch:

> Transparency alone does not improve governance. Real improvements require that the public be able to hold governments accountable for the decisions they make. ... In very repressive environments, transparency can offer little more than an empty gesture that may even allow an abusive or corrupt government to act more brazenly and openly as it violates its citizens' rights or mismanages public funds.[74]

What is true at the government level is equally applicable to those corporate, trust and chimeric structures which exist by virtue of government action and in whose continued availability and evolution governments acquiesce.

Tax battles

On 12 December 2016, Oxfam published its report 'Tax Battles: the Dangerous Global Race to the Bottom on Corporate Tax'[75] identifying 'the world's 15 worst corporate tax havens' – described as having 'taken the no-to-low tax environment to an extreme, ratcheting up the competition to new levels'[76] – and setting itself the task of revealing 'how these tax havens are leading a global race to the bottom on corporate tax that is starving countries out of billions of dollars needed to tackle poverty and inequality.'[77]

As set out in the report, the world's worst tax havens, in order of significance are: (1) Bermuda, (2) the Cayman Islands, (3) the Netherlands, (4) Switzerland, (5) Singapore, (6) Ireland, (7) Luxembourg, (8) Curaçao, (9) Hong Kong, (10) Cyprus, (11) Bahamas, (12) Jersey, (13) Barbados, (14) Mauritius and (15) the British Virgin Islands. The United Kingdom does not feature on the list, but four territories for whose good governance the United

---

73   Human Rights Watch, 'Extractive Industries: A New Accountability Agenda – Human Rights and the Extractive Industries Transparency Initiative' (*Human Rights Watch*, 21 May 2013) <www.hrw.org/news/2013/05/21/extractive-industries-new-accountability-agenda> accessed 12 April 2017 ('Extractive Industries').
74   Human Rights Watch, 'Extractive Industries' (n 73).
75   Esmé Berkhout, 'Tax Battles' (n 64); and see Oxfam, 'World's Worst Corporate Tax Havens Exposed – Oxfam Report Reveals Dangerous Race to the Bottom on Corporate Tax' (*Oxfam*, 12 December 2016) <www.oxfam.org/en/pressroom/pressreleases/2016-12-12/worlds-worst-corporate-tax-havens-exposed-oxfam-report-reveals> accessed 12 April 2017 ('World's Worst').
76   Esmé Berkhout, 'Tax Battles' (n 64) 16.
77   Oxfam, 'World's Worst' (n 76).

Kingdom is ultimately responsible do appear: the Cayman Islands, Jersey, Bermuda and the British Virgin Islands.[78] Oxfam acknowledges that the current, often politicised, basis upon which tax havens are defined is inadequate. It notes that the list to be produced by the European Union in 2017 will exclude any EU Member State – and hence the Netherlands, Luxembourg, Ireland and Cyprus will not appear – leaving open the question of whether the United Kingdom and the Crown Dependencies (the Isle of Man, Jersey and Guernsey) will be included post-Brexit. Oxfam draws attention to the fact that the G20's focus on transparency rather than on internal tax policies would exclude what Oxfam regards as many of the worst tax havens, including Bermuda, the Netherlands, Switzerland and Singapore) and calls for the setting of global criteria, objective and free from political interference.

From the perspective of human rights and corporate governance, the report's tacit acknowledgement of the human rights impact is instructive, though the words 'human rights' appear nowhere in it. It advocates that companies should:

> Approach their tax responsibility as conduct that goes beyond legal compliance and reflects their broader duties to contribute to the public goods on which companies themselves depend [and] [b]e transparent about their business structures and operations, their tax affairs and tax decision making; assess and publicly report the fiscal, economic and social impacts of their tax-related decisions and practices; and take progressive and measurable steps to improve the sustainable development impact of their tax behaviour.[79]

Were Oxfam to go a step further, and advocate not merely the observance of duties to contribute to public goods but also the obligation to comply with applicable human rights norms, and in particular the 'UN Guiding Principles on Business and Human Rights' (2011),[80] its argument would have a massively increased justification.[81]

---

78   Oxfam however acknowledges that the tax havens are only part of the problem, at a time when countries across the world are reducing levels of corporation tax seeking to attract inward investment. The report quotes the G20 Corporation Tax ranking in stating that the average corporate tax rate across G20 countries was 40 per cent twenty-five years ago and today is lower than 30 per cent. Michael Devereux and others, 'G20 Corporation Tax Ranking' (*Oxford University Centre for Business Taxation*, March 2016) <www.sbs.ox.ac.uk/sites/default/files/Business_Taxation/Docs/Publications/Policy_Papers/g20-corporation-tax-ranking-2016_0.pdf> accessed 12 April 2017.

79   Esmé Berkhout, 'Tax Battles' (n 64) 8.

80   United Nations Office of the High Commissioner for Human Rights, 'UN Guiding Principles on Business and Human Rights: Implementing the United Nations 'Protect, Respect and Remedy' Framework' (2011) UN Doc HR/PUB/11/04.

81   For a review of the arguably failed strategies of the OECD, EU and G20 in relation to tax havens and an exploration of using the UN Guiding Principles on Business and Human Rights as an alternative, targeting the multinational, trans-border corporations, see Chapter 4.

Australia: the hidden billions

> Australia is a vibrant multicultural democracy with a strong record of protecting civil and political rights, but serious human rights issues remain.
>
> (Human Rights Watch)[82]

In its research report 'The Hidden Billions: How Tax Havens Impact Lives at Home and Abroad' issued in June 2016,[83] Oxfam Australia makes the connection between the purely fiscal cost of tax havens and the impact of tax havens on poverty and underdevelopment. The fiscal advantages to multinational corporations, the effect of which is to reduce their tax burden in the very countries in which their real economic activity takes place, strips out revenue from those countries whose infrastructure the multinationals have not created and which they do not sustain and whose people (whom the multinationals have not educated and to whose health and wellbeing they contribute but marginally) form a profitable source of cheap labour.[84] The rules of the market economy by which the tax havens exist are not suited to the needs of civil society:

> Tax avoidance is a direct attack on civil society. Human experience – codified by economic theory – has taught us that there are some things which individuals do well. However, there are things vital to a well-functioning human society that require collective action. Such collective action needs funding and without it, it won't occur. In that sense, tax avoidance and the tax havens that facilitate it are a travesty.[85]

The research report identifies the source of the injustice, and the means by which that injustice is perpetuated, as the use by multinational corporations of tax avoidance structures – 'unchecked power and hidden financial systems in which money is unavailable for essential public services because it sits instead in the coffers of wealthy corporations and individuals.'[86] The report lambasts multinational corporations' ability to operate in secrecy and – significantly from a human rights perspective – highlights their limited accountability and transparency.

---

82 Human Rights Watch, 'World Report 2017: Australia Events of 2016' (Human Rights Watch, 2017) <www.hrw.org/world-report/2017/country-chapters/australia> accessed 12 April 2017.
83 Jamaldeen (n 10).
84 Of the twelve reasons why companies choose to invest in a country, the most important are the quality of the country's infrastructure, the availability of an educated, healthy workforce and social stability. World Economic Forum, 'Global Competitiveness Report 2016–2017' (*World Economic Forum*, 2016) <www.weforum.org/reports/the-global-competitiveness-report-2016-2017-1> accessed 12 April 2017.
85 Tony Bryant, School of Economics, Macquarie University, quoted in Jamaldeen (n 10) 5.
86 Jamaldeen (n 10) 6.

The research report cites twenty tax havens (however classified – it acknowledges the absence of any universally adopted definition[87]) used by Australian-based multinationals, including Mauritius, Singapore, Ireland, the Netherlands, Malaysia (Labuan) and Hong Kong, noting that investment in these twenty tax havens increased by 40 per cent (US$22.7 billion) between 2009 and 2014.

The statistical analysis of Oxfam Australia reveals that in 2014 tax avoidance by Australian multinationals amounted to AU$5–6 billion. Developing countries suffered more. More than one in every US$2 of private foreign investment in developing countries came from a tax haven, which resulted in an estimated US$638 billion in profits being 'shifted' to tax havens. 'The tax on this amount – which has been ripped out of 110 developing countries – is estimated to be around US$172 billion in foregone revenue.' The report samples and seeks by illustrations to quantify in real-world terms the impact on Australia's trading partner states: in a year the Philippines lose 1,700 new classrooms; Ghana loses 1,400 primary school teachers and 600 nurses; and Papua New Guinea loses 1,000 clean toilets. The research report estimates losses in essential public services in developing countries due to Australian-based multinationals using tax havens in 2014: education US$2.1 billion; health and sanitation US$1.5 billion; social protection US$500 million; and gender equality US$32 million.

'The world's poorest people, and women in particular, bear the brunt of harmful tax dodging – they are the human face of tax dodging.'[88]

Oxfam Australia calls for reform of tax laws to promote fiscal transparency. It also supports proposals for national and international public registers of 'the ultimate ownership of companies, foundations and trusts'.[89]

Africa: the looting machine

The connection between taxation scams and human rights abuse in Africa is well-made, but many studies focus on domestic tax concessions and unduly favourable revenue rulings within a country's own taxation system, rather than on the use to which those taxable within such countries make of offshore structures to avoid or evade those responsibilities.[90] The window on

---

87   Table 6 of the Report lists 52 jurisdictions and the international organisations which have (each using their own indicators) identified these as tax havens.

88   Jamaldeen (n 10) 8.

89   Chapter 2 explores how this approach, though logical on the face of it, has in all likelihood no hope of succeeding due to the expansion of beneficial ownership avoidance and the restriction of access to such registered information (however incomplete and potentially misleading that information may be) to fiscal and law enforcement authorities, not available to the general public.

90   See eg East Africa Tax & Governance Network (EATGN), 'Taxing Rights Policies are Human Rights Policies' (*EATGN*, 2016) <www.taxjustice.net/wp-content/uploads/2016/11/Tax-and-Human-Rights-Report.pdf> accessed 12 April 2017.

offshore abuse is, however, opening wider, to expose funds flow to tax havens motivated not just by – or not at all by – the need to minimise taxation, but by the need for simple concealment. This haemorrhaging of wealth has a direct effect on the wellbeing of mass populations, and those cases which do come to light, given the opacity and the imperviousness to civil suits which characterise so many of the available offshore structures, can only be the tip of the iceberg.

In Africa, 'an invisible machine is working to plunder the continent. A looting machine. A coalition of corrupt dictators, unscrupulous large corporations and ruthless banks, all working hand in hand, united by their greed.'[91] This characterisation by Bastian Obermayer and Frederik Obermaier of the systematic plundering of African resources using tax haven structures is supported with examples from the data which they and their colleagues have extracted from the Panama Papers. They sample the use of companies incorporated in the British Virgin Islands, Panama, and Niue linked to corruption scandals in Angola, the Democratic Republic of the Congo, Equatorial Guinea, Malawi, and Mozambique.

Democratic Republic of Congo

The Democratic Republic of Congo ended 2016 in a state of political violence and government repression, including systematic armed attacks on its civilian population.[92]

In March 2017, the non-governmental organisation Global Witness published allegations of systematic corruption in the Democratic Republic of Congo concerning mining and minerals giant Glencore:[93]

> Between 2013 and 2016 mining giant Glencore paid over $75m to Dan Gertler, a controversial businessman accused of bribing senior officials in Democratic Republic of Congo to advance his mining interests … These payments were due to be paid to Congo's state mining company Gécamines under the terms of the original contract it had with Glencore. … A Global Witness investigation found that from 2013 to 2016 Toronto-listed Katanga Mining, majority-owned by Glencore, made 'signature bonus' and other payments totalling over $75 million to Dan Gertler's Africa Horizons company, registered in the Cayman Islands. Under the original contract these payments would have gone to

91   Obermayer and Obermaier, (n 32) ch 18.
92   Human Rights Watch, 'World Report 2017 – Democratic Republic of Congo Events of 2016' (Human Rights Watch, 2017) <www.hrw.org/world-report/2017/country-chapters/democratic-republic-congo> accessed 12 April 2017.
93   Glencore, 'Our Activities around the World' (*Glencore*) <www.glencore.com/who-we-are/about-us/our-activities-around-the-world> accessed 12 April 2017.

Gécamines … Glencore admitted that they were made to Gertler's company.[94]

Though analysed by Global Witness in terms of bribery and corruption, the allegations concerning the use of a Cayman Islands company as the recipient of funds, and this syphoning of assets has obvious tax haven human rights abusive implications. Global Witness comments further: 'Congo has vast natural resource wealth, but corruption, mismanagement and the sale of mines below market value have helped keep it one of the world's poorest countries, consistently languishing near the bottom of the UN Human Development Index.'[95]

Kenya

Respect for human rights in Kenya remained precarious in 2016, with authorities failing to adequately investigate a range of abuses across the country and undermining basic rights to free expression and association. Human rights activists and journalists working on a range of issues face increasing obstacles and harassment. Human rights organizations continue to implicate Kenyan police and military in disappearances and killings of individuals allegedly linked to Al-Shabab.

(Human Rights Watch)[96]

In February 2016 before the Royal Court of Jersey, Windward Trading Limited (a Jersey incorporated company[97]) admitted laundering the proceeds

---

94 Global Witness, 'Glencore Redirected over $75 Million in Mining Payments to Scandal-Hit Friend of Congolese President, Global Witness Reveals' ('Glencore Redirected') (*Global Witness*, 3 March 2017 <www.globalwitness.org/en/press-releases/glencore-redirected-over-75-million-mining-payments-scandal-hit-friend-president-global-witness-reveals> accessed 12 April 2017. It is a matter of concern from a rights-based perspective that possible indicators of such alleged corruption have been in part removed by the decision of the US on 3 February 2017 to repeal the Cardin-Lugar Anti-Corruption Provision of the Dodd-Frank Act 2010 (brought into force in 2016) under which US-listed extractive companies were required to publish details of sums paid to governments in return for rights to natural resource extraction. Global Witness, 'US Congress Votes for Corruption by Overturning Historic Transparency Law in Gift to Big Oil' (*Global Witness*, 3 February 2017) <www.globalwitness.org/en/press-releases/us-congress-votes-corruption-overturning-historic-transparency-law-gift-big-oil> accessed 12 April 2017.
95 Global Witness, 'Glencore Redirected' (n 94).
96 Human Rights Watch, 'World Report 2017 – Kenya Events of 2016' (*Human Rights Watch*, 2017) <www.hrw.org/world-report/2017/country-chapters/kenya> accessed 12 April 2017.
97 Windward Trading Limited registered in Jersey with company number 35512 on 8 August 1986, dissolved 1 October 2016. Details available from the Jersey Financial Services Commission (JFSC) Companies Registry <www.jerseyfsc.org/registry/documentsearch/NameDetail.aspx?Id=21007> accessed 12 April 2017.

of corruption between 29 July 1999 and 19 October 2001. The company's beneficial owner, Samuel Gichuru, was also the Chief Executive of Kenya Power and Lightning Company (KPLC), the Kenyan government's electricity utility company, from November 1984 to February 2003. KPLC had awarded contracts to a number of engineering and energy companies worldwide, who had all made payments to Windward. In his Prosecution conclusions, the Island's former Solicitor General, Howard Sharp QC said:

> Windward Trading received and held the proceeds of criminal conduct perpetrated by its controlling mind and beneficial owner, Samuel Gichuru. The company knowingly enabled Gichuru to obtain substantial bribes paid to Gichuru while he held public office in Kenya. The company played a vital role without which corruption on a grand scale is impossible: money laundering. Gichuru ... accepted bribes from foreign businesses that contracted with KPLC during his term of office and hid them in Jersey. ... Windward served as a bank account [and] formed a barrier between the foreign contractors that paid the bribes and the personal accounts of Gichuru and others who benefited from the corrupt payments.[98]

Over £3 million was repatriated from Jersey to Kenya in March 2017, and illustrative of the impoverishment within Kenya which results from illicit funds flow, and of the Kenyan people's human rights to be fully engaged as citizens, calls were made within the Kenyan Parliament for the funds to be paid over to the Kenyan Independent Electoral Boundaries Commission in order to get more Kenyans actively involved in choosing their leaders.[99]

Uganda

> In February [2016], President Yoweri Museveni, in power for more than 30 years, was declared the winner of the presidential elections. Local observers said the elections were not free and fair, and international

---

98 Bailiwick Express, 'Jersey seizes £3.6m in Kenyan bribery case' *Bailiwick Express* (St Helier, 26 February 2016) <www.bailiwickexpress.com/jsy/news/jersey-confiscates-36m-kenyan-corruption-case/#.WMzV01Ksnct> accessed 12 April 2017.

99 For the Jersey perspective see Bailiwick Express, 'Jersey seizes £3.6m in Kenyan bribery case' (n 98); Bailiwick Express, 'Repatriated £3m could get more Kenyans voting' *Bailiwick Express* (St Helier, 17 March 2017) <www.bailiwickexpress.com/jsy/news/repatriated-3m-could-get-more-kenyans-voting/?utm_medium=email&utm_campaign=Bailiwick%20Express%20News%20-%20Friday%2017%20March&utm_content=Bailiwick%20Express%20News%20-%20Friday%2017%20March+CID_5ac54a91593de57759952c48e3be39eb&utm_source=Email%20marketing%20software&utm_term=Read%20More#.WMzVdFKsnct> accessed 12 April 2017; and for Kenyan comment see Aggrey Mutambo, 'Gichuru and Okemo Lose Sh520 Million Stashed in Jersey Island' *Daily Nation* (Nairobi, 26 February 2016) <www.nation.co.ke/news/Jersey-Island-confiscate-Gichuru-and-Okemo—stashes/1056-3092832-59m5saz/index.html> accessed 12 April 2017.

electoral observers argued the process failed to meet international standards. Violations of freedom of association, expression, assembly, and the use of excessive force by security officials continued during campaigns and into the post-election period. ... The police used unlawful means including live ammunition to prevent peaceful opposition gatherings and protests, at times resulting in loss of life.

(Human Rights Watch)[100]

In its report 'How Can We Survive Here?' issued on 3 February 2014,[101] Human Rights Watch assesses the impact of mining on human rights in Karamoja, Uganda, an area described as 'marked by chronic poverty and the poorest human development indicators in the country.' Encouraged by the Ugandan government, mineral exploration companies have begun to explore and mine the area. Local communities 'are voicing serious fears of land grabs, environmental damage and a lack of information as to how and when they will see improved access to basic services and positive impacts.' Specifically, East African Mining Ltd (a Ugandan company) is accused of riding roughshod over local gold prospectors, having obtained exploration licences for over 2,000 square kilometres of land in Kaabong and Kotido districts in 2012. The Ugandan government has acquiesced in the exclusion of customary land owners from making decisions about the development of their own lands and has proceeded without their consent. From an accountability and funds flow perspective, a not unexpected pattern emerges: East African Mining Ltd is a wholly owned subsidiary of East African Gold PLC, a public company incorporated in Jersey.[102]

Bangladesh: the colour of money

The recent record of Bangladesh in matters of human rights, and the country's current engagement with rights activists, is poor in the extreme:

Bangladesh witnessed a spate of violent attacks against secular bloggers, academics, gay rights activists, foreigners, and members of religious minorities in 2016. ... Bangladesh security forces have a long history of arbitrary arrest, enforced disappearance, and extrajudicial killing ...

---

100 Human Rights Watch, 'World Report 2017: Uganda Events of 2016' (*Human Rights Watch*, 2017) <www.hrw.org/world-report/2017/country-chapters/uganda> accessed 12 April 2017.

101 Human Rights Watch, 'How Can We Survive Here? The Impact of Mining on Human Rights in Karamoja, Uganda' (*Human Rights Watch*, 2014) <www.hrw.org/sites/default/files/reports/uganda0214_ForUpload.pdf> accessed 12 April 2017.

102 East African Gold PLC registered in Jersey with company number 111813 on 9 November 2012. Details available from the JFSC Companies Registry: <www.jerseyfsc.org/registry/documentsearch/NameDetail.aspx?Id=289208> accessed 12 April 2017.

Human rights groups in Bangladesh face constant obstacles, including escalating harassment and surveillance by police.[103]

Human Rights Watch identifies general areas of abuse which more or less cover the entire human rights spectrum: attacks on civil society and on freedom of expression; low health and safety standards in the workplace; minorities; environment; labour rights; women's and girls' rights; overseas workers; refugees; sexual orientation and gender identity; and abuse of process in war crime trials. All apparently committed while the international community averted its gaze, and progressed with impunity.[104] Against this lamentable background, it is unremarkable that in March 2017 at a seminar in Dhaka organised by the Policy Research Institute[105] it was stated that the '[c]olour of the money does not matter as long as that money flows into my country. From that point of view, the world's major tax havens can be a good source of investment for us.'[106]

China: embracing tax havens

More than three decades after pledging to 'reform and open up,' there are few signs the Chinese Communist Party intends to change its authoritarian posture. Under the leadership of President Xi Jinping, who will remain in power until 2022 and possibly beyond, the outlook for fundamental human rights, including freedoms of expression, assembly, association and religion, remains dire.

(Human Rights Watch)[107]

103 Human Rights Watch, 'World Report 2017: Bangladesh Events of 2016' ('World Report 2017: Bangladesh') (Human Rights Watch, 2017) <www.hrw.org/world-report/2017/country-chapters/bangladesh> accessed 12 April 2017.
104 Human Rights Watch, 'World Report 2017 – Bangladesh' (n 103).
105 Seminar 'Improving Investment Climate: Key Policy Reforms and Institutional Priorities' reported in 'Seminar Goes to Bat for Bangladesh to Welcome Foreign Direct Investment from Tax Havens' *The Financial Express* (Dhaka 18 March 2017) <www.thefinancial express-bd.com/2017/03/18/64713/BD-needs-to-welcome-FDI-from-tax-havens> accessed 12 April 2017.
106 Syed Nasim Manzur, former President of the Metropolitan Chamber of Commerce and Industry. In this he was supported expressly by the Chairman of the Bangladesh Investment Development Authority, Kazi M. Aminul Islam: 'We have certain criteria for investment in this country and if they can fulfil those criteria, we would welcome investment from such tax havens.' Mr Manzur cited that in 2016 the fourth largest FDI source for Vietnam was the British Virgin Islands, and the largest that year for India was Mauritius. Quoted in *The Financial Express* (n 105).
107 Human Rights Watch, 'World Report 2017: China Events of 2016' (*Human Rights Watch*, 2017) <www.hrw.org/world-report/2017/country-chapters/china-and-tibet> accessed 12 April 2017. The report glaringly omits any reference to offshoring or the use of tax havens by Chinese citizens and entities.

Against this background of human rights abuse, China has openly embraced the structuring and fund flow possibilities afforded by tax havens. Doing business through offshore centres has become standard procedure among Chinese companies and entrepreneurs. Offshore havens feature frequently in corruption cases involving Chinese businesses. The Bank of China has revealed in a 2011 report on capital flight[108] that since the mid-1990s, state-owned companies and other public officials have moved more than US$120 billion away from China, the bulk of this passing through the British Virgin Islands.[109] This may be a massive underestimate:

> As the country has moved from an insular communist system to a social-ist/capitalist hybrid, China has become a leading market for offshore havens that peddle secrecy, tax shelters and streamlined international deal making. ... By some estimates, between [US]$1 trillion and $4 trillion in untraced assets have left the country since 2000.[110]

Conclusions

Tax havens have evolved from retirement centres for the tax averse into complex finance centres where private and commercial wealth is in the order of trillions of dollars. Not only is an evolutionary process at work in the established havens, but new havens may spontaneously generate in jurisdictions which, according to received wisdom, are nothing of the kind. Tax havens are not confined to palm-fringed micro-states.

Yet tax havens have eluded definition, not helped by the use of terms which themselves pre-determine the outcome: *tax havens, low tax areas, secrecy jurisdictions, offshore finance centre, international finance centre*. This has resulted in a great deal of finger pointing between the tax havens, each claiming regulatory and ethical superiority, and in consequence has frustrated attempts to regulate them externally or to name and shame and promote self-regulation from within. The tax havens, having been captured by their own finance sectors, are impaled on Morton's Fork, unable to shed their tax haven status. Even if holed below the water line they will go down with all colours flying. That is their inescapable destiny. But they are not sunk yet,

---

108 Bank of China <www.documentcloud.org/documents/1008119-bankofchinareporton-capitalflight.html> accessed 12 April 2017 (in Chinese).
109 Olesen and Hudson (n 30).
110 Marina Walker Guevara and others, 'Leaked Records Reveal Offshore Holdings of China's Elite' *ICIJ* (Washington DC, 21 January 2014) <www.icij.org/offshore/leaked-records-reveal-offshore-holdings-chinas-elite> accessed 12 April 2017. The ICIJ has released the names of more than 37,000 offshore clients from China, Hong Kong and Taiwan connected to companies and trusts in ten tax havens. Mar Cabra and Marina Walker Guevara, 'Unlocking China's Secrets' *ICIJ* (Washington DC, 23 January 2014) <www.icij.org/offshore/unlocking-chinas-secrets> accessed 12 April 2017.

and examples abound of massive use being made of them, in many cases consciously and deliberately by states whose human rights records are dire.

At a time when human rights observance is in decline, with feigned allegiance to laws and institutions, the role of tax havens often goes unrecognised.

From a human rights perspective, the characteristics in issue are not necessarily tax-based or financial, though there is no doubt that these are siren calls. This completely misses the point. The point is funds flow, opacity and an absence of accountability. A jurisdiction whose legislation may or may not be regarded as being human rights compliant within its borders, but whose domestic compliance does not extend to the effects of that legislation external to that state, and/or whose legislation intentionally promotes, facilitates and ensures accountability avoidance is one of low or zero accountability, and, as such, human rights abusive.

Bibliography

Legislation and regulations

Criminal Finances Bill 2016 (United Kingdom)
Dodd-Frank Act 2010 (United States)
General Corporation Act 1899 (Delaware, United States)
Landesverwaltung Fürstentum (Liechtenstein) <www.gesetze.li> accessed 10 April 2017
The Law of 31 July 1929 (Luxembourg)

International treaty

African Charter on Human and Peoples' Rights 1981

United Nations documents

United Nations Human Rights Council, 'Report of the Independent Expert on the Question of Human Rights and Extreme Poverty, Magdalena Sepulveda Carmona' (17 March 2011) UN Doc A/HRC/17/34
United Nations Office of the High Commissioner for Human Rights, 'UN Guiding Principles on Business and Human Rights: Implementing the United Nations 'Protect, Respect and Remedy' Framework' (2011) UN Doc HR/PUB/11/04

Other

Communiqué, G20 Finance Ministers and Central Bank Governors' Meeting Washington, April 15, 2016 (*University of Toronto G20 Information Centre*, 15 April 2016) <www.g20.utoronto.ca/2016/160415-finance.html> accessed 11 April 2017
HC Deb 21 February 2017, vol 621, col 597–978

Justice Committee, *Crown Dependencies: Developments since 2010* (HC Tenth Report of Session 2013–14)

Richards ET, Minister of Finance, '2017–18 Budget Statement: In Support of the Estimates of Revenue and Expenditure' (Government of Bermuda, 24 February 2017) <www.gov.bm/sites/default/files/7333_2017%20Budget%20Statement_Final_Portal.pdf> accessed 11 April 2017

United Arab Emirates Ministry of Finance, 'Issuing Tax Domicile Certificate' (United Arab Emirates) <www.mof.gov.ae/En/mservices/VTAX/Pages/ServiceCardTax.aspx> accessed 11 April 2017

Secondary sources

Allen & Overy, 'The Transitory Period for 1929 Holding Companies Ending on 31 December 2010' (30 September 2010) <www.allenovery.com/publications/en-gb/Pages/The-transitory-period-for-1929-holding-companies-ending-on-31-December-2010.aspx> accessed 10 April 2017

Al-Hussein ZR, 'Hate is Being Mainstreamed – Global Update by the High Commissioner' (*United Nations Office of the High Commissioner for Human Rights*, 13 June 2016) <www.ohchr.org/EN/NewsEvents/Pages/GlobalhumanrightsupdatebyHC.aspx> accessed 12 April 2017

Bailey W and Liu EX, 'Incorporation in Offshore Financial Centers: Naughty or Nice?' (*Cornell University*, 15 April 2014) <https://courses.cit.cornell.edu/wbb1/papers/BL_OFC_15Apr2014.pdf> accessed 11 April 2017

Bailiwick Express, 'Jersey seizes £3.6m in Kenyan bribery case' *Bailiwick Express* (St Helier, 26 February 2016) <www.bailiwickexpress.com/jsy/news/jersey-confiscates-36m-kenyan-corruption-case/#.WMzV01Ksnct> accessed 12 April 2017

——, 'Repatriated £3m could get more Kenyans voting' *Bailiwick Express* (St Helier, 17 March 2017) <www.bailiwickexpress.com/jsy/news/repatriated-3m-could-get-more-kenyans-voting/?utm_medium=email&utm_campaign=Bailiwick%20Express%20News%20-%20Friday%2017%20March&utm_content=Bailiwick%20Express%20News%20-%20Friday%2017%20March+CID_5ac54a91593de57759952c48e3be39eb&utm_source=Email%20marketing%20software&utm_term=Read%20More#.WMzVdFKsnct> accessed 12 April 2017

Bank of China <www.documentcloud.org/documents/1008119-bankofchinareportoncapitalflight.html> accessed 12 April 2017 (in Chinese)

Beckford G and others, 'NZ at Heart of Panama Money-go-round' (*Radio New Zealand*, 9 May 2016) <www.radionz.co.nz/news/panama-papers/303356/nz-at-heart-of-panama-money-go-round> accessed 11 April 2017

Berkhout E, 'Tax Battles: the Dangerous Global Race to the Bottom on Corporate Tax' ('Tax Battles') (Oxfam, 12 December 2016) <www.oxfam.org/sites/www.oxfam.org/files/bp-race-to-bottom-corporate-tax-121216-en.pdf> accessed 12 April 2017

Bullough O, 'The Fall of Jersey: How a Tax Haven Goes Bust' *The Guardian* (London, 8 December 2015) <www.theguardian.com/uk-news/2015/dec/08/fall-of-jersey-how-tax-haven-goes-bust> accessed 11 April 2017

Cabra M and Walker Guevara M, 'Unlocking China's Secrets' *ICIJ* (Washington DC, 23 January 2014) <www.icij.org/offshore/unlocking-chinas-secrets> accessed 12 April 2017

Collier J, 'Turn Down the Heat, Switch on the Light: A Rational Analysis of Tax Havens, Tax Policy and Tax Politics' (2013) IEA Current Controversies Paper #44 <www.iea.org.uk/sites/default/files/publications/files/Turn%20down%20the %20heat,%20switch%20on%20the%20light.pdf> accessed 11 April 2017

Collier P, 'In Pursuit of the $21 Trillion' (*Prospect Magazine*, 27 March 2013) <www.prospectmagazine.co.uk> accessed 11 April 2017 (article no longer available online)

Devereux M and others, 'G20 Corporation Tax Ranking' (*Oxford University Centre for Business Taxation*, March 2016) <www.sbs.ox.ac.uk/sites/default/files/ Business_Taxation/Docs/Publications/Policy_Papers/g20-corporation-tax-ranking-2016_0.pdf> accessed 12 April 2017

Dharmapala D, 'What Problems and Opportunities Are Created by Tax Havens?' [Winter 2008] 24 *O Rev Econ Policy* 4 <https://academic.oup.com/oxrep/ article-abstract/24/4/661/547359/What-problems-and-opportunities-are-created-by-tax> accessed 11 April 2017

Drucker J, 'The World's Favorite New Tax Haven is the United States' *Bloomberg Businessweek* (New York City, 27 January 2016) <www.bloomberg.com/news/ articles/2016-01-27/the-world-s-favorite-new-tax-haven-is-the-united-states> accessed 11 April 2017

Dufey G and Giddy I, *The International Money Market* (Prentice-Hall 1978)

East Africa Tax & Governance Network, 'Taxing Rights Policies are Human Rights Policies' (*EATGN*, 2016) <www.taxjustice.net/wp-content/uploads/2016/11/ Tax-and-Human-Rights-Report.pdf> accessed 12 April 2017

The Economist, 'The Missing $20 Trillion' (*The Economist*, 16 February 2013) <www.economist.com/news/leaders/21571873-how-stop-companies-and-people-dodging-tax-delaware-well-grand-cayman-missing-20> accessed 11 April 2017

Eriksson A, 'EU Tax Haven List Could Name US' *EU Observer* (Brussels, 16 September 2016) <https://euobserver.com/economic/135109> accessed 11 April 2017

European Parliament, 'EU List of Tax Havens Likely by End 2017, Says EU Commissioner, Pierre Moscovici' *European Parliament News* (Brussels, 7 December 2016) <www.europarl.europa.eu/news/en/news-room/ 20161205 IPR54576/eu-list-of-tax-havens-likely-by-end-2017-says-eu-commissioner-pierre-moscovici> accessed 11 April 2017

Experts for Expats, 'Non-Dom (Non-domiciled) Tax for Residents in the UK' (*Experts for Expats*, last updated 27 October 2016) <www.expertsforexpats.com/ expat-tax/non-dom-non-domiciled-tax-in-the-uk> accessed 11 April 2017

The Financial Express, 'Seminar Goes to Bat for Bangladesh to Welcome Foreign Direct Investment from Tax Havens' *The Financial Express* (Dhaka, 18 March 2017) <www.thefinancialexpress-bd.com/2017/03/18/64713/BD-needs-to-welcome-FDI-from-tax-havens> accessed 12 April 2017

Frieden K and Hogroian F, 'State Tax Haven Legislation: A Misguided Approach to a Global Issue' ('State Tax Haven Legislation') (*State Taxation Research Institute*, February 2016) <http://cost.org/WorkArea/DownloadAsset.aspx?id=92483> accessed 11 April 2017

Gearty C, 'Human Rights' in Adam Kuper and Jessica Kuper (eds), *The Social Science Encyclopaedia* (3rd edn, Routledge, 2004)

Glencore, 'Our Activities around the World' (*Glencore*) <www.glencore.com/who-we-are/about-us/our-activities-around-the-world> accessed 12 April 2017

Global Witness, 'US Congress Votes for Corruption by Overturning Historic Transparency Law in Gift to Big Oil' (*Global Witness*, 3 February 2017) <www.globalwitness.org/en/press-releases/us-congress-votes-corruption-overturning-historic-transparency-law-gift-big-oil> accessed 12 April 2017

——, 'Glencore Redirected over $75 Million in Mining Payments to Scandal-Hit Friend of Congolese President, Global Witness Reveals' ('Glencore Redirected') (*Global Witness*, 3 March 2017 <www.globalwitness.org/en/press-releases/glencore-redirected-over-75-million-mining-payments-scandal-hit-friend-president-global-witness-reveals> accessed 12 April 2017

Harrington B, 'Why Tax Havens Are Political and Economic Disasters' *The Atlantic* (Washington DC, 28 July 2016) <www.theatlantic.com/business/archive/2016/07/tax-haven-curse/491411> accessed 12 April 2017

Human Rights Watch, 'Extractive Industries: A New Accountability Agenda – Human Rights and the Extractive Industries Transparency Initiative' (*Human Rights Watch*, 21 May 2013) <www.hrw.org/news/2013/05/21/extractive-industries-new-accountability-agenda> accessed 12 April 2017

——, 'How Can We Survive Here? The Impact of Mining on Human Rights in Karamoja, Uganda' (*Human Rights Watch*, 2014) <www.hrw.org/sites/ default/ files/reports/uganda0214_ForUpload.pdf> accessed 12 April 2017

——, 'World Report 2017: Australia Events of 2016' (*Human Rights Watch*, 2017) <www.hrw.org/world-report/2017/country-chapters/australia> accessed 12 April 2017

——, 'World Report 2017 – Democratic Republic of Congo Events of 2016' (*Human Rights Watch*, 2017) <www.hrw.org/world-report/2017/country-chapters/democratic-republic-congo> accessed 12 April 2017

——, 'World Report 2017 – Kenya Events of 2016' (*Human Rights Watch*, 2017) <www.hrw.org/world-report/2017/country-chapters/kenya> accessed 12 April 2017

——, 'World Report 2017: Uganda Events of 2016' (*Human Rights Watch*, 2017) <www.hrw.org/world-report/2017/country-chapters/uganda> accessed 12 April 2017

——, 'World Report 2017: Bangladesh Events of 2016' ('World Report 2017: Bangladesh') (*Human Rights Watch*, 2017) <www.hrw.org/world-report/2017/country-chapters/bangladesh> accessed 12 April 2017

——, 'World Report 2017: China Events of 2016' (*Human Rights Watch*, 2017) <www.hrw.org/world report/2017/country-chapters/china-and-tibet> accessed 12 April

International Consortium of Investigative Journalism, 'The Panama Papers: Politicians, Criminals and the Rogue Industry that Hides their Cash' (*ICIJ*, 2016) <https://panamapapers.icij.org> accessed 10 April 2017

Jamaldeen M, 'The Hidden Billions: How Tax Havens Impact Lives of at Home and Abroad' (Oxfam Australia, June 2016) <www.oxfam.org.au/wp-content/uploads/2016/06/OXF003-Tax-Havens-Report-FA2-WEB.pdf> accessed 10 April 2017

Jersey Financial Services Commission Companies Registry <www.jerseyfsc.org/registry/documentsearch/NameDetail.aspx?Id=21007> accessed 12 April 2017

——, <www.jerseyfsc.org/registry/documentsearch/NameDetail.aspx?Id=289208> accessed 12 April 2017

JX Nippon Oil & Gas Exploration Corporation, 'First Oil from Finucane South Field, North West Shelf, Australia' (*JX Nippon Oil & Gas Exploration Corporation*, 24 May 2013) <www.nex.jx-group.co.jp/english/newsrelease/2013/20130524_01.html> accessed 11 April 2017

'Liechtenstein in Zahlen 2017' (Amt für Statistik Fürstentum Liechtenstein, November 2016) (in German) <www.llv.li/files/as/fl-in-zahlen-deutsch-2017.pdf> accessed 10 April 2017

Littlewood M, 'Using New Zealand as a Tax Haven: How is it done? Could it be stopped? Should it be stopped?' (11 April 2016) <https://ssrn.com/abstract=2761993> accessed 11 April 2017

Magnoni S and Youdina K, '5 Things to Know about the Decline of Human Rights' (*World Economic Forum*, 9 December 2016) <www.weforum.org/agenda/2016/12/decline-of-human-rights-civic-spaces> accessed 12 April 2017

Major K, 'George Osborne is Trying to Turn Post-Brexit Britain into a Tax Haven – and It Won't Benefit Anyone Except the Elite' *The Independent* (London, 4 July 2016) <www.independent.co.uk/voices/george-osborne-is-trying-to-turn-post-brexit-britain-into-a-tax-haven-and-it-wont-benefit-anyone-a7119211.html> accessed 11 April 2017

McCauley RN, Upper C and Villar A, 'Highlights of the BIS International Statistics' (September 2013) Bank for Int'l Settlements QR <www.bis.org/publ/qtrpdf/r_qt1309b.pdf> accessed 24 April 2017

Mohindra N, 'In Defence of 'Tax Havens' *Financial Post* (Toronto, 8 June 2016) <http://business.financialpost.com/fp-comment/in-defence-of-tax-havens> accessed 11 April 2017

Mutambo A, 'Gichuru and Okemo Lose Sh520 Million Stashed in Jersey Island' *Daily Nation* (Nairobi, 26 February 2016) <www.nation.co.ke/news/Jersey-Island-confiscate-Gichuru-and-Okemo—stashes/1056-3092832-59m5saz/index.html> accessed 12 April 2017

Nisen M, 'How Nike Solved Its Sweatshop Problem' (*Business Insider*, 9 May 2013) <www.businessinsider.com/how-nike-solved-its-sweatshop-problem-2013-5> accessed 11 April 2017

Obermayer B and Obermaier F, *The Panama Papers: Breaking the Story of How the Rich and Powerful Hide their Money* (Oneworld, 2016)

Oil & Gas Industry Today, 'Vanuatu Oil & Gas Companies News Topics' (*Oil & Gas Industry Today*) <http://oilandgas.einnews.com/category/oil-gas-companies/vanuatu> accessed 11 April 2017

Olesen A and Hudson M, 'China's Scandal-Torn Oil Industry Embraces Tax Havens' *ICIJ* (Washington DC, 22 January 2014) <www.icij.org/offshore/chinas-scandal-torn-oil-industry-embraces-tax-havens> accessed 11 April 2017

Organisation for Economic Co-operation and Development, 'Tax Transparency 2016: Report on Progress' (*OECD Global Forum on Transparency and Exchange of Information for Tax Purposes,* 2016) <www.oecd.org/tax/transparency/GF-annual-report-2016.pdf> accessed 11 April 2017

——, 'Common Reporting Standards' (*OECD Global Forum on Transparency and Exchange of Information for Tax Purposes*) <www.oecd.org/tax/automatic-exchange/common-reporting-standard> accessed 11 April 2017

——, 'Convention on Mutual Administrative Assistance in Tax Matters' (*OECD*, last updated March 2017) <www.oecd.org/tax/exchange-of-tax-information/convention-on-mutual-administrative-assistance-in-tax-matters.htm> accessed 11 April 2017

Oxfam, 'World's Worst Corporate Tax Havens Exposed – Oxfam Report Reveals Dangerous Race to the Bottom on Corporate Tax' (*Oxfam*, 12 December 2016) <www.oxfam.org/en/pressroom/pressreleases/2016-12-12/worlds-worst-corporate-tax-havens-exposed-oxfam-report-reveals> accessed 12 April 2017

Palan R, *The Offshore World: Sovereign Markets, Virtual Places and Nomad Millionaires* ('The Offshore World') (Cornell University Press, 2003)

——, 'History of Tax Havens' (*History and Policy*, 1 October 2009) <www.historyandpolicy.org/policy-papers/papers/history-of-tax-havens> accessed 10 April 2017

Palan R, Murphy R and Chavagneux C, *Tax Havens: How Globalization Really Works* (Cornell University Press, 2010)

Phillips R and others, 'Offshore Shell Games 2016: The Use of Offshore Tax Havens by Fortune 500 Companies' (*US Public Interest Research Group Education Fund, Citizens for Tax Justice, and the Institute on Taxation and Economic Policy*, 2016) <http://ctj.org/ctjreports/2016/10/offshore_shell_games_2016.php> accessed 11 April 2017

Rixtel A, 'Highlights of the BIS International Statistics' (2013) Bank Intl Settlements QR <www.bis.org/publ/qtrpdf/r_qt1309b.pdf> accessed 11 April 2017

Rosenzweig AH, 'Why Are There Tax Havens?' (2010) 52 Wm & Mary L Rev 923 <http://scholarship.law.wm.edu/wmlr/vol52/iss3/5> accessed 11 April 2017

Salomon M, 'Why Should it Matter that Others Have More? Poverty, Inequality and the Potential of International Human Rights Law' (2010) LSE Working Papers 15/2010

Seligman J, 'A Brief History of Delaware's General Corporation Law of 1899' [1976] 1 Del J Corp L 2

Shaer M, Hudson M and Williams M, 'Sun and Shadows: How an Island Paradise Became a Haven for Dirty Money' (*ICIJ*, 9 June 2014) <www.icij.org/offshore/sun-and-shadows-how-island-paradise-became-haven-dirty-money> accessed 10 April 2017

Sharman JC, 'South Pacific Tax Havens: Leaders in the Race to the Bottom or Laggards in the Race to the Top?' [2005] 29 Accounting Forum 311–23

Shaxson N, *Treasure Islands: Uncovering the Damage of Offshore Banking and Tax Havens* (Palgrave Macmillan 2011)

——, 'What is a Tax Haven?' *The Guardian* (London, 9 January 2011). <www.theguardian.com/business/2011/jan/09/explainer-what-is-tax-haven> accessed 11 April 2017

Shaxson N and Christensen J, 'The Finance Curse: How Oversized Financial Centres Attack Democracy and Corrupt Economies' (*Tax Justice Network* May 2013) 67<www.taxjustice.net/cms/upload/pdf/Finance_Curse_Final.pdf> accessed 11 April 2017

Simpson JA and Weiner ESC, *Oxford English Dictionary* (2nd edn, 1989) vol 9

Solly M, *Anatomy of a Tax Haven: The Isle of Man* (Shearwater Press 1975)

Syvret S, 'Why? Of Tax-Dodging, Child Abuse and the Oppression of an Honest Police Chief: Graham Power's Statement – Part 2' (Ex-Senator Stuart Syvret Blog, 27 June 2012) <http://freespeechoffshore.nl/stuartsyvretblog/2012/06> accessed 11 April 2017

Tax Justice Network, 'Financial Secrecy Index' (*Tax Justice Network*) <www.financialsecrecyindex.com> accessed 11 April 2017

——, 'Will the OECD Tax Haven Blacklist Be Another Whitewash?' (*Tax Justice Network,* 20 July 2016) <www.taxjustice.net/2016/07/20/oecd-another-go-hopeless-politicised-tax-haven-blacklisting> accessed 11 April 2017

Vannin E, 'David Cameron: Crown Dependency Tax Haven Banner "Not Fair"' *BBC News* (Isle of Man, 10 September 2013) <www.bbc.co.uk/news/world-europe-isle-of-man-24034768> accessed 11 April 2017

Vanuatu Revenue Review, 'Tugeta Yumi Bildim Vanuatu: Overview of Consultation Paper: The case for Revenue Reform and Modernisation (*Revenue Review,* September 2016) <http://revenuereview.gov.vu/images/Publications/Overview_Document_V5_-_final_20_sept_2016.pdf> accessed 11 April 2017

Walker Guevara M and others, 'Leaked records Reveal Offshore Holdings of China's Elite' *ICIJ* (Washington DC, 21 January 2014) <www.icij.org/offshore/leaked-records-reveal-offshore-holdings-chinas-elite> accessed 12 April 2017

Walter K, *Barmherzigkeit: Grundbegriff des Evangeliums – Schlüssel christlichen Lebens* (Verlag Herder GmbH, 2012)

Wintour P, 'Tax Havens Have No Economic Justification Say Top Economists' *The Guardian* (London, 9 May 2016) <www.theguardian.com/world/2016/may/09/tax-havens-have-no-economic-justification-say-top-economists> accessed 12 April 2017

World Economic Forum, 'Global Competitiveness Report 2016–2017' (*World Economic Forum,* 2016) <www.weforum.org/reports/the-global-competitive-ness-report-2016-2017-1> accessed 12 April 2017

——, 'The Global Risks Report 2017' (*World Economic Forum,* 11 January 2017) <www.weforum.org/reports/the-global-risks-report-2017> accessed 12 April 2017

Zoromé A, 'Concept of Offshore Financial Centers: In Search of an Operational Definition' (April 2007) IMF Working Paper WP/07/87 <www.imf.org/external/pubs/ft/wp/2007/wp0787.pdf> accessed 10 April 2017

Zucman G, *The Hidden Wealth of Nations: The Scourge of Tax Havens* (Teresa Lavender Fagan tr, University of Chicago Press, 2013)

2 Offshore structures

Accountability avoidance

Introduction

In terms of human rights accountability, offshore structures are the brick wall against which the human rights enforcer bangs their head to no avail. These structures are designed to conceal their true ownership, the extent of their wealth and their purpose, and may even remove the concept of beneficial ownership altogether.

The proliferation of such structures has been tax driven, and the collateral effects on anti-money laundering and the countering of terrorist financing have since the turn of the century become widely debated.[1] The elephant in the room is the human rights abuse which these structures facilitate.

This chapter illustrates some of the more prominent structures available in the tax havens (many of these having close equivalents in mainstream onshore jurisdictions also). In many cases, a structure as familiar as a company or a trust, not in itself unique to tax havens, is in the hands of tax haven governments and professionals morphed into something lacking transparency, expressly anonymous and asset protective and, from a right-based perspective, potentially abusive. These chimeric entities sit amidst well-understood structures universally acknowledged to be legitimate, yet in most respects share none, or hardly any, of the legal characteristics of those familiar forms. They are not entities which have evolved to serve a social need – the development of trusts and uses, the commercial pressure for limited liability trading structures – but are wholly artificial.[2]

---

1 For a recent statistical overview from a money laundering and tax evasion perspective see Alex Marriage, 'Secret Structures, Hidden Crimes: Urgent Steps to Address Hidden Ownership, Money Laundering and Tax Evasion from Developing Countries' *(European Network on Debt and Development*, 2013) <http://eurodad.org/files/integration/2013/01/Secret-structures-hidden-crimes-web.pdf> accessed 16 April 2017.

2 They serve to illustrate the proposition articulated over twenty years ago that '[t]he structures of power and interest and the forces at work in the international economy and within developing countries themselves pull remorselessly in the opposite direction to a basic rights agenda.' David Beetham, 'What Future for Economic and Social Rights?' (1995) XLIII Political Studies 41, 56.

Without a reasonably detailed knowledge of these, any human rights tax haven abuse assessment would be incomplete. If an ownership structure has even one of these elements, the question must be asked – why? Is this merely the expression of a legitimate desire for personal or commercial confidentiality, or is it accountability avoidance?

This chapter does not deal with the illegitimate, criminal use of such structures, but instead seeks to assess the impact of such structures on human rights accountability when they are used in jurisdictions where they are not merely legal but where their use is actively encouraged both by government and the private sector.[3]

Such a structure is a creature of the state, created under the laws which give it its form and which by virtue of themselves not being repealed sustain its existence. Modern human rights thinking is that these state creations – and their related entities – must themselves be bound, on the basis of subsidiarity, by those human rights norms which bind the state itself:[4] the

---

3   '[I]nequality is not the result of some accidental deviation from neo-liberal capitalism, but rather a deliberate product of the international political economy.' Margot Salomon, *Why Should it Matter that Others Have More? – Poverty, Inequality and the Potential of International Human Rights Law* (2010) LSE Legal Studies Working Paper No. 15/2010, 10 <https://papers.ssrn.com/sol3/papers.cfm?abstract_id=1711657> accessed 16 April 2017.

4   See the discussion on transnational State responsibility in the context of business structures in 'Who will be accountable? Human Rights and the Post-2015 Development Agenda':

Under international human rights law, States are primarily accountable for respecting and protecting the rights of those within their jurisdiction. The proliferation of actors in international development – from business enterprises and multilateral economic institutions to private foundations – has made it necessary to develop a more multidimensional approach to accountability. … The bond between State and citizen is now at the centre of a more elaborate web of interrelated responsibilities involving actors above, below and beyond the State.

Office of the United Nations High Commissioner for Human Rights, 'Who Will Be Accountable? Human Rights and the Post-2015 Development Agenda (2013)' (*Office of the United Nations High Commissioner for Human Rights,* 2013) <www.ohchr.org/Documents/Publications/WhoWillBeAccountable.pdf> accessed 15 April 2017.

This is further emphasised by the Committee on Economic, Social and Cultural Rights at its meeting on 20-24 February 2017 adopting United Nations Committee on Economic, Social and Cultural Rights (UNCESCR), 'General Comment on State Obligations under the International Covenant on Economic, Social and Cultural Rights in the Context of Business Activities [Draft Prepared by Olivier De Schutter and Zdzislaw Kedzia, Rapporteurs]' (17 October 2016) UN Doc E/C.12/60/R.1 ('General Comment: Business Activities'):

35. The extraterritorial obligation to protect requires States Parties to also pay close attention to the adverse impacts outside their territories of the activities and operations of business entities that are domiciled in their jurisdiction. … 38. In discharging their duty to regulate business activities with potential adverse impact on Covenant rights, States Parties may also require such businesses to ensure that other related entities, such as subsidiaries, suppliers, franchisees, or investors, comply with the requirements under the Covenant.

state cannot promote an entity the human rights accountability of which is at odds with those of the state itself:

> The State duty to protect is a standard of conduct. Therefore, States are not per se responsible for human rights abuse by private actors. However, States may breach their international human rights law obligations where such abuse can be attributed to them, or where they fail to take appropriate steps to prevent, investigate, punish and redress private actors' abuse. While States generally have discretion in deciding upon these steps, they should consider the full range of permissible preventative and remedial measures, including policies, legislation, regulations and adjudication. States also have the duty to protect and promote the rule of law, including by taking measures to ensure equality before the law, fairness in its application, and by providing for adequate accountability, legal certainty, and procedural and legal transparency.[5]

How therefore are such structures – entirely legitimate in the jurisdiction in which they are formed – to be assessed in light of applicable international human rights norms, bearing in mind that 'a party may not invoke the provisions of its internal law as justification for its failure to perform a treaty'?[6] And what responsibility do the tax havens have to take cognisance of the international human rights consequences of the structures whose existence they facilitate?

Tools of abuse

The following tools of abuse are wholly or in part common to many of the tax haven structures, and in most cases have been consciously applied in domestic legislation:

- The structures are subject to artificially low levels of domestic taxation, or are wholly exempt from income and capital taxes or customs duties.
- Reciprocal enforcement of foreign judgments in domestic courts is limited or dis-applied altogether (and domestic court proceedings may be held in secret).

---

5   Foundational Principle 1, United Nations Human Rights Council, 'Report of the Special Representative of the Secretary General on the Issue of Human Rights and Transnational Corporations and Other Business Enterprises, John Ruggie: Guiding Principles on Business and Human Rights: Implementing the United Nations "Protect, Respect and Remedy" Framework' (21 March 2011) UN Doc A/HRC/17/31 ('the Ruggie Principles').
6   Vienna Convention on the Law of Treaties (adopted 23 May 1969, entered into force 27 January 1980) 1155 UNTS 331, Article 27.

- Limitation periods (the time within which a claim may be brought, at the expiration of which that right is extinguished) may be so short as to preclude in practice the preparation and filing of a claim.
- Foreign rules on forced heirship (a system common in civil law jurisdictions whereby heirs have a fixed entitlement to the property of the deceased, regardless of the deceased's preferences to the contrary) are dis-applied.
- Domestic remedies relating to fraudulent transfers (the transfer of property into a structure which either intentionally defeats or is deemed in law to defeat the interests of legitimate creditors and other claimants) are dis-applied.
- The structure may be aggressively asset protective, and assets held within it may not be capable of being alienated or passed by bankruptcy, insolvency or liquidation; or liable to be seized, sold, attached, or otherwise taken in execution by process of law.
- A structure may be an 'orphan' with no beneficial owner, in law or in equity.
- The requirement to place details of the structure, its existence, its finances, and its activities in the public domain (in the form of a publicly accessible register) may be minimal or entirely absent.
- Structures which under generally accepted legal principles have a limited life span (such as private trusts) may be given perpetual existence.
- Fiduciary responsibilities of those administering or managing structures – be they directors, trustees or any other responsible officer – may be dis-applied, or, if applied, those otherwise responsible may, through a combination of manipulated limitation periods and indulgences, be deemed not culpable, or culpable but absolved.
- The structure may take a form unknown under generally accepted legal principles, or may have the power to shape-shift.

The structures

Structures may be corporate in nature, having a legal personality separate from that of their participants, or may be relationship based, such as the interaction between settlors, trustees and beneficiaries. In the tax havens these distinctions become blurred. Elements essential to the creation and sustainability of structures – members of corporations, beneficiaries of trusts – may be eliminated. What results are structures best described as chimera: they sit inside the body of law by which they are ostensibly identified and to which apparently they belong, but share none of its DNA. When is a company not a company? When is a trust not a trust? And what possible social purpose could such chimera serve within those jurisdictions? The answer is that there is no domestic social benefit, other than foreign earnings generated by their tax haven service providers. Many of the structures have been commissioned by tax haven governments to provide them with a competitive edge in attracting those customers for whom privacy, secrecy, or (dropping the jaded euphemisms) accountability avoidance is a priority.[7]

This chapter samples some of those tax haven structures, showing how the generic form has been mutated to meet market needs:[8]

- Generic corporations
  - Nominee directors, nominee shareholders
  - Absence of information on public record – Seychelles IBC
  - Bahamas Executive Entities
- Generic trusts
  - Charitable trusts
  - Non-charitable purpose trusts
    - ○ Isle of Man Purpose Trusts
  - Cayman STAR Trusts
  - BVI VISTA Trusts
- Foundations
  - Liechtenstein Private Benefit Foundation
  - Panama Private Foundation
  - Nevis Multiform Foundation

Generic corporations

A corporation can take a number of forms – public or private, limited by shares or by guarantee (or by both), with directors or (in the case of a limited liability company – LLC) without. The key in all cases is that the corporation has a legal personality which is separate from its members. Also key, in general terms, is that the property held by a corporation is owned by that corporation, and is not held directly by the members of the corporation – it is the simplest of concepts: the members own the company; the company owns the assets. Corporations owe their existence to the state and this fact alone has in the context of international human rights spawned a vast literature and body of soft law on what standards of corporate governance must be applied in order that a corporation, bound by proxy as it were to observe the human rights obligations of the state which has enacted the legislation which creates it and which by not repealing that legislation sustains it, is not used as a vehicle of abuse.[9]

---

7   For a review of tax haven structures from the perspective of taxation and globalisation, see Ronen Palan, Richard Murphy, and Christian Chavagneux, *Tax Havens: How Globalization Really Works* (Cornell University Press, 2010), ch 3.

8   See Appendix 1 for an example of a generic offshore archetype.

9   See the 'Ruggie Principles' (n 5). United Nations Economic and Social Council, 'Statement on the Obligations of States Parties Regarding the Corporate Sector and Economic, Social and Cultural Rights' (12 July 2011) UN Doc E/C.12/2011/1; UNCE-SCR, 'General Comment: Business Activities' (n 4); Nadia Bernaz, *Business and Human Rights: History, Law and Policy – Bridging the Accountability Gap* (Routledge, 2017), ch 7 'International Soft Law Initiatives on Business and Human Rights'.

This chapter is focused more narrowly on the ways in which tax havens manipulate the generic corporate structure to promote concealment.[10] The dangers are compounded by the sheer volume of companies formed within, or formed elsewhere but managed and controlled within, the tax havens. Motivated by a combination of the need for low taxation, for privacy (or concealment), for local legitimacy of the structures, thousands upon thousands seek to use corporate structures in and from the tax havens.[11]

Nominee directors, nominee shareholders

The simplest form of concealment is to employ nominee shareholders and nominee directors of corporations.[12] It is a strategy widely used and, until

10   It must however not be overlooked that unaccountability and a lack of oversight in the matter of company formation is by no means exclusive to the tax havens. See Tom Bergin and Stephen Grey, 'Insight – How UK Company Formation Agents Fuel Fraud' *Reuters* (United Kingdom, 18 March 2016) <http://uk.reuters.com/article/uk-regulations-agents-insight-idUKKCN0WK17W> accessed 16 April 2017. This has ostensibly been addressed in the UK with effect from 30 June 2016 by the introduction of the Register of People with Significant Control. United Kingdom Government, Department for Business, Innovation & Skills, '"People with Significant Control" Companies House Register Goes Live' (*gov.uk*, 30 June 2016) <www.gov.uk/government/news/people-with-significant-control-companies-house-register-goes-live> accessed 16 April 2017; United Kingdom Government, Companies House, 'Summary Guide for Companies – Register of People with Significant Control' (*gov.uk*, 27 January 2016) <www.gov.uk/government/publications/guidance-to-the-people-with-significant-control-requirements-for-companies-and-li mited-liability-partnerships> accessed 16 April 2017.The full statutory guidance takes no account of the tax haven technique of separating ownership and control, or of avoiding beneficial ownership altogether: United Kingdom Government, Department for Business, Innovation & Skills, 'Statutory Guidance on the Meaning of "Significant Influence or Control" over Companies in the Context of the Register of People with Significant Control' (*gov.uk*, 14 April 2016) <www.gov.uk/government/uploads/system/uploads/attachment_data/file/523120/PSC_statutory_guidance_companies.pdf> accessed 16 April 2017.
11   See Appendix 2. Though the tide may be turning. Eg The British Virgin Islands. On 19 January 2017 bvinews.com reported that company incorporation dropped 35% in the third quarter of 2016 compared to the corresponding quarter in 2015. In his Budget speech on 16 January 2017, BVI Premier and Finance Minister Dr D Orlando Smith said: 'We are currently facing some headwinds in our financial services sector, and we need to retool', blaming 'global regulatory challenges, new restrictive banking practices, negative media and perceptions'. Aspects of internationally acknowledged standards of corporate governance did not feature in the debate. BVI News Online, 'More Bad News for Financial Services: 35% Drop' (*bvinews.com*, 19 January 2017) <http://bvinews.com/new/more-bad-news-for-financial-services-35-drop> accessed 16 April 2017.
12   David Leigh, Harold Frayman and James Ball, 'How the Nominee Trick Works' *ICIJ* (Washington DC, 25 November 2012) <www.icij.org/offshore/how-nominee-trick-done> accessed 16 April 2017. An indication of the potential scale of the nominee business was shown in a joint investigation by the ICIJ, the BBC and The Guardian newspaper (UK) in 2012, which unmasked 28 nominee directors who between them held more than 21,500 directorships: David Leigh, Harold Frayman and James Ball, 'Front Men Disguise

recent years with the growing awareness of drug trafficking and international terrorism, had not aroused significant interest.[13]

A simple company limited by shares is controlled by its directors who are answerable to the shareholders. The shareholders as such do not take part in the day-to-day management and control of the company. They have the right to vote in general meetings of the company, and the extent to which their consent is required, if at all, to proposed management decisions, will be set out in the company's constitutional documents. The issue is not therefore one of undue empowerment of shareholders through the use of nominees, but of the inability of any third party accurately to position the company within a wider framework. If, in addition to there being nominee shareholders in place, the directors are themselves de facto (when not de juris) nominees the problem is compounded. Those truly pulling the strings are invisible and seemingly inviolable. Corporate responsibility becomes opaque, and the cross-border activities of such companies as potential members of a network of similar institutions under common ownership cannot be successfully investigated:[14] 'Currently, we regulate the birth certificates of people far more closely than the birth certificates of companies'.[15]

Statutory checks on money laundering, drug trafficking and anti-terrorism[16] are fine and necessary in themselves, but from an international human rights perspective the inability of those who in practical terms only nominally manage and control trading companies to influence in any meaningful way the activities of those companies is an open door to human rights abuse. Financial services regulators may try to stem the tide (for example, the Isle of Man Government Financial Services Authority[17] has ultimate authority over those who administer companies, requires them to have more than a

the Offshore Game's Real Players' *ICIJ* (Washington DC) <www.icij.org/front-men-disguise-offshore-players> accessed 16 April 2017. See also Gerard Ryle and Stefan Candea, 'Faux Corporate Directors Stand in for Fraudsters, Despots and Spies' *ICIJ* (Washington DC, 4 July 2013) <www.icij.org/offshore/faux-corporate-directors-stand-fraudsters-despots-and-spies> accessed 16 April 2017.

13   See Chapter 3 for the critique by the G20 of this planning in its High-Level Principles on Beneficial Ownership Transparency.

14   See Chapter 3 for a fuller discussion on beneficial ownership avoidance.

15   Paul Collier, 'In Pursuit of the $21 Trillion' [2013] *Prospect Magazine* www.prospect-magazine.co.uk (article no longer available online).

16   For example, see the Anti-Money Laundering and Countering the Financing of Terrorism Requirements Guidance issued by the Isle of Man Government Financial Services Authority, 'AML/CFT Requirements and Guidance' (*The Isle of Man Financial Services Authority*) <www.iomfsa.im/handbooks/guides/AML/amlcftrequirementsguidance.xml> accessed 16 April 2017 and Cayman Islands Monetary Authority, 'Guidance Notes on the Prevention and Detection of Money Laundering and Terrorist Financing in the Cayman Islands' (*Cayman Islands Monetary Authority*) <www.cimoney.com.ky/AML_CFT/aml_cft.aspx?id=144> accessed 16 April 2017.

17   Isle of Man Financial Services Authority, 'www.iomfsa.im' (*Isle of Man Financial Services Authority*) <www.iomfsa.im> accessed 16 April 2017.

working knowledge of such companies' activities,[18] and seeks to limit the number of directorships which any one person may hold), but in practice there are not enough hours in the day – in a lifetime – for those holding multiple directorships to be made and kept fully aware of each company's trading activities.

Absence of information on public record – Seychelles IBC

Many tax havens have very loose public filing requirements for companies (an extreme example being the Principality of Liechtenstein, which has no companies registry at all[19]), and the Seychelles International Business Company ('Seychelles IBC') serves as an example. Seychelles IBCs originated in 1994[20] and are now governed by the International Business Companies Act 2016.[21]

The Seychelles IBC has very wide trading powers, which it need not specify, though is not permitted to trade within the Seychelles itself. Neither meetings of members nor board meetings of directors are required. The use of nominee shareholders is common. Its accounts are not publicly filed, and there is no audit requirement. Details of directors and shareholders are maintained by the company itself, but these are neither available for public access nor filed publicly. There is no 'annual return' (an annual report commonly found in mainstream jurisdictions, filed at the relevant companies registry, which provides details of officers and members). There is no requirement to file publicly details of any mortgages or charges against the company. The Seychelles IBC is wholly exempt from taxation in the Seychelles.

The Seychelles IBC is therefore typical of the opacity afforded to many corporate forms in the tax havens, concealing purpose, governance, ownership, financial and accounting status, and, above all, accountability.

---

18   Financial Services Act 2008<https://legislation.gov.im/cms/images/LEGISLATION/PRINCIPAL/2008/2008-0008/FinancialServicesAct2008_8.pdf> accessed 16 April 2017; Isle of Man Financial Services Authority, 'Financial Services Rule Book' (2016) <www.iomfsa.im/lib/docs/iomfsa/consultations/financialservicesrulebook20131.pdf> accessed 16 April 2017.

19   Liechtenstein Chamber of Commerce and Industry, 'Commercial Registry' (*Liechtenstein Chamber of Commerce and Industry*, 15 September 2015) <www.lihk.li/CFDOCS/cms/cmsout/index.cfm?u=1&GroupID=20&meID=75> accessed 16 April 2017.

20   International Business Companies Act 1994 (repealed).

21   <www.seylii.org/sc/legislation/act/2016/15> accessed 23 April 2017. Since 1994 it is estimated that the Seychelles has registered around 180,000 IBCs, with over 18,000 in 2015 alone. The Seychelles IBC is ranked fourth in the global tax-exempt company market (the first three rankings being the US State of Delaware, the British Virgin Islands and the Republic of Panama. See Peter Burian, 'Seychelles: Beating the Odds' [2016] *Offshore Investment* <www.offshoreinvestment.com/seychelles-beating-the-odds-archive> accessed 17 April 2017 (subscription service only).

Bahamas Executive Entities

Bahamas Executive Entities ('BEE') are a bizarre, artificial creation, unique to the Bahamas, the design of which was commissioned by the Bahamian Government from leading London lawyers in 2010 to fill what the Government believed to be a gap in the offshore products market.[22]

BEEs were introduced under The Executive Entities Act 2011,[23] with the intention of facilitating the establishment, operation, management, and termination of a new private wealth structure. A BEE is defined as 'a legal person established by a Charter to perform only executive functions and registered in accordance with the Act' and is 'able to sue and be sued in its own name'.

The BEE is therefore simply a vehicle to carry out executive functions, primarily in wealth and asset holding structures. Executive Functions are defined in s 2 as:

> any powers and duties of an executive, administrative, supervisory, fiduciary and office holding nature including, but not limited to, the powers and duties of –
> (i) an enforcer, protector, trustee, investment advisor and the holder of any other office of any trust, and
> (ii) the holder of any office of any legal person;
> the ownership, management and holding of (i) executive entity assets; and (ii) trust assets.

The BEE is created by a founder, and may have officers and a supervisory council. It has unlimited capacity and is of perpetual existence.

No estate, inheritance, succession or gift tax, rate, duty, levy, or other charge is payable by a founder or any other person with respect to any interest given to or received from a BEE. The BEE is statutorily immune to foreign forced heirship rights, challenges to fraudulent dispositions, or the application reciprocally of foreign judgments.

In practice this means that if assets have been transferred into the ownership of a BEE, the validity of that transfer cannot be challenged. This opens the possibility that anyone seeking to avoid their accountability for an international human rights breach – including breaches of corporate governance

---

22 Danielle Levy, 'Lawrence Graham Seeks to Revolutionise Offshore Trust Structures' (*Citywire*, 23 April 2010) <http://citywire.co.uk/wealth-manager/news/lawrence-graham-seeks-to-revolutionise-offshore-trust-structures/a395505/print?section=wealth-manager> accessed 17 April 2017.

23 <http://laws.bahamas.gov.bs/cms/images/LEGISLATION/PRINCIPAL/2011/2011-0052/ExecutiveEntitiesAct2011_1.pdf> accessed 23 April 2017, together with the Executive Entities Regulations 2012, SI 13 of 2012 <http://laws.bahamas.gov.bs/cms/images/LEGISLATION/SUBORDINATE/2012/2012-0013/ExecutiveEntities_Regulations2012_1.pdf> accessed 23 April 2017.

standards on the Ruggie Principles[24] – has a clear home run: the transfer may clearly have been made with the express intent to defraud a known or ascertainable creditor (the victims of the breach) by denuding the abuser of substantial assets, but no foreign judgment upholding a claim brought on this ground will have any effect on the BEE in the Bahamas, and no claim based on a fraudulent transfer can be brought against the BEE in the Bahamas courts.[25]

Fundamentally, from a human rights accountability perspective, a BEE is an 'orphan' structure: there are no shareholders or members of any kind, and no beneficiaries. It is the corporate equivalent of the non-charitable purpose trust.

Generic trusts

Trusts are a long-established vehicle in common law jurisdictions and approximate roughly to foundations under civil law. They are a means whereby funds can be alienated by a donor, held by persons whom the donor trusts to deal with them fairly and responsibly, for the benefit of named individuals (or for charitable purposes). A simple discretionary trust is a triangular structure, the three points being the donor (or 'settlor/grantor'), the trustees themselves, and the beneficiaries for whom the trustees hold the assets. The trustees do not themselves benefit from the funds placed in the trust by the donor.[26] The beneficiaries do not 'own' the trust funds, but they do have a right to be considered as and when the trustees exercise their discretion whether or not to make payments from the trust fund to any one of them. Trusts are not required to be publicly registered, and all details remain confidential.[27] Taking advantage of the division in common law

24   (n 5).
25   This sits uneasily with the role of the Bahamas as a founding member in June 2015 of the Association of Integrity Commissions and Anti-Corruption Bodies in the Commonwealth Caribbean (the other members being Antigua and Barbuda, Barbados, Belize, Dominica, Grenada, Guyana, Jamaica, Saint Lucia, St Kitts and Nevis, St Vincent and the Grenadines, and Trinidad and Tobago) The Commonwealth, 'Caribbean Integrity Commissions Form New Commonwealth Body to Fight Corruption' (*The Commonwealth*, 25 June 2015) <https://shar.es/1QVznK> accessed 17 April 2017; and see Bruce Zagaris, 'Changes in International Regulatory Regimes on Caribbean Corporate, Financial Regulatory and Transparency Law' (2016) 263 *Offshore Investment* <www.offshoreinvestment.com/ changes-in-international-regulatory-regimes-on-caribbean-corporate-financial-regulatory-and-transparency-law> accessed 17 April 2017 (subscription only service).
26   Though they may receive a fee for their work.
27   A further refinement common in tax haven trusts is that the name of the Settlor/Grantor does not appear in the trust deed itself. The trust takes the form of a 'declaration' whereby the Trustees state that they hold and have held the trust fund since a given date. The identity of the settlor remains confidential to them. In the hands of less scrupulous trust practitioners, a sham settlor may be used – truly the settlor of a trust having on its face trust funds of, say, $100, but not the source of the bulk of the after-settled trust fund. This device is also common in the case of Foundations where the Founder is in many cases a service provider acting as a man of straw.

jurisdictions between legal ownership (in simple terms, the name on the property) and equitable ownership (those entitled to benefit from the property), individuals using trusts can alienate property rights and distance themselves from creditors[28] and transfer responsibility for the management of the property to the trustees.

Arguments for the registration of trusts continue to be put forward, which would at least aid in initial identification of their existence even if the substantive details of the trust themselves were to remain confidential, but there appears globally to be an absence of political will not merely to overcome the difficulties of forcing those in a private, equitable relationship (the settlor and the trustees, together with any beneficiaries) to place this on public record but also how to determine (and enforce) what information such registers should contain.[29]

In the tax havens, this long-established trust device has morphed into many artificial forms, some of which – for example, the non-charitable purpose trusts which have no beneficiaries of any kind – are wholly counter-intuitive. The driving force behind the populating of this legal freak show has, as with the re-engineering of corporate forms, been the desire for secrecy (more euphemistically characterised as an assertion of privacy rights) and the avoidance – or outright evasion – of taxation. But the collateral effect has been a rupture in the accountability which is fundamental to the operation of the international human rights continuum.[30]

Charitable trusts

On the face of it, a trust for charitable purposes offers little scope for concealment. The literature on charitable trusts is extensive, and a detailed consideration of them is outside the scope of this work. The Isle of Man serves as an illustration.

The technical and artificial meaning attached under English law to the words 'charity' and 'charitable' do not apply under Isle of Man law, which is

---

28   A number of tax haven structures specifically exclude the rights of creditors who would otherwise be in a position to bring an action in respect of fraudulent transfers (eg the Nevis Multiform Foundation). In others, this right of action is not extinguished. In the Isle of Man, for example, the principle that a transfer made with the intention of defeating a just creditor (ie a current debtor or a debt falling due on a known future date) is void and of no effect became hard law under the Fraudulent Assignments Act 1736 <www.legislation.gov.im/cms/images/LEGISLATION/PRINCIPAL/1736/1736-0002/FraudulentAssignmentsAct1736_1.pdf> accessed 23 April 2017 (the Act remains in full force and effect today).

29   See Andres Knobel, 'The Case for Registering Trusts – and How to Do It' (*The Tax Justice Network*) <www.taxjustice.net/wp-content/uploads/2013/04/Registration-of-Trusts_AK.pdf> accessed 17 April 2017.

30   In a fiscal context, see Andres Knobel (edited by Nicholas Shaxson), 'Trusts: Weapons of Mass Injustice?' (13 February 2017) <www.taxjustice.net/wp-content/uploads/2017/02/Trusts-Weapons-of-Mass-Injustice-Final-12-FEB-2017.pdf> accessed 17 April 2017.

more liberal 'and in any event not narrower' than that of England:[31] never-theless, a clear charitable intention is necessary, and in this regard English, Scottish and Irish cases are treated by Isle of Man courts as guides to those courts in deciding what is charitable.[32]

Charitable status may be obtained by trusts, companies and foundations. However, regard must be had to the provisions of the Charities Registration Act 1989[33] which provides that any institution which in the Isle of Man takes or uses any name, style, title, or description implying or otherwise pretend-ing that it is a charity, or which holds itself out as a charity, is guilty of an offence unless it files a statement in the prescribed form at the General Registry in the Isle of Man.[34] The Chief Registrar has the power to refuse the filing if he is of the opinion that the institution is not established for charita-ble purposes, does not have a substantial connection with the Isle of Man, or has a name which is undesirable or misleading.[35]

These hurdles once overcome, should the donor of the charitable trust choose at the outset that the trust is to be revocable,[36] the property in the trust is alienated only for its duration. The unscrupulous may make merely token distributions within the Isle of Man, in order to maintain a real connection and hence registration, while preserving the bulk of the charita-ble trust fund for ultimate return to the donor upon its being revoked. This pattern of potential abuse is in no way unique to the Isle of Man.

The potential to 'warehouse' assets in plain sight within a socially worthy medium, only later to have them 'returned to sender' represents accounta-bility avoidance in its purest form.

Non-charitable purpose trusts[37]

The non-charitable purpose trust (NCPT) takes concealment to a new and dangerous level, by not simply hiding the identity of a beneficial owner, but by abolishing the concept of beneficial ownership altogether.

Traditionally, a trust in which the beneficiaries could not be clearly iden-tified, or for purposes which were not charitable (and so capable of benefitting persons identified not by name but by classification), would be void. The NCPT takes the triangle and cuts off the third corner.

---

31   *Costain, Re* (1961) 1961–71 MLR 1, 7 (Deemster Kneale).
32   *Ring, Re* (1962) 1961–71 MLR 60, 66 (Deemster Kneale).
33   <www.legislation.gov.im/cms/images/LEGISLATION/PRINCIPAL/1989/1989-0011/CharitiesRegistrationAct1989_1.pdf> accessed 23 April 2017.
34   s 1.
35   s 3(1).
36   Assuming this is not regarded by the Chief Registrar or by HM Attorney General in the Isle of Man as a bar in itself to charitable status (ss 3–4).
37   See Chapter 3 'Beneficial Ownership Avoidance' for a fuller treatment of this topic.

At common law, a non-charitable purpose trust would be void for want of identifiable beneficiaries to enforce it and for breach of the rule against perpetuities.

NCPTs are now available worldwide in both offshore and onshore jurisdictions under legislation which bears a universal similarity.[38]

ISLE OF MAN PURPOSE TRUST[39]

In the Isle of Man, NCPTs are among the longest established. The Purpose Trusts Act 1996[40] provides for the creation of NCPTs. The purpose must be certain, reasonable and possible; and must not be unlawful, contrary to public policy or immoral.[41]

The following are *not* capable of being regarded as NCPTs:

- those made for the benefit of a particular person (whether or not immediately ascertainable);
- those made for the benefit of some aggregate of persons identified by reference to some personal relationship; or
- those made for charitable purposes.

The purpose of the trust itself is not the issue: anything lawful, compatible with public policy, and moral will suffice. The purpose may be – and most often is – simply to hold the shares in a company. The issue is that *there are no beneficiaries*. It is not simply that individuals do not 'own' the trust fund but would have the right to be considered eligible for distributions to be made to them. There is no one who owns the trust fund. For the duration of the NCPT,[42] although the legal title to the assets in the trust is held in the names of the trustees, there is no beneficial owner. Non-charitable purpose trusts under the Purpose Trusts Act 1996 have the following characteristics:

- The trust must be created by deed or by a will which is capable of being, and which is, admitted to probate in the Isle of Man (or in the alternative in respect of which letters of administration are capable of being and are granted) (s1(1)(b)).
- There must be two or more trustees, of whom at least one must be a person falling to one of the categories designated under the Act: an

---

38 See Appendix 3.
39 For a review of NCPTs and beneficial ownership avoidance, see Chapter 3.
40 <www.legislation.gov.im/cms/images/LEGISLATION/PRINCIPAL/1996/1996-0009/PurposeTrustsAct1996_1.pdf> accessed 23 April 2017.
41 s 1(1)(a).
42 A maximum of 80 years – s 1(1).

Advocate, a foreign registered legal practitioner, a qualified auditor, a member of the Chartered Institute of Management Accountants, a member of the Institute of Chartered Secretaries and Administrators, a fellow or associate member of the Institute of Bankers, or a trust corporation (ss 1(1)(c) and 9(1)).

- To enforce the trust there must be an 'enforcer'. The trust instrument must provide for the enforcer to have an absolute right of access to any information or document which relates to the trust, the assets of the trust or to the administration of the trust (ss 1(1)(d)(i) and 1(1)(e)).
- The trust instrument must specify the event upon the happening of which the trust terminates and must provide for the disposition of surplus assets of the trust upon its termination (s 1(1)(f)).
- The designated person must keep a copy of the trust (including supplemental instruments), a register (specifying the creator of the trust, its purpose and the details of the enforcer), and trust accounts. These accounts are to be open to inspection by the Attorney General (or anyone authorised by the Attorney General). Public inspection is, however, not required (s2).
- Should the enforcer die or become incapable, the Attorney General must be informed, and he may apply to the High Court of Justice of the Isle of Man to appoint a successor (s 3).
- No land or any interest in land in the Isle of Man may be held, directly or indirectly, in a purpose trust (s 5).

At the end of the trust period, the trust funds, which is now regarded no longer as a trust fund (because the trust has terminated) but as surplus assets, pass to an individual or institution ('the recipient of surplus') who is either named in the purpose trust deed or who can be identified through the use of a formula.

This opens up various planning possibilities, including:

- Holding shares in a company which can then be voted in accordance with the terms of the trust (of particular importance in circumstances where an individual may not wish beneficially to own such assets).
- Protection of subsidiaries where a parent company borrows – the shares of the subsidiary are placed in trust until the loan is repaid, thereby protecting the subsidiary from creditors of its parent.
- Protection of the lender where a parent company borrows – the shares of the subsidiary can be placed in trust until the loan is repaid, thereby preventing the ownership of the subsidiary from changing.
- Capital financing and securitisation projects in which the trust assets are off the balance sheet of one or more parties to the transaction.

The practical effect is substantial. It is common to find that the entire issued share capital in a company, 'ABC Limited', is held in a NCPT. *ABC Limited therefore has no beneficial owner while the NCPT is in existence.*[43] The recipient of surplus may be the very company ('Parent Limited') of which ABC Limited would have been a subsidiary, but which Parent Limited prefers to keep off balance sheet. Investigating the books of Parent Limited during the life of the purpose trust will give no indication whatsoever of the existence of ABC Limited. Yet ABC Limited is destined to become the property of Parent Limited. Until that time, Parent Limited has no legal responsibility for the good governance of, or any economic connection with, ABC Limited.

A common use of ABC Limited would be to place under its ownership hazardous assets, such as bulk cargo tankers or brown field, toxic development sites; or politically sensitive projects such as mining or rain forest development: ABC Limited has by its very nature limited liability, and apart from the assets which it holds has no means to satisfy any claims which could be brought against it. Parent Limited, which will ultimately benefit from any profits and capital gains made by ABC Limited, remains wholly invisible and inviolate throughout.

Cayman STAR Trusts

Cayman STAR Trusts derive their name from the Special Trusts (Alternative Regime) Law 1997, now replaced by Part VIII Trusts Law (2011 Revision)[44] as amended by the Trusts (Amendment) Law 2016 with effect from 24 October 2016,[45] which introduced the concept of private purpose trusts into a jurisdiction which up to that point recognised trusts only for beneficiaries or for charitable purposes, drawing its strength from English common law.

It is another example of an artificial construction – no doubt justified locally as an evolutionary step – to serve the demands of the burgeoning Cayman finance and fiduciaries industries and to provide what is perceived to be a competitive edge.

The Cayman STAR Trust shares many of the characteristics of a noncharitable purpose trust, save that beneficiaries are possible. There is no

---

43 The initiative taken by the United Kingdom Government under the Small Business Enterprise and Employment Act 2015 [<www.legislation.gov.uk/ukpga/2015/26/contents> accessed 23 April 2017] to establish a register of people with significant control would be wholly thwarted by this. United Kingdom Government, Companies House, 'Keeping Your People with Significant Control (PSC) Register' (*gov.uk*, 6 April 2016) <www.gov.uk/government/news/keeping-your-people-with-significant-control-psc-register> accessed 17 April 2017.

44 <https://laws-in-force.judicial.ky/WebSearchFileView.aspx?fileView=T\Trusts Law (2011 Revision).pdf and https://laws-in-force.judicial.ky/WebSearchFileView.aspx?fileView= T\Trusts (Amendment) Law, 2016.PDF> accessed 23 April 2017 (subscription only website).

45 Access to Cayman Islands legislation and to the decisions of its Courts is obtainable on subscription from Cayman Islands Judicial Administration <www.judicial.ky> accessed 17 April 2017.

limitation on the number of beneficiaries or of purposes (whether charitable or not). One such purpose can be wholly self-referring: the preservation of the trust assets. The trust is enforced by an Enforcer – again a similarity with the non-charitable purpose trust – to the exclusion, however, of any rights in equity of the beneficiaries themselves to seek to enforce its terms, to have information concerning the trust disclosed to them, or to challenge the trust in any way. The Cayman STAR Trust is, if desired, perpetual, and because it is open to constant re-interpretation by the trustees (with or without Court assistance) it can never fail or be held void ab initio for perceived uncertainty.

The beneficiaries will have a right to be considered by the trustees for a distribution, but have no means to enforce this – men and women of straw in any human rights enforcement action seeking to attach trust assets. The Enforcer has no proprietary rights, in law or in equity, in the trust assets and exists merely to monitor decisions of the trustees the parameters of which they themselves have set.

In terms of accountability therefore, the settlor of a Cayman STAR Trust can warehouse assets within the trust for any purpose, and section off assets for beneficiaries who have no means of influencing the administration of the trust; generation following generation. Those assets held for a purpose will have no beneficial owner in any sense of the words and in addition will, from a corporate perspective, be 'off balance sheet'. In consequence, they will be completely un-attachable. As there is no requirement for Cayman STAR Trusts to be registered publicly, even their very existence is concealed.

The Cayman STAR Trust may hold shares in a private trust company (that is, a company established solely to act as trustee of a particular trust), and it is not beyond the bounds of imagination that this itself may be the trustee of a non-charitable purpose trust. Thus is the ownerless itself made ownerless, ad infinitum.

BVI VISTA Trusts

The VISTA[46] trust is created and subject to the Virgin Islands Special Trusts Act 2003, as amended most recently in 2013.[47] It is a creation of statute, unique to the BVI, and hence not naturally occurring in any accepted body of trust law. Specifically designed for, and confined to, the holding of company shares, it has therefore the chimeric qualities of many of these genetically engineered tax haven structures.

It is a long-established principle of trust law that a trustee is under a duty of care and must act prudently when making decisions concerning the assets

---

46 VISTA is simply the acronym for the Act.
47 Virgin Islands Special Trusts Act 2003 <www.bvifsc.vg/Portals/2/Virgin%20 Islands%20Special%20Trusts%20Act,%202003.pdf> accessed 23 April 2017 and Virgin Islands Special Trusts (Amendment) Act 2013 <www.bvifsc.vg/Portals/2/Virgin%20 Islands%20Special%20Trusts%20(Amendment)%20Act,%202013.pdf> accessed 23 April 2017.

in a trust fund.[48] In the case of trustees holding shares in a company, their duty to act as prudent businesspersons is paramount: speculative, bordering on reckless, behaviour by trustee shareholders is a breach of their fiduciary duty. Similarly, speculative or reckless conduct on the part of the directors of the company, who have its management and control, can be monitored by the trustee shareholders and reined in when felt not to be in the best commercial interests of the company or of its stakeholders. Those stakeholders include not only the shareholders themselves, but also the likes of creditors, suppliers, and the company's customer base (not forgetting overriding principles of good corporate governance).

In the case of a VISTA trust, this principle is dis-applied. It is a form of trust for holding shares in companies where it is intended that the shares will be held indefinitely, and the trustee is not intended, other than in special and defined circumstances, to intervene in the conduct of the affairs of the underlying company or companies. The trustees as shareholders, regardless of any countervailing provisions of BVI company law (as VISTA applies only to BVI companies), have no management responsibility, leaving the directors with unconstrained authority. The trustees have a statutory duty to retain the shares. Even the appointment of directors is limited by 'office of director' rules contained in the trust deed which specify how the trustee shareholders must exercise their votes in respect of the appointment, removal, and remuneration of directors. All authority is therefore vested in the directors.

The shareholder trustees have no fiduciary duty in relation to the assets or affairs of the company.[49] Though the VISTA trust is permitted only to hold shares in a BVI company and no other assets, there is no restriction on the assets which the BVI company itself may hold; which may of course include shares in non-BVI companies.

For a period of up to 20 years, the trustees are denied the right under the long-established common law rule in *Saunders v Vautier* 1841[50] to vary or terminate the trust.[51]

---

48   In some jurisdictions this equitable principle has been enshrined as a statutory duty of care: Trustee Act 2000 (United Kingdom) <www.legislation.gov.uk/ukpga/2000/29/contents> accessed 23 April 2017, pt 1; Trustee Act 2001 (Isle of Man) <https://legislation.gov.im/cms/images/LEGISLATION/PRINCIPAL/2001/2001-0018/TrusteeAct2001_1.pdf> accessed 23 April 2017, pt 1.

49   In one jurisdiction, the Isle of Man, the rule is diametrically opposed to this. The position of creditors in relation to assets owned by a company that is itself wholly owned by a trust is subject to the *corporate-trust fusion principle* established on 19 September 2002 in *Re Poyiadjis* 2001–03 MLR 316. Under the corporate-trust fusion principle where trustees hold 100% of the issued share capital in a company, and may even themselves be the directors of that company, their fiduciary responsibility in relation to the shares extends to the company's own assets, requiring that those assets be dealt with as if directly held in the trust itself.

50   [1841] EWHC J82, [1841] 4 Beav 115.

51   Exceptionally, if an 'interested person' (eg a beneficiary) calls upon the VISTA trustee to intervene in the company's affairs, then the trustee must do so if the interested person has a 'permitted ground of complaint' which must be specified in the trust instrument.

No trust deed under BVI law is subject to public registration.

One of the marketing advantages claimed for the VISTA trust is the creation of blind trusts for politicians, who can thereby distance themselves from the companies in which they have a financial interest and easily refute accusations that they abuse their position of influence.

In terms of human rights accountability, this claimed advantage is pernicious. Any entity or individual which or who but for the VISTA trust would hold shares directly in a human rights abusive corporation remains with clean hands throughout and will be wholly absolved from responsibility in the company's affairs as only the directors are empowered.

Foundations

Foundations, once in offshore terms the preserve of Liechtenstein (Stiftungen), are now available globally, and what was originally the preserve of civil law is now a form recognised by and promoted within common law jurisdictions.[52]

Unlike a trust, which has no legal personality of its own (a trust exists in the relationship between the settlor, trustees and beneficiaries) a foundation is a legal entity, with the capacity – like a corporation – to govern itself. Unlike a corporation, it has no shareholders or other form of participation, but, in common with a trust, has beneficiaries. It is an 'orphan' structure.

As a state creation, a foundation registers its creation with that state, though in many cases the register is not available for public inspection, or merely to the extent that the name of the foundation is accessible.

As with a trust, a foundation exists in order to hold a fund, which can comprise any form of property. A foundation itself does not trade, but by holding shares in trading entities this limitation is of no practical effect. The assets transferred to a foundation may come from any person, and not merely the founder identified in the constitutional documents of the foundation itself. This is reflected in the fact that it is very common for the founder to be a professional fiduciary.

The purpose of the foundation is contained in its constitution. It is common for the founder to have powers reserved under which the founder can amend the purpose and amend the identity (or percentage entitlement) of the beneficiaries, in much the same way as the objects of a company and the rights attaching to its shares can be mutated over time. Entitlement to benefit can therefore pass from group to group, each supplanting its predecessor, and prominence may be given to a particular individual, wholly secretly.

Unlike a trust, which is open to attack as a sham – on the basis that the settlor did not have a true intent to create it, that those intended to benefit

52 See Appendix 4.

and the funds to be settled are insufficiently identified (the 'three certainties'), the existence and validity of a foundation once registered is beyond challenge. Because the founder has in many jurisdiction wide powers in relation to the administration of the foundation and of disposition, the difficulty often encountered by over-zealous and possessive settlors of trusts, who while acquiescing in the transfer of assets to trustees nevertheless seek still to control those assets (which eliminates one of the three certainties and fatally wounds the trust), is entirely absent.

The more common uses of foundations (and the motivations for using foundations) relevant to human rights abuse include tax and estate planning, asset protection planning, maintenance of corporate control, assistance to charities, separation of voting and economic benefits in investment holding companies, ownership of private trust companies, operation of employee share option schemes and holding assets off-balance sheet.

Liechtenstein Private Benefit Foundation

The Liechtenstein Foundation, the archetype upon which all later foundation laws have been based and by the degree of their divergence from which archetype the radicalisation of this offshore structure can be assessed, are created under Personen und Gesellschaftsrecht 1926 as most recently amended (the new foundations law) by the Stiftungs Gesetz 2009.[53]

A private-benefit foundation may be purely to benefit a family, or may be in a mixed form which serves both the family and other charitable and non-charitable purposes. The foundation itself cannot in general terms trade, but may hold the shares in a trading company – and as such is then designated a holding foundation. The minimum foundation capital is 30,000 euros, Swiss francs or US dollars.

In the case of private benefit foundations, registration is not required – the foundation has legal personality upon being established. All that is required of the foundation is that it give notice of its formation – its name and purpose, details of its Liechtenstein-based registered agent and the identity of the members of the foundation council (the body which administers and represents the foundation). No beneficiary details need be notified. Nothing held at the Liechtenstein Land and Public Register Office is made available to the public: all that it is permitted to reveal to third parties is that the unregistered foundation exists.

---

53 LGBl. 2008 no 220 <www.gesetze.li> accessed 23 April 2017 (Further amended, but not germane to this topic, by the Gesetz vom 1. Dezember 2016 über die Abänderung des Personen- und Gesellschaftsrechts). For a useful overview see Marxer & Partner Rechtsanwälte, 'The Liechtenstein Foundation' (*Marxer & Partner Rechtsanwälte*, 2010) <www.marxerpartner.com/fileadmin/user_upload/marxerpartner/pdf-downloads/ Die_Stiftung_Broschuere_eng.pdf> accessed 17 April 2017.

It is common for a fiduciary to act as founder, its name appearing in the documentation establishing the foundation, which means that the actual founder has the option of remaining anonymous. The actual founder may sit on the foundation council and may be a beneficiary (possibly the sole beneficiary).

The foundation is of perpetual duration but this irrevocability on the part of the actual founder can be countered by provisions in the foundation's articles that the founder retains the right both to revoke and to amend – not only its administrative provisions, but also the identity of the beneficiaries. Dissolution (in most cases at the instance of the foundation council) is also an option. On a revocation or dissolution, the assets within the foundation pass to the actual founder as ultimate beneficiary (unless other provisions have been included to the contrary). Alternatively, the re-domiciliation of the foundation is permitted, subject to the laws of the foreign jurisdiction allowing the foundation to re-domicile as a continuing entity not deemed to have been liquidated and re-established.

There is no audit requirement, unless the private benefit foundation were voluntarily to submit to the supervision of the Foundation Supervisory Authority.[54] However, a control body may at the founder's option be appointed to verify annually that the foundation assets are being managed and distributed in accordance with the purpose(s) of the foundation: the control body can be the founder him or herself, an auditor appointed by the Court, or a specialist adviser.

The new Liechtenstein foundation law places particular emphasis on good corporate governance, which in the case of private benefit foundations focuses on internal management controls and the information rights of beneficiaries, and in the case of those which have submitted voluntarily to supervision by the Foundation Supervisory Authority to provide the Authority upon request with information and with access to the foundation's books.

Forced heirship avoidance is absent. Every contribution to the assets of a foundation is open to challenge by the donor's heirs, where those heirs have forced heirship rights (either under the law of Liechtenstein itself or under foreign law, in which case the provisions of the Liechtenstein Private International Law Act will be applied). A claim against the foundation for payment of the relevant compulsory portion has to be made to the Princely Court of Justice.[55]

Liechtenstein has extremely limited provisions for the recognition and enforceability of foreign judgments (Switzerland and Austria), and this lack

---

54   Amt für justiz, Fürstentum Liechenstein, 'Stiftungsaufsichstbehörde' (*Amt für justiz, Fürstentum Liechenstein*) <www.stifa.li/en> accessed 17 April 2017.

55   Fürstliche Gerichte Fürstentum Liechenstein, 'News' (*Fürstliche Gerichte Fürstentum Liechenstein*) <www.gerichte.li> accessed 17 April 2017.

of reciprocity is seen as an advantage for foundations, against which an action must, but for these minor exceptions, be brought in the Liechtenstein courts. Significantly, and positively, there is no provision which would automatically prevent the re-litigation before the Liechtenstein courts of a foreign, non-reciprocal judgment.

Asset protection is contemplated in the new law, but in a conscious effort to weight the rights of legitimate creditors against the rights of the founder and of the foundation. There is no duty to preserve the foundation assets, but no distribution is permitted if as a result the foundation were left with funds inadequate to meet its debts. Claims against the foundation, if successful, will attach to foundation assets; but successful claims against the founder or against beneficiaries in their personal capacities will not.

Panama Private Foundation

Panama Private Foundations ('PPF') are a creation of La Ley por la cual Se Regulan las Fundaciones de Interés Privado 1995 ('Law by which Private Interest Foundations Are Regulated').[56] There are no restrictions on the purposes for which they may be formed, but they cannot engage in commercial or for profit activities as a day-to-day activity.

A PPF may take effect on its incorporation or may instead become active on a later event, such as the death of the founder. The asset minimum upon incorporation is a lowly US$10,000. Any inheritance laws in the jurisdiction where the founder or any of the beneficiaries are domiciled are dis-applied. Equally, in the event of any judgment or other seizure of assets of the founder, the assets of the PPF are inviolate. Unlike the Bahamian BEE, for example, the transfer of assets into a PPF is open to challenge by creditors on the basis that it was done fraudulently to defeat the rights of those creditors, but subject to a limitation period of three years from the date on which the transfer of those assets was made (bearing in mind that such a transfer can occur throughout the life of the PPF) – beyond that date, no claims will be heard before the Panamanian courts. In respect of non-Panamanian assets, the PPF is tax exempt in Panama.

The administrative workings of the PPF are found in its Charter, in which the names of the founder, the foundation council and (if appointed) protector are contained. Only the names of the founder and council members need be made public – the option exists that the protector may be appointed privately. The beneficiary provisions are contained in its Regulations, which are wholly private.

A PPF is subject[57] to a state duty of confidentiality, without limit as to time, which binds not only the members of the foundation council and any protec-

---

56 <http://docs.panama.justia.com/federales/leyes/25-de-1995-jun-14-1995.pdf> accessed 17 April 2017.
57 La Ley por la cual Se Regulan las Fundaciones de Interés Privado 1995 (n 56) art 35.

tor, but also any person in a civil service or private capacity who has knowledge of the activities of the PPF. Violation of this duty incurs a six-month jail sentence plus a fine of US$50,000 in addition to any civil penalties.

Nevis Multiform Foundation

The Nevis Multiform Foundation is a creation of the Nevis Multiform Foundations Ordinance 2004.[58] It is the ultimate chameleon, and it has the ability to designate itself as a trust, a company, a limited liability company, or a general or limited partnership.[59] If none of these forms is specified, then the foundation is governed by the terms of the Ordinance as a foundation plain and simple; but if so designated, then the relevant laws of Nevis apply to each designated form.

The multiform foundation throughout its life is a shape-shifter. Only one multiform may be adopted at a time, but following establishment or, as the case may be, continuation or transformation or conversion or consolidation or merger, a stated multiform may be changed by amendment to the constitution, together with, if appropriate, a change in name.

There may be any purpose, or more than one purpose, whatsoever, be it charitable or non-charitable, commercial or non-commercial, so long as not contrary to public policy in Nevis. There is no requirement to have a beneficiary.[60]

Nevis is robust in its defence of the multiform foundation. No multiform foundation governed by the law of Nevis, and no subscription of property to a multiform foundation which is valid under the law of Nevis, is void, voidable, or liable to be set aside or defective in any manner by reference to the law of a foreign jurisdiction.[61] Expressly, the fact that the laws of any foreign jurisdiction prohibit or do not recognise the concept of a foundation, a multiform foundation or any stated multiform will be disregarded.

In many jurisdictions, heirs have fixed rights to the deceased's estate – a civil law concept known as 'forced heirship'. In the case of multiform foundations these rights are expunged.

There is a state duty of confidentiality,[62] without limit as to time, which binds any person in possession of or having control over any information relating to the multiform foundation. Violation of this duty incurs a six-month jail sentence or a fine of US$50,000, or both, in addition to any civil penalties. Further, the Confidential Relationships Act, No.2 of 1985 of St Christopher and Nevis[63] applies to every multiform foundation established

---

58   <www.liburddash.com/legislation/MFO,%202004.pdf> accessed 23 April 2017.
59   Nevis Multiform Foundations Ordinance 2004 s 10.
60   Nevis Multiform Foundations Ordinance 2004 s 11.
61   Nevis Multiform Foundations Ordinance 2004 s 46.
62   Nevis Multiform Foundations Ordinance 2004 s 113.
63   <www.nexus.ua/images/legislation/Nevis_Confidential_1985.pdf> accessed 23 April 2017.

under the Ordinance. All judicial proceedings, other than criminal proceedings, relating to multiform foundations are to be heard in camera (that is, without members of the public present), and no details of the proceedings are to be published by any person without leave of the Court.

Hard wired into the ordinance is a wide range of asset protective features:[64]

- The multiform foundation itself and the beneficiaries are tax exempt in Nevis.
- There is a right to silence: a person may refuse to answer any question put to him or her pursuant to any provision of the Ordinance if that person's answer would or might tend to expose that person, or the spouse of that person, to proceedings under the law of Nevis or elsewhere for an offence or for the recovery of any penalty.
- Acting honestly, in the opinion of the Court, is a full defence to an action against any member of the foundation's management for negligence, default, or breach of duty.
- Notwithstanding that it is proved beyond reasonable doubt by a creditor that a multiform foundation was subscribed to by or on behalf of a subscriber with principal intent to defraud the creditor of the subscriber and did at the time such subscription take place render the subscriber insolvent or without property by which that creditor's claim (if successful) could have been satisfied, such subscription will not be regarded by the Court as void or voidable, and the multiform foundation shall instead be liable to satisfy the creditor's claim. Such liability is, however, limited to the extent of the interest that the subscriber had in the property representing or comprising the subscription prior to subscription.
- If a creditor has a cause of action (wherever this arises, and not merely in Nevis) against a subscriber to the multiform foundation, and the subscription into the multiform foundation was made more than one year after that cause arose, the matter is time barred. If the subscription is made within that year, the creditor must commence the action no later than six months from the date of the subscription, or be time barred.
- No assets or property of the multiform foundation available for distribution to a beneficiary are to be alienated or pass by bankruptcy, insolvency or liquidation or be liable to be seized, sold, attached, or taken in execution by process of law.[65]
- The constitution of a multiform foundation may provide that any beneficiary, creditor of the beneficiary, trustee-in-bankruptcy, or liquidator of the beneficiary shall forfeit his beneficial entitlement in the event that he or any creditor of the beneficiary, trustee-in-bankruptcy, or liquidator of

---

64 Nevis Multiform Foundations Ordinance 2004 pt XV.
65 Multiform Foundations Ordinance 2004 s 47(1).

the beneficiary challenges the creation of the multiform foundation, any subscriptions to the multiform foundation, the constitution or any provision thereof, or any decision of the management board or the supervisory board.

- No foreign judgment against the multiform foundation, its management, or the beneficiaries will be enforced in Nevis.
- The Statute of Elizabeth[66] (enactment entitled 13 Elizabeth 1 Ch 5 (1571)) which renders void any fraudulent transfer of property, and which would otherwise apply under the laws of Nevis, has no application to any multiform foundation which takes the form of a trust, nor to any subscription to such a multiform foundation.

From a human rights perspective, a Nevis multiform foundation is opaque and unassailable.[67]

Conclusions

Offshore structures are designed to conceal their true ownership, the extent of their wealth, and their purpose. They may even remove the concept of beneficial ownership altogether. Either derived from traditional legal forms but mutated, or artificially designed, these are chimeric entities. They have evolved to serve no domestic social need.

The presence of such an element in an ownership structure begs the question, why? Do they serve to provide personal or commercial confidentiality, or is instead their true function accountability avoidance?

Many tax havens, often as their raison d'être, have in the past denied and continue to deny public access to beneficial ownership information. They have corrupted their own traditional legal forms and promoted trusts without beneficiaries, companies without members. They have adopted legislation such as the laws on foundations with which they have no historical jurisprudential connection, and have commissioned and are today blatantly commissioning legislation from international legal experts with the express intention of creating orphan structures.

Their abusive role remains unrecognised and unchallenged; obscured – indeed, eclipsed – by the global debate on tax evasion, money laundering and the financing of terrorism. But there can be no doubt: these structures are the global engines of human rights abuse.

---

66 Wikipedia, 'Fraudulent Conveyances Act 1571,' (*Wikipedia*, 27 February 2017) <https://en.wikipedia.org/wiki/Fraudulent_Conveyances_Act_1571> accessed 19 April 2017.

67 Notwithstanding that St Kitts and Nevis is a founder member in June 2015 of the Association of Integrity Commissions and Anti-Corruption Bodies in the Commonwealth Caribbean. See The Commonwealth (n 25).

APPENDIX 1

An offshore archetype

Drawing the threads together, a generic archetype can be constructed, as in Figure 2.1 below.[68] The archetype has the following characteristics:

- 'Overlord' can be an individual or a corporation.
- 'Overlord' is the Settlor both of the Charitable Trust and of the Purpose Trust.
- The Nominee Shareholders and the Nominee Directors[69] will have given appropriate contractual undertakings as to the manner in which they will discharge their duties towards their clients.
- The Charitable Trust may or may not be revocable, and if revocable the assets placed in it are liable to be returned to 'Overlord' at any given moment.
- The recipient of the ultimate surplus on the termination of the Purpose Trust may be designated as XYZ Limited, which is wholly beneficially owned by 'Overlord'.
- Asset Holding Company #1 deals in the buying and selling of stocks, generating cash gains which are held in an offshore bank account; and some percentage of which will be distributed in the Isle of Man to justify the Charitable Trust's registered status – the balance being held for reinvestment or on deposit.
- Asset Holding Company #2 is engaged in hazardous mining operations with which neither 'Overlord' nor XYZ Limited wishes to be associated. The Purpose Trust is designed to terminate once the hazard has passed and the project is 'clean'.
- Depending on the jurisdiction of its incorporation, the Asset Holding Company may be wholly immune to the enforceability of fraudulent transfer, forced heirship and insolvency claims and to the reciprocal enforcement of foreign judgments generally.
- XYZ Limited may function as a 'headquarters company' and as such may have any number of trading operations (not shown in the diagram) in other jurisdictions with which the jurisdiction of its incorporation has

---

68 Drawn on the assumption that each element has been validly created and is not (on the basis of characteristics unique to that particular actor) in danger of being rendered at the instance of a third party void or otherwise compromised.

69 For the purpose of this structure the term Nominee Directors is used to designate professionals who supply their services as directors of the companies concerned, and who are personally fully liable for the manner in which they discharge their fiduciary duties as directors; but who nonetheless permit their judgment to be influenced by or to be subject to the absolute control of 'Overlord' or the Charitable Trustees or the Purpose Trustees as the case may be as their client, adopting in this way a de facto nominee position.

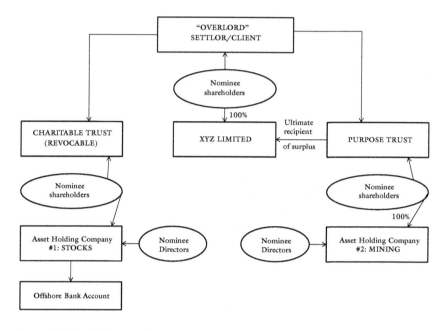

Figure 2.1 An offshore archetype

double taxation treaties ('DTT'); and therefore, because it is liable to taxation in its home jurisdiction, it is liable to pay little or no tax at all on its profits in those DTT jurisdictions.

- XYZ Limited may be a company incorporated in a jurisdiction in which neither the details of its directors nor of any indebtedness by way of charges or debentures needs to be filed publicly.
- As a further refinement, if a Bahamian BEE, XYZ Limited will have no shareholders (nominee or otherwise) and will free float as an 'orphan' structure.
- The accounts of companies formed in most offshore jurisdictions are not required to be filed publicly.
- The individual elements of the archetype may be subject to low or zero taxation.

In summary, the archetype has no substantial commercial connection with the jurisdiction of its creation apart from the fact that elements within it are subject to the laws of that jurisdiction. Its beneficial owners and purpose are obscured. Its hollow shell elements stand between those who would seek to enforce commercial and human rights accountability and those whose purpose in establishing the archetype ought to render them accountable.

APPENDIX 2

Table 2.1 Numbers of companies incorporated in tax havens (sampled)

Jurisdiction	Companies	As at date	Source
British Virgin Islands	447,503	30 September 2016	www.bvifsc.vg/Portals/2/2016%20 Statistical%20Bulletin%20Qtr%203.pdf
Bahamas	461,600	31 December 2013	Registrar General's Department Revenue Estimates 2013 www.bahamas.gov.bs
Cayman Islands	98,838	31 December 2015	www.ciregistry.gov.ky/portal/pls/ portal/docs/1/12364405.PDF
Delaware, USA	1,181,000	31 December 2015	Delaware Division of Corporations 2015 Annual Report https://corp.delaware.gov/ Corporations_2015%20Annual%20 Report.pdf
Guernsey	19,468	31 December 2015	Guernsey Registry Statistics www.guernseyregistry.com/article/ 117152/Quarterly-Register-Statistics-2015
Isle of Man	27,168	31 December 2016	www.gov.im/about-the-government/ departments/economic-development/ central-registry/companies-registry/ statistics/
Jersey	33,533	31 December 2015	www.jerseyfsc.org/pdf/JFSC_ ANNUAL_REPORT_2015.pdf
Liechtenstein	Not available	Not available	The Liechtenstein Chamber of Commerce and Industry does not keep a register of companieswww.lihk.li/CFDOCS/ cms/cmsout/index.cfm?u=1&Group ID=20&meID=75
Malta	68,676	31 December 2014	www.fbsmalta.com/5503/malta-registry-of-companies-surpasses-5000-company-mark/
Seychelles	69,954	31 December 2014	http://sterlingoffshore.com/offshore-company/seychelles-international-business-company-seychelles-ibc/

APPENDIX 3

Table 2.2 Non-charitable purpose trust jurisdictions (sampled)

Jurisdiction	Statute
British Virgin Islands	Trustee Act (Cap. 303) as amended by Trustee (Amendment) Act 2013
Barbados	International Trusts Act 1995
Cayman Islands	Introduced into the Cayman Islands via the Special Trusts (Alternative Regime) Law 1997, now embedded in Part VIII of the Trusts Law (2011 Revision)
Cook Islands[a]	International Trusts Amendment Act 1995–96, s 8
Guernsey	Trusts (Guernsey) Law 2007, s 12
Isle of Man	Purpose Trusts Act 1996
Jersey	Trusts (Jersey) Law 1984 (as amended by Trusts (Amendment No. 3) (Jersey) Law 1996 with effect from 24 May 1996)
Labuan	Labuan Trusts Act 1996 (as amended, 2010) s 11A
Mauritius	Trusts Act 2001, s 19
Niue	Trustee Companies Act 1994, s 31
Samoa	Trusts Act 2014, s 66
Turks and Caicos Islands	Trusts Ordinance 2016
USA, Delaware	Del. Code tit. 12, s 3556
USA, New Hampshire	N.H. Rev. Stat. s 564-B
USA, South Dakota	South Dakota Codified Laws ss 55-1-20
USA, Wyoming	Wyo. Stat. ss 4-10-410

Note: [a]Pacific Islands Legal Information Institute <www.paclii.org> accessed 23 April 2017.

APPENDIX 4

Table 2.3 Foundation jurisdictions (sampled)

Jurisdiction	Statute
Anguilla	Anguilla Foundation Act 2008
Austria	Privatstiftungsgesetz 1993
Bahamas	Foundations Act 2004 (amended 2007)
Barbados	Foundations Act 2013-2
Cook Islands	Cook Islands Foundations Act 2012
Denmark	Danish Foundation Act
Guernsey	Foundations (Guernsey) Law 2012
Isle of Man	Foundations Act 2011
Jersey	Foundations (Jersey) Law 2009
Liechtenstein	Personen und Gesellschaftsrecht 1926; Stiftungs Gesetz 2009
Malta	Act XIII of 2007
Mauritius	Foundations Act 2012
Netherlands Antilles	National Ordinance Regarding Foundations 1998; Civil Code, Book 2 2004 ('Stichting Particulier Fonds')
Nevis	Multiform Foundation Ordinance 2004
Panama	La Ley por la cual Se Regulan las Fundaciones de Interés Privado 1995 ('Law by which Private Interest Foundations Are Regulated')
Seychelles	Foundations Act 2009

Bibliography

Cases

Costain, Re (1961) 1961–71 MLR 1
Poyiadjis, Re (2002) 2001–03 MLR 316
Ring, Re (1962) 1961–71 MLR 60
Saunders v Vautier [1841] EWHC J82, 4 Beav 115

Legislation and regulations

Charities Registration Act 1989 <www.legislation.gov.im/cms/images/LEGISLATION/PRINCIPAL/1989/1989-0011/CharitiesRegistrationAct1989_1.pdf> accessed 23 April 2017 (Isle of Man)
Confidential Relationships Act, No 2 of 1985 <www.nexus.ua/images/legislation/Nevis_Confidential_1985.pdf> accessed 23 April 2017 (St Kitts and Nevis)
The Executive Entities Act 2011 <http://laws.bahamas.gov.bs/cms/images/LEGISLATION/PRINCIPAL/2011/2011-0052/ExecutiveEntitiesAct2011_1.pdf> accessed 23 April 2017 (The Bahamas)
Executive Entities Regulations 2012, SI 13 of 2012 <http://laws.bahamas.gov.bs/cms/images/LEGISLATION/SUBORDINATE/2012/2012-0013/ExecutiveEntitiesRegulations2012_1.pdf> accessed 23 April 2017 (The Bahamas)
Financial Services Act 2008 <https://legislation.gov.im/cms/images/LEGISLATION/PRINCIPAL/2008/2008-0008/FinancialServicesAct2008_8.pdf> accessed 23 April 2017 (Isle of Man)
Fraudulent Assignments Act 1736 <www.legislation.gov.im/cms/images/LEGISLATION/PRINCIPAL/1736/1736-0002/FraudulentAssignmentsAct1736_1.pdf> accessed 23 April 2017 (Isle of Man)
Gesetz vom 1. Dezember 2016 über die Abänderung des Personen- und Gesellschaftsrechts (Liechtenstein)
International Business Companies Act 1994 (repealed) (Seychelles)
International Business Companies Act 2016 <www.seylii.org/sc/legislation/act/2016/15> accessed 23 April 2017 (Seychelles)
La Ley de Fundaciones de Panamá ('Law by which Private Interest Foundations Are Regulated') <http://docs.panama.justia.com/federales/leyes/25-de-1995-jun-14-1995.pdf> accessed 17 April 20171995
Nevis Multiform Foundations Ordinance 2004 <www.liburddash.com/legislation/MFO,%202004.pdf> accessed 23 April 2017(St Kitts and Nevis)
Personen und Gesellschaftsrecht 1926 (Liechenstein)
Purpose Trusts Act 1996 <www.legislation.gov.im/cms/images/LEGISLATION/PRINCIPAL/1996/1996-0009/PurposeTrustsAct1996_1.pdf> accessed 23 April 2017 (Isle of Man)
Small Business Enterprise and Employment Act 2015 <www.legislation.gov.uk/ukpga/2015/26/contents> accessed 23 April 2017 (United Kingdom)
Special Trusts (Alternative Regime) Law 1997 (Cayman Islands)
Stiftungs Gesetz 2009 <www.gesetze.li> accessed 23 April 2017 (Liechtenstein)
Trustee Act 2000 <www.legislation.gov.uk/ukpga/2000/29/contents> accessed 23 April 2017 (United Kingdom)
Trustee Act 2001 <https://legislation.gov.im/cms/images/LEGISLATION/

PRINCIPAL/2001/2001-0018/TrusteeAct2001_1.pdf> accessed 23 April 2017 (Isle of Man)

Trusts (Amendment) Law 2016 <www.judicial.ky> accessed 17 April 2017 (Cayman Islands)

Trusts Law (as amended 2011) <www.judicial.ky> accessed 17 April 2017 (Cayman Islands)

Virgin Islands Special Trusts Act 2003 <www.bvifsc.vg/Portals/2/Virgin%20 Islands%20Special%20Trusts%20Act,%202003.pdf> accessed 23 April 2017

Virgin Islands Special Trusts (Amendment) Act 2013 <www.bvifsc.vg/Portals/2/ Virgin%20Islands%20Special%20Trusts%20(Amendment)%20Act,%202013.pdf> accessed 23 April 2017

International treaties

Vienna Convention on the Law of Treaties (adopted 23 May 1969, entered into force 27 January 1980) 1155 UNTS 331

United Nations documents

United Nations Committee on Economic, Social and Cultural Rights, 'General Comment on State Obligations under the International Covenant on Economic, Social and Cultural Rights in the Context of Business Activities [Draft Prepared by Olivier De Schutter and Zdzislaw Kedzia, Rapporteurs]' (2016) UN Doc E/C.12/60/R.1

United Nations Economic and Social Council, 'Statement on the Obligations of States Parties Regarding the Corporate Sector and Economic, Social and Cultural Rights' (2011) UN Doc E/C.12/2011/1

United Nations Human Rights Council, 'Report of the Special Representative of the Secretary General on the Issue of Human Rights and Transnational Corporations and Other Business Enterprises, John Ruggie: Guiding Principles on Business and Human Rights: Implementing the United Nations "Protect, Respect and Remedy" Framework' (2011) UN Doc A/HRC/17/31

Secondary sources

Amt für justiz, Fürstentum Liechenstein, 'Stiftungsaufsichstbehörde' (*Amt für justiz, Fürstentum Liechenstein*) <www.stifa.li/en> accessed 17 April 2017

Beetham D, 'What Future for Economic and Social Rights?' (1995) XLIII Political Studies 41

Bergin T and Grey S, 'Insight – How UK Company Formation Agents Fuel Fraud' *Reuters* (United Kingdom, 18 March 2016)

Bernaz N, *Business and Human Rights: History, Law and Policy – Bridging the Accountability Gap* (Routledge, 2017)

Burian P, 'Seychelles: Beating the Odds' [2016] *Offshore Investment* <www.offshore investment.com/seychelles-beating-the-odds-archive> accessed 17 April 2017

BVI News Online, 'More Bad News for Financial Services: 35% Drop' (*bvinews.com*, 19 January 2017) <http://bvinews.com/new/more-bad-news-for-financial-services-35-drop> accessed 16 April 2017

'Cayman Islands Judicial Administration' (*Cayman Islands Judicial Administration*) <www.judicial.ky> accessed 17 April 2017

Cayman Islands Monetary Authority, 'Guidance Notes on the Prevention and Detection of Money Laundering and Terrorist Financing in the Cayman Islands' (*Cayman Islands Monetary Authority*) <www.cimoney.com.ky/AML_CFT/ aml_cft.aspx?id=144> accessed 16 April 2017

Collier P, 'In Pursuit of the $21 Trillion' [2013] *Prospect Magazine* <www.prospect-magazine.co.uk>

The Commonwealth, 'Caribbean Integrity Commissions Form New Commonwealth Body to Fight Corruption' (*The Commonwealth*, 25 June 2015) <https://shar.es/ 1QVznK> accessed 17 April 2017

Fürstliche Gerichte Fürstentum Liechenstein, 'News' (*Fürstliche Gerichte Fürstentum Liechenstein*) <www.gerichte.li> accessed 17 April 2017

Isle of Man Financial Services Authority, 'Financial Services Rule Book' (2016) <www.iomfsa.im/lib/docs/iomfsa/consultations/financialservicesrule-book20131.pdf> accessed 16 April 2017

——, 'AML/CFT Requirements and Guidance' (*Isle of Man Financial Services Authority*) <www.iomfsa.im/handbooks/guides/AML/amlcftrequirementsguid-ance.xml> accessed 16 April 2017

——, 'Isle of Man Financial Services Authority' (*Isle of Man Financial Services Authority*) <www.iomfsa.im> accessed 16 April 2017

Knobel A, 'The Case for Registering Trusts – and How to Do It' (*The Tax Justice Network*) <www.taxjustice.net/wp-content/uploads/2013/04/Registration-of-Trusts_AK.pdf> accessed 17 April 2017

Knobel A (Shaxson N ed), 'Trusts: Weapons of Mass Injustice?' (13 February 2017) <www.taxjustice.net/wp-content/uploads/2017/02/Trusts-Weapons-of-Mass-Injustice-Final-12-FEB-2017.pdf> accessed 17 April 2017

Leigh D, Frayman H and Ball J, 'How the Nominee Trick Works' *ICIJ* (Washington DC, 25 November 2012) <www.icij.org/offshore/how-nominee-trick-done> accessed 16 April 2017

——, 'Front Men Disguise the Offshore Game's Real Players' *ICIJ* (Washington DC) <www.icij.org/front-men-disguise-offshore-players> accessed 16 April 2017

Levy D, 'Lawrence Graham Seeks to Revolutionise Offshore Trust Structures' (*Citywire*, 23 April 2010) <http://citywire.co.uk/wealth-manager/news/ lawrence-graham-seeks-to-revolutionise-offshore-trust-structures/a395505/ print?section=wealth-manager> accessed 17 April 2017

Liechtenstein Chamber of Commerce and Industry, 'Commercial Registry' (*Liechtenstein Chamber of Commerce and Industry*, 15 September 2015) <www.lihk.li/CFDOCS/cms/cmsout/index.cfm?u=1&GroupID=20&meID=75 > accessed 16 April 2017

Marriage A, 'Secret Structures, Hidden Crimes: Urgent Steps to Address Hidden Ownership, Money Laundering and Tax Evasion from Developing Countries' (*European Network on Debt and Development*, 2013) <http://eurodad.org/files/ integration/2013/01/Secret-structures-hidden-crimes-web.pdf> accessed 16 April 2017

Marxer & Partner Rechtsanwälte, 'The Liechtenstein Foundation' (*Marxer & Partner Rechtsanwälte*, 2010) <www.marxerpartner.com/fileadmin/ user_ upload/marxerpartner/pdf-downloads/Die_Stiftung_Broschuere_eng.pdf> accessed 17 April 2017

Office of the United Nations High Commissioner for Human Rights, 'Who Will Be Accountable? Human Rights and the Post-2015 Development Agenda' (*Office of the United Nations High Commissioner for Human Rights*, 2013) <www.ohchr.org/Documents/Publications/WhoWillBeAccountable.pdf> accessed 15 April 2017

Pacific Islands Legal Information Institute <www.paclii.org> accessed 23 April 2017

Palan R, Murphy R and Chavagneux C, *Tax Havens: How Globalization Really Works* (Cornell University Press, 2010)

Ryle G and Candea S, 'Faux Corporate Directors Stand in for Fraudsters, Despots and Spies' *ICIJ* (Washington DC, 4 July 2013) <www.icij.org/offshore/faux-corporate-directors-stand-fraudsters-despots-and-spies> accessed 16 April 2017

Salomon M, 'Why Should It Matter That Others Have More? – Poverty, Inequality and the Potential of International Human Rights Law' (2010) LSE Legal Studies Working Paper 15/2010, 10

United Kingdom Government, Companies House, 'Summary Guide for Companies – Register of People with Significant Control' (*gov.uk*, 27 January 2016) <www.gov.uk/government/publications/guidance-to-the-people-with-significant-control-requirements-for-companies-and-limited-liability-partnerships> accessed 16 April 2017

——, 'Keeping Your People with Significant Control (PSC) Register' (*gov.uk*, 6 April 2016) <www.gov.uk/government/news/keeping-your-people-with-significant-control-psc-register> accessed 17 April 2017

United Kingdom Government, Department for Business, Innovation & Skills, 'Statutory Guidance on the Meaning of "Significant Influence or Control" over Companies in the Context of the Register of People with Significant Control' (*gov.uk*, 14 April 2016) <www.gov.uk/government/uploads/system/uploads/attachment_data/file/523120/PSC_statutory_guidance_companies.pdf> accessed 16 April 2017

——, '"People with Significant Control" Companies House Register Goes Live' (*gov.uk*, 30 June 2016) <www.gov.uk/government/news/people-with-significant-control-companies-house-register-goes-live> accessed 16 April 2017

Wikipedia, 'Fraudulent Conveyances Act 1571' (*Wikipedia*, 27 February 2017) <https://en.wikipedia.org/wiki/Fraudulent_Conveyances_Act_1571> accessed 19 April 2017

Zagaris B, 'Changes in International Regulatory Regimes on Caribbean Corporate, Financial Regulatory and Transparency Law' (2016) 263 *Offshore Investment* <www.offshoreinvestment.com/changes in-international-regulatory-regimes-on-caribbean-corporate-financial-regulatory-and-transparency-law> accessed 17 April 2017

3   Beneficial ownership avoidance

Introduction[1]

In a post-2008 Great Recession world of increasingly complex criminality, corruption, doctrinal fanaticism, and state terrorism, just as the distinction between legitimate tax avoidance and illegitimate tax evasion has been blurred, so the distinction between privacy and confidentially, on the one hand, and secrecy and concealment, on the other, has ceased to resonate. Hence there has been a global initiative to identify beneficial owners. The new mantra is that 'someone, somewhere must know who owns something or everything'.[2]

From an international human rights perspective, the trend towards accountability avoidance[3] is hugely magnified by what amounts to a global fiduciary services drive towards the creation of 'orphaned' structures, which as such have no beneficial owners, and no one therefore to hold accountable. By analogy with tax avoidance,[4] the current thinking on beneficial ownership is not correctly targeted and appears half-hearted (though whether from an inability to appreciate the significance of the problem, or because of an unspoken satisfaction with the perceived benefits of concealment is moot). On occasion, human rights have been invoked not to force the disclosure of

---

1   This chapter is based on 'Beneficial Ownership of Companies – G20 High Level Principles – a Paper Tiger?' a paper delivered by the author at the 107th Annual Conference of the Society of Legal Scholars, held at St Catherine's College, Oxford on 7 September 2016.
2   Finding out who, where and why is an immense task: tens of thousands of people in more than 170 countries and territories are linked to offshore companies and trusts: Marina Walker Guevara and others, 'Who Uses the Offshore World' (*ICIJ*, 16 April 2013) <www.icij.org/offshore/who-uses-offshore-world> accessed 25 April 2017. Names behind secret companies and trusts have been released by the ICIJ in its *Offshore Leaks Database*. Marina Walker Guevara, 'ICIJ Releases Offshore Leaks Database Revealing Names Behind Secret Companies, Trusts' (*ICIJ*, 14 June 2013) <www.icij.org/offshore/icij-releases-offshore-leaks-database-revealing-names-behind-secret-companies-trusts> accessed 25 April 2017; Mar Cabra, 'Map: The Offshore Leaks Revelations' (*ICIJ*, 23 January 2014) <www.icij.org/offshore/map-offshore-leaks-revelations> accessed 25 April 2017.
3   Chapter 2.
4   Chapter 4.

information the withholding of which could facilitate abuse, but on the grounds of privacy to prevent that very disclosure.[5]

This chapter focuses on the G20 High-Level Principles on Beneficial Ownership Transparency ('Principles'), on state implementation responses (using the Isle of Man[6] as a case study) and on how a very simple, inexpensive offshore device, the non-charitable purpose trust, can be used to render the application of the G20 principles – and accountability in human rights terms – legally impossible. The political will behind beneficial ownership disclosure measures may not be what it appears.

The thesis is simple, but potent. Worldwide, efforts are being made to implement enforcement mechanisms for identifying the beneficial owners of companies (and other 'legal persons' such as limited liability companies (LLCs), foundations etc.), and the policies driving this initiative are found in the Principles.

This chapter reviews to what extent, if any, implementation legislation which focuses on the registration and disclosure of beneficial owners is effective in practice, and how sincere such political initiative is, using the Companies (Beneficial Ownership) Act 2012 of the Isle of Man as a case study: politically compelling, but in the face of a robust avoidance culture, inevitably toothless in its application.

Using an Isle of Man non-charitable purpose trust as a case study, the chapter shows that in fact no enforcement mechanism – no matter how robustly crafted – will be of the slightest use if the structure under investigation has in fact no beneficial owner at all. When they get there, the cupboard is bare. This, by analogy with current accountability thinking, is *beneficial ownership avoidance*.

Various tax havens have introduced 'orphan' structures which, by definition, have no beneficial owners at all, the Bahamas Executive Entity introduced under The Executive Entities Act 2011,[7] being arguably the most

---

5   For example, the approach in the United Kingdom of Her Majesty's Revenue and Customs in relation to the exemption from disclosure under the Common Reporting Standard of information held by charities. See Alice Sharman, 'HMRC Revises Common Reporting Standard on Human Rights' (*Civil Society News*, 23 January 2017) <www.civil society.co.uk/news/hmrc-revises-common-reporting-standard-guidance-over human-rights-implications.html> accessed 27 April 2017 and United Kingdom Government, Her Majesty's Revenue and Customs, 'HMRC Internal Manual: International Exchange of Information Manual: IEIM 406000: Charities: Protection on Human Rights Grounds' (*gov.uk*, 27 April 2017) <www.gov.uk/hmrc-internal-manuals/international-exchange-of-information/ieim406000> accessed 27 April 2017.

6   For an overview of the political, economic and legal structure of the Isle of Man see Paul Beckett, 'Isle of Man' in *European Cross-Border Estate Planning* (Sweet & Maxwell, London, first published 1995, current edition 2017) and Paul Beckett, 'Isle of Man' in *Digest of Commercial Laws of the World* (Thomson Reuters, USA, 2016)

7   <http://laws.bahamas.gov.bs/cms/images/LEGISLATION/PRINCIPAL/2011/2011-0052/ExecutiveEntitiesAct2011_1.pdf> accessed 27 April 2017, together with the Executive Entities Regulations 2012 <http://laws.bahamas.gov.bs/cms/images/LEGISLATION/SUBORDINATE/2012/2012-0013/ExecutiveEntitiesRegulations 2012_1.pdf> accessed 27 April 2017.

blatant.[8] But the universality of non-charitable purpose trusts, their continuing spread, and the undisguised enthusiasm for ownership avoidance on the part of those jurisdictions which have adopted them is the strongest illustration of the phenomenon.

Beneficial ownership avoidance counter-initiatives

When from the mid-nineteenth century onwards ever more elaborate corporate structures were evolving, the underlying principle was to promote trade through the limitation of liability of those beneficially interested who would otherwise have been financially exposed. In our own time, these structures are increasingly used to conceal the identity of those beneficial owners, and this concealment is, in the hands of the unscrupulous, a cloak of invisibility thrown over tax evasion, bribery and corruption, fraud, the financing of terrorism, and the abuse of internationally recognised human rights norms.[9]

It is a decade since the Financial Action Task Force[10] in 'The Misuse of Corporate Vehicles Including Trust and Company Service Providers' (13 October 2006)[11] identified the concealment of true beneficial ownership as that which fuelled the engine of abuse:

> Despite the important and legitimate roles corporate entities, including corporations, trusts, foundations and partnerships with limited liability, play in the global economy, they may, under certain conditions, be used for illicit purposes. The present study's prime aim has been to seek to identify in respect of corporate vehicles areas of vulnerability for money laundering and terrorist financing, along with evidence of their misuse. Faced with the vast scope of a general project on corporate vehicle misuse the study focuses on what is considered to be the most significant feature of their misuse – the hiding of the true beneficial owner.

8   Discussed in Chapter 2.
9   'From a human rights perspective, effective access to public information is a precondition for exercising other human rights. Exercise of the right to participation depends on transparency and access to complete, up-to-date and comprehensible information.' United Nations Human Rights Council, 'Report of the Independent Expert on the Question of Human Rights and Extreme Poverty, Magdalena Sepulveda Carmona' (17 March 2011) UN Doc A/HRC/17/34.
10   The Financial Action Task Force (FATF) is an independent inter-governmental body that develops and promotes policies to protect the global financial system against money laundering, terrorist financing and the financing of proliferation of weapons of mass destruction. The FATF Recommendations are recognised as the global anti-money laundering (AML) and counter-terrorist financing (CFT) standard. 'Financial Action Task Force' (*Financial Action Task Force*) <www.fatf-gafi.org> accessed 27 April 2017.
11   (*Financial Action Task Force*) <www.fatf-gafi.org/media/fatf/documents/reports/ Misuse%20of%20Corporate%20Vehicles%20including%20Trusts%20and%20Company%20 Services%20Providers.pdf> accessed 30 April 2017, Executive Summary.

The flywheel turns only slowly. In October 2014, the Financial Action Task Force was again intoning:

1. Corporate vehicles[12] – such as companies, trusts, foundations, partnerships, and other types of legal persons and arrangements – conduct a wide variety of commercial and entrepreneurial activities. However, despite the essential and legitimate role that corporate vehicles play in the global economy, under certain conditions, they have been misused for illicit purposes, including money laundering (ML), bribery and corruption, insider dealings, tax fraud, terrorist financing (TF), and other illegal activities. This is because, for criminals trying to circumvent anti-money laundering (AML) and counter-terrorist financing (CTF) measures, corporate vehicles are an attractive way to disguise and convert the proceeds of crime before introducing them into the financial system. 2. The misuse of corporate vehicles could be significantly reduced if information regarding both the legal owner and the beneficial owner, the source of the corporate vehicle's assets, and its activities were readily available to the authorities. Legal and beneficial ownership information can assist law enforcement and other competent authorities by identifying those natural persons who may be responsible for the underlying activity of concern, or who may have relevant information to further an investigation. This allows the authorities to 'follow the money' in financial investigations involving suspect accounts/assets held by corporate vehicles. In particular, beneficial ownership information can also help locate a given person's assets within a jurisdiction. However, countries face significant challenges when implementing measures to ensure the timely availability of accurate beneficial owner information. This is particularly challenging when it involves legal persons and legal arrangements spread across multiple jurisdictions.
…
88. … [C]orporate vehicles are increasingly attractive to criminals for the purpose of disguising their identity and distancing themselves from their illicit assets. Increasing the transparency of corporate vehicles is an effective way to prevent their misuse for criminal purposes, including for the commission of offenses such as money laundering or terrorism financing, corruption, tax fraud, trafficking and other organized crime related offences.[13]

12 The FATF in this paper uses the term corporate vehicles to mean *legal persons* and *legal arrangements,* as defined in the glossary of the FATF Recommendations 2012 (updated to June 2016). Financial Action Task Force, 'FATF Recommendations 2012' (*Financial Action Task Force,* 16 February 2012) <www.fatf-gafi.org/publications/fatfrecommendations/documents/fatf-recommendations.html> accessed 30 April 2017.
13 Financial Action Task Force, 'FATF Guidance on Transparency and Beneficial Ownership' (*Financial Action Task Force,* October 2014) <www.fatf-gafi.org/media/fatf/documents/reports/Guidance-transparency-beneficial-ownership.pdf> accessed 30 April 2017 (citation omitted) paras 1, 2, 88.

On 24 March 2011, the Stolen Asset Recovery (StAR) Initiative of the World Bank and the United Nations Office on Drugs and Crime issued their report, *The Puppet Masters: How the Corrupt Use Legal Structures to Hide Stolen Assets and What to Do About It*,[14] commenting:[15]

> 'We need to put corporate transparency back on the national and international agenda,' said Emile van der Does de Willebois, World Bank Senior Financial Sector Specialist who led the StAR research team. 'It is important for governments to increase the transparency of their legal entities and arrangements and at the same time improve the capacity of law enforcement.'
>
> The report ... examines how bribes, embezzled state assets and other criminal proceeds are being hidden via legal structures – shell companies, foundations, trusts and others. The study also provides policy makers with practical recommendations on how to step up ongoing international efforts to uncover flows of criminal funds and prevent criminals from misusing shell companies and other legal entities.
>
> The study explains how corrupt public officials and their associates conceal their connection to ill-gotten funds by exploiting legal and institutional loopholes that allow opacity in companies, foundations, and trust-like structures. It also lists obstacles to investigating and establishing the origin and ownership of stolen assets: the difficulty of identifying where legal entities operate and have business relationships, lack of access to information on beneficial ownership, and the use of complex and multi-jurisdictional corporate structures.

The introduction to *The Puppet Masters* makes clear the extent of the problems of establishing transparency and the urgent social need to do so:

> Corruption is estimated to be at least a $40 billion dollar a year business. Every day, funds destined for schools, healthcare, and infrastructure in the world's most fragile economies are siphoned off and stashed away in the world's financial centers and tax havens. Corruption, like a disease, is eating away at the foundation of people's faith in government. It undermines the stability and security of nations. So it is a development challenge in more ways than one: it directly affects development assistance, but it also undermines the preconditions for growth and equity. We need mobilization at the highest level so that corruption is tackled

---

14   Emile van der Does de Willebois and others (World Bank Publications, 2011) (*The Puppet Masters*).

15   The World Bank, 'Corrupt Money Concealed in Shell Companies and Other Opaque Legal Entities, Finds New StAR Study' (*The World Bank*, 24 October 2011) <www.world bank.org/en/news/press-release/2011/10/24/corrupt-money-concealed-in-shell-companies-and-other-opaque-legal-entities-finds-new-star-study> accessed 30 April 2017.

effectively. This report, *The Puppet Masters*, deals with the corporate and financial structures that form the building blocks of hidden money trails. In particular, it focuses on the ease with which corrupt actors hide their interests behind a corporate veil and the difficulties investigators face in trying to lift that veil.

G20: Brisbane November 2014, Washington DC April 2016, Hangzhou September 2016

The 2014 G20 Brisbane Summit endorsed the initiative by the Financial Action Task Force ('FATF') in 2012 to set the benchmarks for the determination of beneficial ownership.[16]

Following the November 2014 G20 Brisbane Summit, the Leaders issued their Communiqué under which they adopted the High-Level Principles (Section 4 below):

> 14. We endorse the 2015–16 G20 Anti-Corruption Action Plan that will support growth and resilience. Our actions are building cooperation and networks, including to enhance mutual legal assistance, recovery of the proceeds of corruption and denial of safe haven to corrupt officials. We commit to improve the transparency of the public and private sectors, and of beneficial ownership by implementing the G20 High Level Principles on Beneficial Ownership Transparency.[17]

In the Communiqué[18] issued on 27 April 2016 following the meeting of G20 Finance Ministers and Central Bank Governors in Washington DC that month, beneficial ownership and the need for transparency featured prominently:

> 8. The G20 reiterates the high priority it attaches to financial transparency and effective implementation of the standards on transparency by all, in particular with regard to the beneficial ownership of legal persons and legal arrangements. Improving the transparency of the beneficial ownership of legal persons and legal arrangements is vital to

16 Now central in the context of taxation also to the exchange of information on request (EIOR) and to the automatic exchange of information (AEOI) embodied in the Common Reporting Standard (CRS) – see the discussion on this in the Organisation for Economic Co-operation and Development (OECD), 'OECD Secretary-General's Report to G20 Finance Ministers, April 2016' (*OECD*, April 2016) <www.oecd.org/tax/oecd-secretary-general-tax-report-g20-finance-ministers-april-2016.pdf> accessed 30 April 2017.

17 'G20 High-Level Principles on Beneficial Ownership Transparency' (*Australian Government, Attorney General's Department*, 2014) <www.ag.gov.au/ CrimeAnd Corruption/AntiCorruption/Documents/G20High-LevelPrinciplesOnBeneficial OwnershipTransparency.pdf> accessed 30 April 2017.

18 <www.g20.utoronto.ca/2016/160415-finance.html> accessed 20 May 2017.

protect the integrity of the international financial system, and to prevent misuse of these entities and arrangements for corruption, tax evasion, terrorist financing and money laundering. The G20 reiterates that it is essential that all countries and jurisdictions fully implement the FATF standards on transparency and beneficial ownership of legal persons and legal arrangements and we express our determination to lead by example in this regard. We particularly stress the importance of countries and jurisdictions improving the availability of beneficial ownership information to, and its international exchange between, competent authorities for the purposes of tackling tax evasion, terrorist financing and money laundering. We ask the FATF and the Global Forum on Transparency and Exchange of Information for Tax Purposes to make initial proposals by our October meeting on ways to improve the implementation of the international standards on transparency, including on the availability of beneficial ownership information, and its international exchange.

The G20 Leaders remain largely 'human rights blind', and in repeating themselves in their Communiqué issued on 5 September 2016 following the Hangzhou Summit they state:

> 20. Financial transparency and effective implementation of the standards on transparency by all, in particular with regard to the beneficial ownership of legal persons and legal arrangements, is vital to protecting the integrity of the international financial system, and to preventing misuse of these entities and arrangements for corruption, tax evasion, terrorist financing and money laundering.[19]

Distilling their approach in the form of the G20 Anti-Corruption Action Plan 2017–2018, they state:

> Beneficial ownership: Transparency over beneficial ownership is critical to preventing and exposing corruption and illicit finance. We will fully implement the FATF Recommendations on Transparency and Beneficial Ownership of Legal Persons[20] and our Action Plans to implement the G20 High Level Principles on Beneficial Ownership Transparency. The G20 will further promote the identification of the true beneficial ownership and control of companies and legal arrangements, including trusts, wherever they are located. We will encourage and support other countries to implement beneficial ownership standards and best practice. We

---

19 'G20 Leaders' Communiqué: Hangzhou Summit, Hangzhou' (*University of Toronto*, 5 September 2016) <www.g20.utoronto.ca/2016/160905-communique.html> accessed 30 April 2017 (Hangzhou Communiqué).
20 FATF Guidance on Transparency and Beneficial Ownership (n 13) makes no mention of beneficial ownership avoidance mechanisms.

will promote the utilisation of beneficial ownership information to tackle corruption and related money laundering.[21]

Significantly, however, in that same Communiqué the G20 Leaders unwittingly revealed their understanding of how their fiscally based agenda interacts with human rights observance. They propose to combat corruption and illicit finance flows 'while fully respecting international law, human rights and the rule of law as well as the sovereignty of each country'.[22] They appear blind to the fact that it is not the means of combatting these abuses which may impact adversely on human rights, but the abuses themselves.

The 2014 G20 High-Level Principles on Beneficial Ownership Transparency[23]

From the outset, the High-Level Principles make the assumption that legal structures and arrangements have a beneficial owner. It seems beyond their grasp that beneficial ownership may indeed be absent. The agenda, however, is apparently limited to the role of ultimate beneficial owner as ultimate tax payer, the exchange of beneficial ownership information being characterised as desirable for the purposes of protecting 'the integrity and transparency of the global financial system' as if for no other.[24]

In its introduction to the Principles issued following the 2014 Brisbane summit the G20 states:

> The G20 considers financial transparency, in particular the transparency of beneficial ownership of legal persons and arrangements, is a high priority. The G20 Leaders' Declaration from St Petersburg states, 'We encourage all countries to tackle the risks raised by the opacity of legal

---

21 'G20 Anti-Corruption Action Plan 2017–2018: 2016 Hangzhou Summit: Hangzhou, September 5, 2016' (*University of Toronto*, 2016) <www.g20.utoronto.ca/2016/160905-anticorruption.html> accessed 30 April 2017.

22 Hangzhou Communiqué (n 19) para 22.

23 All G20 Australia 2014 materials are available from the 'G20 Information Centre' (*University of Toronto, Munk School of Global Affairs*) <www.g20.utoronto.ca> accessed 30 April 2017.

24 Reflected at each G20 summit in the OECD Secretary General's Report to G20 Leaders November 2014 (Brisbane) <www.oecd.org/g20/topics/taxation/OECD-secretary-general-report-tax-matters-brisbane-november-2014.pdf> accessed 20 May 2017 and to the G20 Finance Ministers in April 2016 (Washington DC). OECD, 'OECD Secretary-General's Report to G20 Finance Ministers, April 2016' (n 16) (as updated in OECD, 'OECD Secretary-General Report to G20 Finance Ministers: Chengdu People's Republic of China 23–24 July 2016' (*OECD*, 2016) <www.oecd.org/ctp/oecd-secretary-general-tax-report-g20-finance-ministers-july-2016.pdf> accessed 30 April 2017. And see OECD, 'G20/OECD Principles of Corporate Governance' (*University of Toronto*, September 2015) <www.g20.utoronto.ca/2015/G20-OECD-Principles-of-Corporate-Governance.pdf> accessed 30 April 2017.

persons and legal arrangements'. In order to maintain the momentum, Leaders called upon Finance Ministers to update them by the 2014 G20 Leaders' Summit on the steps taken by G20 countries 'to meet FATF standards regarding the beneficial ownership of companies and other legal arrangements such as trusts by G20 countries leading by example.' At their meeting in Sydney in 2014, Finance Ministers and Central Bank Governors requested the ACWG provide them with an update before their April meeting on concrete actions the G20 could take to lead by example on beneficial ownership transparency and the implementation of relevant FATF standards. Following the G20 ACWG meeting in Sydney, ACWG co-chairs reported to Finance Ministers and Central Bank Governors that the ACWG agreed that G20 countries will lead by example by developing G20 High-Level Principles on Beneficial Ownership Transparency that will set out concrete measures G20 countries will take to prevent the misuse of and ensure transparency of legal persons and legal arrangements. Improving the transparency of legal persons and arrangements is important to protect the integrity and transparency of the global financial system. Preventing the misuse of these entities for illicit purposes such as corruption, tax evasion and money laundering supports the G20 objectives of increasing growth through private sector investment.

The G20 is committed to leading by example by endorsing a set of core principles on the transparency of beneficial ownership of legal persons and arrangements that are applicable across G20 work streams. These principles build on existing international instruments and standards, and allow sufficient flexibility too for our different constitutional and legal frameworks.

There are ten Principles, recommendations in which range from the specific to the merely aspirational:

1   Countries should have a definition of 'beneficial owner' that captures the natural person(s) who ultimately owns or controls the legal person or legal arrangement.
2   Countries should assess the existing and emerging risks associated with different types of legal persons and arrangements, which should be addressed from a domestic and international perspective.
   a.   Appropriate information on the results of the risk assessments should be shared with competent authorities, financial institutions and designated non-financial businesses and professions (DNFBPs) and, as appropriate, other jurisdictions.
   b.   Effective and proportionate measures should be taken to mitigate the risks identified.
   c.   Countries should identify high-risk sectors, and enhanced due diligence could be appropriately considered for such sectors.

3   Countries should ensure that legal persons maintain beneficial ownership information onshore and that information is adequate, accurate, and current.

4   Countries should ensure that competent authorities (including law enforcement and prosecutorial authorities, supervisory authorities, tax authorities and financial intelligence units) have timely access to adequate, accurate and current information regarding the beneficial ownership of legal persons. Countries could implement this, for example, through central registries of beneficial ownership of legal persons or other appropriate mechanisms.

5   Countries should ensure that trustees of express trusts maintain adequate, accurate and current beneficial ownership information, including information of settlors, the protector (if any), trustees and beneficiaries. These measures should also apply to other legal arrangements with a structure or function similar to express trusts.

6   Countries should ensure that competent authorities (including law enforcement and prosecutorial authorities, supervisory authorities, tax authorities and financial intelligence units) have timely access to adequate, accurate and current information regarding the beneficial ownership of legal arrangements.

7   Countries should require financial institutions and DNFBPs, including trust and company service providers, to identify and take reasonable measures, including taking into account country risks, to verify the beneficial ownership of their customers.
   a.   Countries should consider facilitating access to beneficial ownership information by financial institutions and DNFBPs.
   b.   Countries should ensure effective supervision of these obligations, including the establishment and enforcement of effective, proportionate and dissuasive sanctions for non-compliance.

8   Countries should ensure that their national authorities cooperate effectively domestically and internationally. Countries should also ensure that their competent authorities participate in information exchange on beneficial ownership with international counterparts in a timely and effective manner.

9   Countries should support G20 efforts to combat tax evasion by ensuring that beneficial ownership information is accessible to their tax authorities and can be exchanged with relevant international counterparts in a timely and effective manner.

10 Countries should address the misuse of legal persons and legal arrangements which may obstruct transparency, including:
   a.   prohibiting the ongoing use of bearer shares and the creation of new bearer shares, or taking other effective measures to ensure that bearer shares and bearer share warrants are not misused; and
   b.   taking effective measures to ensure that legal persons which allow nominee shareholders or nominee directors are not misused.

The ten Principles appear to resonate with an almost biblical authority, as if carried down the mountain on stone tablets, but on closer examination are less than they seem – though are almost certainly what the G20 intended them to be.

The Principles suffer from a degree of abstraction, stemming from the use of the term 'beneficial ownership' without any attempt to define this. There is no proposal for a formula – merely the exhortation that '[c]ountries should have a definition of "beneficial owner" that captures the natural person(s) who ultimately owns or controls the legal person or legal arrangement'.

The Principles overlap and repeat each other. The ten Principles, when edited to remove these overlaps and repetitions, amount to no more than a call for risk assessment, registration (access to this being restricted to state-designated taxation and law enforcement authorities), and information exchanges between states.

Reference to the curbing of the use of bearer shares and controls on nominee shareholders and nominee directors, which have been for the past fifty years the most obvious, most easily identifiable and least sophisticated of beneficial ownership avoidance structures, indicates how superficial an understanding the G20 has of the subtleties and complexities of the modern approach to avoidance.

Without addressing these weaknesses, the G20 in July 2016 issued its 'Progress Report on the Implementation of the G20/OECD High-Level Principles of Corporate Governance'.[25] Unaware that ownership may be entirely absent, the report states:

> Disclosure of ownership should be provided once certain thresholds of ownership are passed. Such disclosure might include data on major shareholders and others that, directly or indirectly, significantly influence or control or may significantly influence or control the company through, for example, special voting rights, shareholder agreements, the ownership of controlling or large blocks of shares, significant cross share-holding relationships and cross guarantees.[26]

The Report does, however, concede that 'empirical work indicates that in a number of jurisdictions, a large number of firms fail to report ownership data and in particular share ownership by management and members of the board. Moreover, enforcement can be weak and regulations unclear.'[27]

---

25   OECD, (*University of Toronto*, July 2016) <www.g20.utoronto.ca/2016/g20-oecd-progress-report-corporate-governance.pdf> accessed 23 April 2017.

26   s 5.2.1.3 para 222.

27   s 5.2.1.3 para 223. For the full text of s 5.2.1.3 dealing with major share ownership, including beneficial owners and voting rights, see Appendix 3.

Sidelined and defeated by a non-charitable purpose trust[28]

A trust is a simple triangle. A Settlor, wishing to benefit a Beneficiary, transfers property to a Trustee, who takes that property into their name but who holds it for the benefit of the Beneficiary.

The Beneficiary has no rights of ownership in law over the property, and the Trustee has no right to benefit from the property either in law or in equity. The Beneficiary has an expectation that in equity they will receive the property (or the income it generates, or both).[29]

The 'three certainties' which are required for the creation and constitution of a trust are thereby present – certainty of having an intention to create a trust, certainty as to what property is to be placed in the trust, and certainty of the identity of who will benefit. It is possible for the beneficiary, instead of being a person, to be a charitable cause – something which can objectively be identified even though at any one time no individual is in mind.

This analysis falls asunder in the case of a non-charitable purpose trust, under which for the duration of such trusts there is a complete absence of beneficial ownership of any asset held (for example, shares in a company) because such a trust cannot be for the benefit any individual or identifiable group of legal or moral persons, but exists simply for its own stated purpose. That purpose may simply be the holding of the very shares in a company which form the trust fund – Ouroborus conceptualised as an equitable Möbius curve.[30]

Dis-applying the concept of beneficial ownership means there is no possibility of transparency. The Principles – and in particular Principle 5 on trust

---

28   See the discussion of non-charitable purpose trusts in Chapter 2. For further beneficial ownership avoidance structuring possibilities, see Appendix 2.

29   This simple equitable truth has not proved apparent, for example, to the European Union. In their Directive (EU) 2015/849 of the European Parliament and of the Council of 20 May 2015 on the prevention of the use of the financial system for the purposes of money laundering or terrorist financing, amending Regulation (EU) No 648/2012 of the European Parliament and of the Council [known as the EU 4th Money Laundering Directive], and repealing Directive 2005/60/EC of the European Parliament and of the Council and Commission Directive 2006/70/EC (Text with EEA relevance) [2015] OJ L141, 5.6.2015, 'beneficial owner' in relation to trusts is identified as the settlor, trustees, beneficiaries and protector (art 3(6)(b) and art 31(1)). Not only is this wholly at odds with the equitable principles which give rise to trusts, it takes no account of beneficial ownership avoidance strategies using non-charitable purpose trusts, seemingly unaware that such trusts having no beneficiaries are widely available. Indeed, the concept of beneficial ownership avoidance is entirely absent from the Directive.

30   For example the use of a non-charitable purpose trust to hold special purpose vehicles – that is, companies set up to perform a specific task or to hold a specific asset – used in off-balance sheet transactions where the beneficial interest in a special purpose vehicle may be said to be "ownerless" – see the discussion by Carey Olsen of Jersey non-charitable purpose trusts in this context: 'A Guide to Non-Charitable Purpose Trusts in Jersey' (*Carey Olsen*, 23 March 2017) <www.careyolsen.com/downloads/Non_charitable_purpose_trusts_in_Jersey.pdf> accessed 30 April 2017.

structures[31] – can be wholly sidelined and disclosure of beneficial ownership defeated.

Case study 1:[32] The Isle of Man Purpose Trusts Act 1996[33]

Purpose trusts are not trusts in the classical sense and are designed to be used as adjuncts to taxation planning structures and risk avoidance in various ways, including:

- holding shares in a company which can then be voted in accordance with the terms of the trust (of particular importance in circumstances where an individual may not wish beneficially to own such assets);
- protection of subsidiaries where a parent company borrows – the shares of the subsidiary are placed in trust until the loan is repaid, thereby protecting the subsidiary from creditors of its parent;
- protection of the lender where a parent company borrows – the shares of the subsidiary can be placed in a purpose trust until the loan is repaid, thereby preventing the ownership of the subsidiary from changing;
- capital financing and securitisation projects in which the trust assets are off the balance sheet of one or more parties to the transaction; or
- holding toxic or high risk assets (e.g. untreated brownfield development sites; bulk carriers) in a special purpose vehicle the shares in which are held in a purpose trust.

At common law, a non-charitable purpose trust would be void for want of identifiable beneficiaries to enforce it and for breach of the rule against perpetuities.[34] The Act provides for the creation of purpose trusts. The purpose must be certain, reasonable and possible: and must not be unlawful, contrary to public policy or immoral (s 1(1)(a)).

---

31 '5. Countries should ensure that trustees of express trusts maintain adequate, accurate and current beneficial ownership information, including information of settlors, the protector (if any) trustees and beneficiaries. These measures should also apply to other legal arrangements with a structure or function similar to express trusts.'

32 The Isle of Man is merely one of an increasing number of jurisdictions which within the past twenty years have introduced legislation supporting the creation of non-charitable purpose trusts. This is a global phenomenon. See Appendix 1, which samples some of these.

33 <http://legislation.gov.im/cms/images/LEGISLATION/PRINCIPAL/1996/1996-0009/PurposeTrustsAct1996_1.pdf> accessed 30 April 2017. The Act came into force on 22 May 1996.

34 Note that the rule against perpetuities, under which property in trust (other than one for exclusively charitable purposes) had to vest in the beneficiaries within a fixed period of time, has been abolished in certain jurisdictions including the Isle of Man: Perpetuities and Accumulations Act 1968 (as amended) <https://legislation.gov.im/cms/images/LEGISLATION/PRINCIPAL/1968/1968-0008/PerpetuitiesandAccumulationsAct1968_2.pdf> accessed 30 April 2017, s 1A.

The following are not capable of being regarded as purpose trusts (s 9(1)), those made:

- for the benefit of a particular person (whether or not immediately ascertainable);
- for the benefit of some aggregate of persons identified by reference to some personal relationship; or
- for charitable purposes.

The operational mechanics of an Isle of Man purpose trust do not differ in any material respect from the mechanics of similar structures in other jurisdictions.[35]

The crucial issue is that any asset held under a purpose trust is not beneficially owned. Not until after the purpose trust has terminated will ownership of those assets once again be possible, in the form of the distribution of a surplus. Those future recipients of surplus, even if identified in the purpose trust deed itself (by name or by the use of a formula from which identity can be deduced) are in no sense beneficiaries. Their status is activated only after the event.[36]

No principles of beneficial ownership tracing and declaration are of the slightest utility if there are in fact no beneficial owners.

Case study 2: beneficial ownership disclosure in the Isle of Man

The obstacles to and limitations on the drive to identify beneficial ownership can be illustrated by the efforts of the Isle of Man. The principal legislation is found in the Companies (Beneficial Ownership) Act 2012[37] ('the 2012 Act') with the exceptions to those provisions being found in the Companies (Beneficial Ownership) (Exemptions) Order 2013[38] which came into operation on 1 September 2013.[39]

---

35 See Chapter 2 for an account of the structural mechanics.
36 They are therefore invisible, and wholly outside the scope of, eg, (1) the OECD's Common Reporting Standard [OECD, 'Standard for Automatic Exchange of Financial Account Information in Tax Matters' (*OECD*, 14 July 211AD) <www.oecd.org/ctp/exchange-of-tax-information/standard-for-automatic-exchange-of-financial-account-information-for-tax-matters-9789264216525-en.htm> accessed 30 April 2017]; and (2) the United Kingdom's PSC (people with significant control) regime [United Kingdom Government, Companies House, 'PSC Requirements for Companies and Limited Liability Partnerships' (*gov.uk*, 27 January 2016) <www.gov.uk/government/publications/guidance-to-the-people-with-significant-control-requirements-for-companies-and-limited-liability-partnerships> accessed 30 April 2017].
37 <https://legislation.gov.im/cms/images/LEGISLATION/PRINCIPAL/2012/2012-0009/CompaniesBeneficialOwnershipAct2012_2.pdf> accessed 30 April 2017.
38 <www.tynwald.org.im/links/tls/SD/2013/2013-SD-0235.pdf> accessed 30 April 2017.
39 The Act applies to companies formed under the Companies Acts 1931 to 2004 (including

The meaning of 'beneficial ownership'

Section 3 (1) of the 2012 Act defines 'beneficial owner' in relation to a member's interest in a company as being the person ultimately beneficially interested in the membership interest. Beneficial ownership may be traced through any number of persons or arrangements of any description.[40]

The scope of the 2012 Act is narrowed firstly by the fact that it applies only to companies, and not to LLCs, Isle of Man Foundations or partnerships, either general or limited. It is further narrowed by its application to only one of the twin company law regimes in the Isle of Man, where companies may be

a protected cell company under the Protected Cell Companies Act 2004, an incorporated cell company under the Incorporated Cell Companies Act 2010 and any company continued in the Isle of Man under the Companies (Transfer of Domicile) Act 1998. Draft legislation has been introduced to widen the range of structures to which disclosure and registration must apply in the form of the Beneficial Ownership Bill 2017 <www.tynwald.org.im/business/bills/Bills/Beneficial_Ownership_Bill_2017.pdf> accessed 30 April 2017.

40   S 3 is as follows:

Meaning of beneficial owner (1) In this Act, 'beneficial owner', in relation to a member's interest in a company means the person ultimately beneficially interested in the membership interest, and 'beneficial ownership' is to be construed accordingly. (2) Beneficial ownership may be traced through any number of persons or arrangements of any description. Clause 4 of the Beneficial Ownership Bill 2017 expands this considerably, attempting also to provide for future definitional flexibility: 4 Meaning of beneficial owner (1) In this Act 'beneficial owner' means a natural person who ultimately owns or controls a legal entity to which this Act applies, in whole or in part, through direct or indirect ownership or control of shares or voting rights or other ownership interest in that entity, or who exercises control via other means, and 'beneficial ownership' is to be construed accordingly. (2) If two or more natural persons each own or control an interest in a legal entity to which this Act applies, each of them is treated for the purposes of this Act as owning or controlling that interest. Example: If two persons jointly own or control a 30% interest in a legal entity, they are each treated as owning the 30% interest and each is a registrable beneficial owner for the purposes of this Act. (3) Beneficial ownership may be traced through any number of persons or arrangements of any description. (4) The [Isle of Man Government Financial Services] Authority may issue guidance about the meaning of 'beneficial ownership', 'ownership', 'control', 'legal ownership' and 'registrable beneficial ownership'. (5) Regard must be had to guidance issued under subsection (4) in interpreting references in this Act to those expressions. (6) The Authority may revise guidance issued under subsection (4) and a reference to guidance includes a reference to revised guidance. (7) Guidance issued under subsection (4) must be published by the Authority on its website or in a manner the Authority considers will bring it to the attention of those likely to be affected by it. (8) The Treasury may by order amend – (a) subsection (1) to revise the meaning of 'beneficial owner'; and (b) subsection (2). (9) An order under subsection (8) must not come into operation unless it is approved by Tynwald.

The Clause (and the Bill in its entirety) nevertheless fails to address the issue of beneficial ownership avoidance.

formed wither under the Companies Acts 1931 to 2004 or the Companies Act 2006.[41]

This logic is continued in section 4(2) of the 2012 Act, which expressly does not apply to a company which is incorporated outside the Isle of Man, listed on a stock or investment exchange recognised by the Isle of Man Treasury, or a collective investment scheme under the Collective Investment Schemes Act 2008.[42]

Requirement to have a Nominated Officer

Each company to which the 2012 Act applies must have a nominated officer who has to be either an individual resident in the Island (though not required to hold any specific qualifications) or a licensed Corporate Service Provider. If there is more than one nominated officer per company, their liability is both joint and several.

Duty of members to keep Nominated Officer informed

If a member of the company whose name appears in the register of share-holders or guarantee members is not a beneficial owner, that person is obliged to inform the nominated officer who the beneficial owner is and to provide a range of details set out in s 8 of the 2012 Act. In the case of an individual, the details required are: name, residential address, nationality, and date of birth. In the case of 'a beneficial owner which has legal personality but is not an individual' all that is required is its name, jurisdiction of formation, legal form and the law by which it is governed, registered office, and (if any) official registered number. (Presumably it has not occurred to the legal draughtsman that defining beneficial ownership as being traced through any number of persons or arrangements of any description but only requiring a member which is holding on behalf of the corporation to give the details set out above misses the point entirely).

Duty of the Nominated Officer

The nominated officer is obliged to inform the company if the officer believes that insufficient detail has been provided and is required to provide

41   The thinking behind restricting the 2012 Act to companies formed under the Companies Acts 1931 to 2004 is that companies formed under the Companies Act 2006 are obliged to have a registered agent and that registered agent must be a Corporate Service Provider. One of the licence conditions of being a CSP is to have information which identifies the beneficial owners of the relevant companies for Anti Money-Laundering purposes. The absence of a registered agent in the case of companies formed under the Companies Acts 1931 to 2004 meant that a separate mechanism had to be introduced.

42   <https://legislation.gov.im/cms/images/LEGISLATION/PRINCIPAL/2008/2008-0007/CollectiveInvestmentSchemesAct2008_4.pdf> accessed 30 April 2017.

the information which he or she holds if served with a Notice by the Isle of Man's Attorney General, the Isle of Man's Chief Constable, the Financial Crimes Unit of the Isle of Man, the Isle of Man Financial Services Authority, the Isle of Man Assessor of Income Tax or Collector of Customs and Excise (or any person appointed by any of these for the purpose of giving the Notice).

Tipping off

The 2012 Act makes it an offence if a person knows that a Notice has been, or is about to be issued to the nominated officer and tips off the ultimate beneficial owner.

Privileged information

Although an Advocate is not required to divulge anything which is subject to legal professional privilege,[43] nevertheless an Advocate may be required to give the name and address of any client. Thus are the boundaries of legal privilege slowly but inexorably rolled back.

How effective is the 2012 Act in practice?

The 2012 Act is rendered largely toothless by the Companies (Beneficial Ownership) (Exemptions) Order 2013 which sets out no fewer than sixteen exemptions.[44] The 2012 Act does not apply *inter alia* to a public company,

---

43 Which the 2012 Act defines as being within the meaning of s 13 Police Powers and Procedures Act 1998 <https://legislation.gov.im/cms/images/LEGISLATION/PRINCIPAL/1998/1998-0009/PolicePowersandProceduresAct1998_3.pdf> accessed 30 April 2017:

> 13 Meaning of 'items subject to legal privilege' (1) Subject to subsection (2), in this Act 'items subject to legal privilege' means – (a) communications between a professional legal adviser and his client or any person representing his client made in connection with the giving of legal advice to the client; (b) communications between a professional legal adviser and his client or any person representing his client or between such an adviser or his client or any such representative and any other person made in connection with or in contemplation of legal proceedings and for the purposes of such proceedings; and (c) items enclosed with or referred to in such communications and made – (i) in connection with the giving of legal advice; or (ii) in connection with or in contemplation of legal proceedings and for the purposes of such proceedings, when they are in the possession of a person who is entitled to possession of them. (2) Items held with the intention of furthering a criminal purpose are not items subject to legal privilege.

44 S 3:

> Exemptions from Act The Companies (Beneficial Ownership) Act 2012 does not apply to a company – (a) which is a public company within the meaning given by section 341 of the Companies Act 1931; (b) which is a registered charity within the meaning given by section 15(1) of the Charities Registration Act 1989; (c) which, by virtue of a licence

a registered charity, a company licensed by the Financial Services Authority under the Financial Services Act 2008, an insurance intermediary or insurance manager, a pension scheme administrator, an online gambling company, a bookmaker or betting office, or a casino.

Companies exempt under the Order are, therefore, in the main those which are already adequately regulated under other legislation; but the whole thrust of establishing a mechanism for the identification of the beneficial ownership of companies was that it would be a single system and not scattered across a whole range of licensing authorities. The system of notification under the 2012 Act is not centralised and is not publicly accessible.

United Kingdom and Isle of Man – commitment to share beneficial ownership information – 12 April 2016[45]

The effectiveness of a recent initiative on the part of the United Kingdom

from the Attorney General under section 18 of the Companies Act 1931, is exempt from the obligation to use the word 'limited' as part of its name; (d) which – (i) is formed for promoting art, science, religion, sport, commerce, charity or any profession (whether or not licensed under section 18 of the Companies Act 1931); and (ii) has confirmed in its annual return most recently submitted to the Department of Economic Development under section 109 of the Companies Act 1931 that its principal trade or business is consistent with the purpose for which it was formed; (e) which is licensed by the Financial Supervision Commission under section 7 of the Financial Services Act 2008 to carry on a regulated activity (within the meaning given by section 3 of that Act); (f) which is in receipt of services provided by the holder of a Class 3 (services to collective investment schemes) or Class 4 (corporate services) licence issued by the Financial Services Authority under section 7 of the Financial Services Act 2008 in accordance with the licence; (g) which is an insurer authorized under section 8 of the Insurance Act 2008 to carry on an insurance business; (h) which is registered under section 25 of the Insurance Act 2008 in the register of insurance intermediaries kept by the Insurance and Pensions Supervisor under that Act; (i) which is registered under section 25 of the Insurance Act 2008 in the register of insurance managers kept by the Insurance and Pensions Supervisor under that Act; (j) which is registered under section 36 of the Retirement Benefit Schemes Act 2000 in the register of scheme administrators kept by the Insurance and Pensions Supervisor under that Act; (k) which is licensed by the Isle of Man Gambling Supervision Commission to conduct online gambling under section 4 of the Online Gambling Regulation Act 2001; (l) which holds a bookmakers' permit granted by the Isle of Man Gambling Supervision Commission under Schedule 1 to the Gaming, Betting and Lotteries Act 1988; (m) which holds a betting office licence granted by the Isle of Man Gambling Supervision Commission under Schedule 1 to the Gaming, Betting and Lotteries Act 1988; (n) which holds a certificate granted by the Isle of Man Gambling Supervision Commission under section 3 of the Gaming (Amendment) Act 1984 authorizing the keeping of controlled machines (within the meaning given by section 1 of that Act) for use on premises specified in the certificate; (o) which holds a casino licence granted by the Council of Ministers under section 3 of the Casino Act 1986; or (p) which is a wholly-owned subsidiary of a company to which the Companies (Beneficial Ownership) Act 2012 does not apply by virtue of this Order.

45   'Exchange of Notes between the Governments of the United Kingdom and the Government of the Isle of Man in Respect of the Sharing of Beneficial Ownership

and Isle of Man government remains to be seen, given the limitation in both jurisdictions on ascertaining beneficial ownership. What 'beneficial ownership' and its identification signify is far from clear in each case.

The initiative takes the form of an Exchange of Notes:

> The Participants recognize the importance of the provision of beneficial ownership information for the prevention and detection of corruption, money laundering, terrorism financing, financing of the proliferation of weapons of mass destruction and other serious and organized crimes. It also recognizes the importance of facilitating timely and secure access for law enforcement agencies to such information whilst ensuring individuals concerned are not informed that a request has been made. ... The Participants will hold adequate, accurate and current beneficial ownership information for corporate and legal entities incorporated in their own jurisdictions. This information will be held in a secure central electronic database. ... Law enforcement authorities of the Participants will have automatic right to the provision of unrestricted and timely ... beneficial ownership information held in the other jurisdiction.

In the Technical Protocol attached to the Exchange of Notes it is made clear that the Isle of Man Database will be maintained by the Isle of Man Companies Registry and will be overseen by the Isle of Man Financial Services Authority. The arrangements are to come into effect no later than 30 June 2017. Whether the Isle of Man Government has fully appreciated the magnitude of the task of introducing 'any necessary legislative regulatory or technical changes'[46] to allow implementation within this timeframe, in light of the current scattering of such information (however superficial) throughout the corpus of Manx statute law, case law, and international treaty obligations is moot.[47]

> Information' <www.gov.uk/government/uploads/system/uploads/attachment_data/file/518321/Sharing-beneficial-ownership-information-exchange-of-information-between-UK-government-and-government-of-Isle-of-Man.pdf> accessed 30 April 2017 ('Exchange of Notes').
>
> 46 'Exchange of Notes' (n 45), Technical Protocol, para 9.
> 47 Sight must not be lost of the fact that the Isle of Man has for decades been bound by the provisions of a number of international human rights documents, all of which – with or without local enabling legislation – are justiciable and may be pleaded before the Courts, and which impact on state incursions into privacy:
>
> - Convention for the Protection of Human Rights and Fundamental Freedoms (the European Convention) 1950 [and the Human Rights Act 2001]
> - International Covenant on Civil and Political Rights 1966
> - International Covenant on Economic, Social and Cultural Rights 1966
> - Convention on the Elimination of All Forms of Discrimination Against Women 1979
> - Convention on the Rights of the Child 1989
>
> In addition, the Isle of Man is under the wing of the United Kingdom as regards its obligations entered into as a member of the world's oldest human rights organisation, the

Even if it were to prove possible to achieve implementation within the suggested timescale, the weakness of this approach is immediately apparent. It is restricted to corporate and legal entities. Such entities are those 'incorporated in the Isle of Man'.[48] Information exchange is restricted to law enforcement agencies and is not made available to the wider public,[49] thereby excluding any general corporate governance review[50] of an entity which is not itself associated with criminal activity in the widest sense of that term. Disclosure of information relating to requests other than to the law enforcement authorities of the United Kingdom and the Isle of Man will itself be criminalised.[51] It takes no account of the fact that legislation such as the Purpose Trusts Act 1996 may be used to remove the concept of beneficial ownership altogether, and this not merely in relation to entities incorporated in the Isle of Man but also to entities incorporated anywhere in the world the shares (or other financial instruments) of which are held under a purpose trust.

International Labour Organization. For an analysis of the representative impact of Isle of Man structures on the international human rights continuum see Chapter 5.

48 Reflecting the limitation found in section 4(2) Companies (Beneficial Ownership) Act 2012 – data on the beneficial ownership of companies incorporated outside the Isle of Man is not held, notwithstanding that the licensed corporate services providers in the Isle of Man provide on a regular basis their services to entities wherever incorporated. Presumably even when this provision is re-enacted to conform to the Technical Protocol of 12 April 2016 this limitation will not be removed.

49 An attempt on the part of the United Kingdom to compel the publication of beneficial ownership registers of companies in Overseas Territories by the insertion of a clause in the Criminal Finances Bill 2017 was defeated in the House of Commons on 21 February 2017. Speaking in the debate, Nigel Mills MP stated:

> The advantage of transparency … is that it puts the information into the public domain so that various NGOs or other bodies can do some of the initial investigation, piece together the corporate chains and links, break the corporate veils, and thereby work out where this money is coming from and where it has got to. I am a little sceptical that our law enforcement bodies will ever have the resources to start that process in the vast majority of cases.

Criminal Finances Bill Deb 21 February 2017 vol 621 col 906–08 <https://hansard. parliament.uk/Commons/2017-02-21/debates/E346156E-E862-4E5B-8233-C17ECF 374C21/CriminalFinancesBill?highlight=beneficial%20ownership# contribution-56833C35-3DAB-46FB-A38C-71E3422E4138> accessed 30 April 2017. 'Nevertheless, it remains the Government's ambition for public registers to become the global standard. If this happens, we would expect the Overseas Territories and Crown Dependencies to follow suit.' 'Companies: Ownership: Written question – 67174' (Secretary of State for Foreign and Commonwealth Affairs, United Kingdom, 8 March 2017) <www.parliament. uk/business/publications/written-questions-answers-statements/written-question/ Commons/2017-03-08/67174> accessed 30 April 2017.

50 For example, as envisaged under the United Nations Office of the High Commissioner for Human Rights, "UN Guiding Principles on Business and Human Rights: Implementing the United Nations 'Protect, Respect and Remedy' Framework" (2011) UN Doc HR/PUB/11/04.

51 Technical Protocol, para 7(vi)(a).

MONEYVAL Mutual Evaluation Report on the Isle of Man December 2016[52]

On 10 October 2012, the Council of Europe's Committee of Ministers passed resolution CM/Res (2012)6 authorising the participation of the Isle of Man in the mutual evaluation process and procedures of the Committee of Experts on the Evaluation of Anti-Money Laundering Measures and the Financing of Terrorism ('MONEYVAL'). This allows the Isle of Man to participate in MONEYVAL's evaluation and follow-up procedures.

The MONEYVAL Fifth Round Mutual Evaluation Report makes extensive updating suggestions (a lesson in itself of how time-consuming and legislatively challenging it is for smaller jurisdictions to incorporate into domestic law a constantly shifting set of international standards) and in Recommendations 24 and 25 provides a highly detailed analysis of the existing statutory (including regulatory) requirements under Isle of Man law in relation to beneficial ownership transparency. Its 190 pages contain no reference to a purpose trust, and are silent on the question of beneficial ownership avoidance structures. As with the approach of the G20, MONEYVAL makes the flawed assumption that there must be a beneficial owner and that the only skill required is to tease out that information and to make it (to a greater or lesser extent) publicly available.

Conclusion

The G20 High-Level Principles on the beneficial ownership of companies are not fit for purpose. They are a paper tiger. They lack specificity as to how to define beneficial ownership, how effectively to gather data, and how to disseminate data broadly. They take no account of beneficial ownership avoidance structures, which simply stop the Principles dead in their tracks.

Lip service is being paid to these flawed Principles in the form of legislation itself hesitant and incomplete. At the same time, seemingly unobserved by the G20 but by no means underutilised, legislation promoting beneficial ownership avoidance is advancing apace, not merely in the tax haven micro nations, unchallenged.

The consequences for the enforcement of international human rights may not be immediately apparent to the observer who focuses on taxation, money laundering, and terrorism, but they are none the less real. Where states themselves facilitate beneficial ownership avoidance, the private actor and the

---

52   Council of Europe, The Committee of Experts on the Evaluation of Anti-Money Laundering Measures and the Financing of Terrorism (MONEYVAL), 'Anti-Money Laundering and Counter-Terrorist Financing Measures: Isle of Man: Fifth Round Mutual Evaluation Report' (*Council of Europe*, 2016) <www.coe.int/t/dghl/monitoring/moneyval/ Evaluations/ round5/MONEYVAL(2016)25_5thR_MER_Isle%20of%20Man.pdf> accessed 25 April 2017.

human rights activist seeking to identify the source of abuse and those who benefit from that abuse are confronted by complicit jurisdictions which are themselves – to the extent that it even crosses the minds of their legislators – the agents of obscurity.

APPENDIX 1

Table 3.1 Non-charitable purpose trust jurisdictions (sampled)

Jurisdiction	Statute
British Virgin Islands	Trustee Act (Cap. 303) as amended by Trustee (Amendment) Act 2013
Barbados	International Trusts Act 1995
Cayman Islands	Introduced into the Cayman Islands via the Special Trusts (Alternative Regime) Law, 1997, now embedded in Part VIII of the Trusts Law (2011 Revision)
Cook Islands[a]	International Trusts Amendment Act 1995–96, s 8
Guernsey	Trusts (Guernsey) Law 2007, s 12
Isle of Man	Purpose Trusts Act 1996
Jersey	Trusts (Jersey) Law 1984 (as amended by Trusts (Amendment No 3) (Jersey) Law 1996 with effect from 24 May 1996)
Labuan	Labuan Trusts Act 1996 (as amended, 2010) Section 11A
Mauritius	Trusts Act 2001, s 19
Niue	Trustee Companies Act 1994, s 31
Samoa	Trusts Act 2014, s 66
Turks and Caicos Islands	Trusts Ordinance 2016
US, Delaware	Del. Code tit. 12, s 3556
US, New Hampshire	N.H. Rev. Stat. s 564-B
US, South Dakota	South Dakota Codified laws ss 55-1-20
US, Wyoming	Wyo. Stat. ss 4-10-410

Note: [a] Pacific Islands Legal Information Institute <www.paclii.org> accessed 1 May 2017.

APPENDIX 2

Sample alternative beneficial ownership avoidance structures

1 *Substitute beneficial ownership*

This occurs where a person holds assets as legal and beneficial owner, not in any trustee, nominee or fiduciary capacity, and not subject to any legally binding option (put or call), but does so on the understanding (reinforced by whatever form of pressure may be threatened or brought to bear) that at any point in time that person may be called upon to transfer those assets to a third party. This may be wholly undetectable. The use and abuse of cryptocurrencies is a contemporary example.[53]

2 *Single premium life assurance policies*

Assets may be held in a single premium life assurance policy (so called because only one initial premium is required) where the premium is paid either in liquid cash or in specie. This is a contractual arrangement, to which universally recognised principles of insurance law apply. The policyholder – who may be a man of straw with no connection to the person whose life is assured – designates those persons to whom the proceeds of the policy will be paid when the life assured dies.[54] They are themselves not the source of funds (initially, this being the policyholder and subsequently the life insurance company whose property the premium becomes). If the asset held

---

53   As the Financial Transparency Coalition observes:

> Bitcoin presents short- and long-term risks to financial crime. Like tax havens and other jurisdictions with lax laws on beneficial ownership, Bitcoin presents criminals with an opportunity to keep their money and their transactions secret. Specifically, Bitcoin users don't need to present an ID to receive a Bitcoin address – or key – so they are not necessarily tied to a flesh and blood person. This means Bitcoin transactions are unidentifiable as long as the user takes care to anonymize his or her IP address.

> Ann Hollingshead, 'Recent Efforts to Regulate Bitcoin Fall Flat' (*Financial Transparency Coalition*, 31 July 2014) <https://financialtransparency.org/recent-efforts-to-regulate-bitcoin-fall-flat> accessed 5 January 2017.

54   In certain jurisdictions the policyholder and the life assured need have no prior connection. The concept of 'insurable interest' which was developed to prevent policies of life assurance from being classified as mere wagers unenforceable at law has been abolished (for example, in the Isle of Man under the Life Assurance (Insurable Interest) Act 2004, which came into force on 1 July 2004. Section 4, which applies in respect of all assurance contracts, whether entered into before or after 1 July 2004, provides in sub-section (2): 'An insurance contract is not void or illegal nor is to be treated as ever having been void or illegal by reason only that the policyholder did not, at the time the contract was entered into, have an insurable interest in the subject of the contract.'

within the single premium life assurance policy is shares in a corporation, the beneficial owner during the life of the policy of those shares is therefore the life assurance company itself, constrained only by the contractual obligation at some future date to transfer some or all of the value of the policy to those persons designated. The persons designated to receive the funds are volunteers, and have no right of ownership in the policy and no right to enforce payment. They are not in any sense the beneficial owners or controllers.[55]

3 'Orphan' entities

The most blatant of the tax haven structures of this kind are Bahamas Executive Entities ('BEE'), a bizarre, artificial creation, unique to The Bahamas, the design of which was commissioned by The Bahamian government from leading London lawyers in 2010 to fill what the Government believed to be a gap in the offshore products market.[56]

BEEs were introduced under The Executive Entities Act 2011,[57] with the intention of facilitating the establishment, operation, management, and termination of a new private wealth structure.

Fundamentally, from a human rights accountability perspective, it is an 'orphan' structure: there are no shareholders or members of any kind, and no beneficiaries. It is the corporate equivalent of the non-charitable purpose trust.[58]

---

55 See also Ronen Palan, Richard Murphy and Christian Chavagneux, *Tax Havens – How Globalization Really Works* (Cornell University Press, 2010) 95–97.

56 Danielle Levy, 'Lawrence Graham Seeks to Revolutionise Offshore Trust Structures' (*Citywire*, 23 April 2010) <http://citywire.co.uk/wealth-manager/news/lawrence-graham-seeks-to-revolutionise-offshore-trust-structures/a395505/print?section=wealth-manager> accessed 5 January 2017.

57 <http://laws.bahamas.gov.bs/cms/images/LEGISLATION/PRINCIPAL/2011/2011-0052/ExecutiveEntitiesAct2011_1.pdf> accessed 1 May 2017, together with the Executive Entities Regulations 2012 <http://laws.bahamas.gov.bs/cms/images/LEGISLATION/SUBORDINATE/2012/2012-0013/ExecutiveEntitiesRegulations2012_1.pdf> accessed 1 May 2017.

58 For a fuller treatment, see Chapter 2.

APPENDIX 3

G20/OECD Progress Report on the Implementation of the G20/OECD High-Level Principles of Corporate Governance July 2016[59]

5.2.1.3 Principle V.A.3: Major share ownership, including beneficial owners, and voting rights.

221. The annotations note that the right to such information should also extend to information about the structure of a group of companies and intra-group relations. Such disclosures should make transparent the objectives, nature and structure of the group.

Likely practices to be examined:

222. Disclosure of ownership data should be provided once certain thresholds of ownership are passed. Such disclosure might include data on major shareholders and others that, directly or indirectly, significantly influence or control or may significantly influence or control the company through, for example, special voting rights, shareholder agreements, the ownership of controlling or large blocks of shares, significant cross shareholding relationships and cross guarantees. It is also good practice to disclose shareholdings of directors, including non-executives.

223. However, empirical work indicates that in a number of jurisdictions, a large number of firms fail to report ownership data and in particular share ownership by management and members of the board. Moreover, enforcement can be weak and regulations unclear. The legal recourse of minority investors can therefore also be frustrated: 'grey' cases may require considerable resources to prove that a regulation has been violated.

224. Company groups are a feature of the corporate governance landscape in many jurisdictions despite usually not having any legal identity. In many cases a group will also include private companies, and cross shareholdings, which makes control of the listed company very opaque. Since group structures might be used to transfer resources to the detriment of minority shareholders, a number of jurisdictions are moving to require improved disclosure and thereby improve implementation of the principle.

225. Particularly for enforcement purposes, and to identify potential conflicts of interest, related party transactions, and insider trading, information about record ownership needs to be complemented with current information about beneficial ownership (in some jurisdictions also termed ultimate owner). In cases where major shareholdings are held through intermediary structures or arrangements, information about the beneficial owners should therefore be

59 (n 25).

obtainable at least by regulatory and enforcement agencies and/or through the judicial process. The reviewer will need to examine whether such arrangements have in fact been effective, and to this end the OECD template Options for Obtaining Beneficial Ownership and Control Information and the Financial Action Task Force's Guidance on Transparency and Beneficial Ownership can serve as reference points. If the arrangements appear effective, criterion 2 can be assessed as fully implemented.

226. Such practices and the intent of the principle suggest the following essential criteria:

i. The corporate governance framework requires disclosure about the recorded owner and holdings of persons who individually or collectively own a substantial (well below controlling) ownership interest in a company: (a) at least annually (eg annual report or shareholder meeting information circular); and (b) on a timely basis as soon as the ownership threshold requiring disclosure has been passed. The disclosure requirement is sufficiently broad enough to apply to complex ownership structures and arrangements, including those that may have been designed to conceal control. There are effective enforcement and remedial mechanisms, and there is widespread implementation of the requirements.

ii. The regulatory system ensures that current information about the beneficial owners should be obtainable at least by regulatory and enforcement agencies and/or through the judicial process, and there is no evidence that such processes have proved ineffective. Where public disclosure of beneficial owners is required, such disclosures should give an accurate view of the ownership and control situation.

iii. The corporate governance framework requires or encourages companies to provide sufficient, timely disclosure about company group structures, significant cross shareholdings and intragroup relations to enable shareholders to understand the control mechanisms of the company. When disclosure is required, there are effective mechanisms for enforcing such standards and effective remedial mechanisms for those who are harmed by inadequate disclosure. Whether it is required or encouraged, disclosure is widespread.

Bibliography

Legislation, regulations, and legislative debates

Beneficial Ownership Bill 2017 <www.tynwald.org.im/business/bills/Bills/Beneficial_Ownership_Bill_2017.pdf> accessed 30 April 2017 (Isle of Man)

Collective Investment Schemes Act 2008 <https://legislation.gov.im/cms/images/LEGISLATION/PRINCIPAL/2008/2008-0007/CollectiveInvestmentSchemesAct2008_4.pdf> accessed 30 April 2017 (Isle of Man)

Companies Act 1931 <https://legislation.gov.im/cms/images/LEGISLATION/PRINCIPAL/1931/1931-0002/CompaniesAct1931_5.pdf> accessed 23 April 2017 (Isle of Man)

Companies Act 2006 <https://legislation.gov.im/cms/images/LEGISLATION/PRINCIPAL/2006/2006-0013/CompaniesAct2006_5.pdf> accessed 23 April 2017(Isle of Man)

Companies (Beneficial Ownership) Act 2012 <https://legislation.gov.im/cms/images/LEGISLATION/PRINCIPAL/2012/2012-0009/CompaniesBeneficialOwnershipAct2012_2.pdf> accessed 30 April 2017 (Isle of Man)

The Companies (Beneficial Ownership) (Exemptions) Order 2013 <www.tynwald.org.im/links/tls/SD/2013/2013-SD-0235.pdf> accessed 30 April 2017 (Isle of Man)

'Companies: Ownership: Written question – 67174' (Secretary of State for Foreign and Commonwealth Affairs, United Kingdom, 8 March 2017) <www.parliament.uk/business/publications/written-questions-answers-statements/written-question/Commons/2017-03-08/67174> accessed 30 April 2017

Companies (Transfer of Domicile) Act 1998 <https://legislation.gov.im/cms/images/LEGISLATION/PRINCIPAL/1998/1998-0006/CompaniesTransferofDomicileAct1998_1.pdf> accessed 23 April 2017 (Isle of Man)

Criminal Finances Bill Deb 21 February 2017 vol 621 col 906–08 <https://hansard.parliament.uk/Commons/2017-02-21/debates/E346156E-E862-4E5B-8233-C17ECF374C21/CriminalFinancesBill?highlight=beneficial%20ownership#contribution-56833C35-3DAB-46FB-A38C-71E3422E4138> accessed 30 April 2017

The Executive Entities Act 2011 <http://laws.bahamas.gov.bs/cms/images/LEGISLATION/PRINCIPAL/2011/2011-0052/ExecutiveEntitiesAct2011_1.pdf> accessed 1 May 2017 (The Bahamas)

Executive Entities Regulations 2012 <http://laws.bahamas.gov.bs/cms/ images/LEGISLATION/SUBORDINATE/2012/2012-0013/ExecutiveEntitiesRegulations2012_1.pdf> accessed 1 May 2017 (The Bahamas)

Financial Services Act 2008 <https://legislation.gov.im/cms/images/LEGISLATION/PRINCIPAL/2008/2008-0008/FinancialServicesAct 2008_8.pdf> accessed 23 April 2017 (Isle of Man)

Human Rights Act 2001 <https://legislation.gov.im/cms/images/LEGISLATION/PRINCIPAL/2001/2001-0001/HumanRightsAct2001_1.pdf> accessed 23 April 2017 (Isle of Man)

Incorporated Cell Companies Act 2010 <https://legislation.gov.im/cms/images/LEGISLATION/PRINCIPAL/2010/2010-0013/IncorporatedCellCompaniesAct2010_1.pdf> accessed 23 April 2017 (Isle of Man)

The Isle of Man Purpose Trusts Act 1996 <http://legislation.gov.im/cms/images/LEGISLATION/PRINCIPAL/1996/1996-0009/PurposeTrustsAct 1996_1.pdf> accessed 30 April 2017

The Life Assurance (Insurable Interest) Act 2004 <https://legislation.gov.im/cms/images/LEGISLATION/PRINCIPAL/2004/2004-0003/LifeAssurance InsurableInterestsAct2004_2.pdf> accessed 23 April 2017 (Isle of Man)

Perpetuities and Accumulations Act 1968 (as amended) <https://legislation.gov.im/cms/images/LEGISLATION/PRINCIPAL/1968/1968-0008/Perpetuitiesand AccumulationsAct1968_2.pdf> accessed 30 April 2017 (Isle of Man)

Police Powers and Procedures Act 1998 <https://legislation.gov.im/cms/images/LEGISLATION/PRINCIPAL/1998/1998-0009/PolicePowersandProcedures Act1998_3.pdf> accessed 30 April 2017 (Isle of Man)

Protected Cell Companies Act 2004 <https://legislation.gov.im/cms/images/LEGISLATION/PRINCIPAL/2004/2004-0001/ProtectedCell CompaniesAct2004_2.pdf> accessed 23 April 2017 (Isle of Man)

Exchange of notes

'Exchange of Notes between the Governments of the United Kingdom and the Government of the Isle of Man in Respect of the Sharing of Beneficial Ownership Information' <www.gov.uk/government/uploads/system/uploads/attachment_data/file/518321/Sharing-beneficial-ownership-information-exchange-of-information-between-UK-government-and-government-of-Isle-of-Man.pdf> accessed 30 April 2017

European directives

Directive (EU) 2015/849 of the European Parliament and of the Council of 20 May 2015 on the prevention of the use of the financial system for the purposes of money laundering or terrorist financing, amending Regulation (EU) No 648/2012 of the European Parliament and of the Council [known as the EU 4th Money Laundering Directive], and repealing Directive 2005/60/EC of the European Parliament and of the Council and Commission Directive 2006/70/EC (Text with EEA relevance) [2015] OJ L141, 5.6.2015

International treaties

Convention for the Protection of Human Rights and Fundamental Freedoms (European Convention on Human Rights, as amended

Convention on the Elimination of All Forms of Discrimination Against Women (adopted 18 December 1979, entered into force 3 September 1981) 1249 UNTS 13

Convention on the Rights of the Child (adopted 20 November 1989, entered into force 2 September 1990) 1577 UNTS 3

International Covenant on Civil and Political Rights (adopted 16 December 1966, entered into force 23 March 1976) 999 UNTS 171

International Covenant on Economic, Social and Cultural Rights (adopted 16 December 1966, entered into force 3 January 1976) 993 UNTS 3

United Nations documents

United Nations Human Rights Council, 'Report of the Independent Expert on the Question of Human Rights and Extreme Poverty, Magdalena Sepulveda Carmona' (17 March 2011) UN Doc A/HRC/17/34

United Nations Office of the High Commissioner for Human Rights, 'UN Guiding Principles on Business and Human Rights: Implementing the United Nations "Protect, Respect and Remedy" Framework' (2011) UN Doc HR/PUB/11/04'

Secondary sources

Beckett P, 'Beneficial Ownership of Companies – G20 High Level Principles – a Paper Tiger?', *107th Annual Conference of the Society of Legal Scholars* (2016)

——, 'Isle of Man', *European Cross-Border Estate Planning* (Sweet & Maxwell, London, first published 1995, current edition 2017)

——, 'Isle of Man', *Digest of Commercial Laws of the World* (Thomson Reuters, USA, 2016)

Cabra M, 'Map: The Offshore Leaks Revelations' (*ICIJ*, 23 January 2014) <www.icij.org/offshore/map-offshore-leaks-revelations> accessed 25 April 2017

Carey Olsen, 'A Guide to Non-Charitable Purpose Trusts in Jersey' (*Carey Olsen*, 23 March 2017) <www.careyolsen.com/downloads/Non_charitable_purpose_trusts_in_Jersey.pdf> accessed 30 April 2017

Council of Europe, The Committee of Experts on the Evaluation of Anti-Money Laundering Measures and the Financing of Terrorism (MONEYVAL), 'Anti-Money Laundering and Counter-Terrorist Financing Measures: Isle of Man: Fifth Round Mutual Evaluation Report' (2016) <www.coe.int/t/dghl/ monitoring/ moneyval/Evaluations/round5/MONEYVAL(2016)25_5thR_MER_Isle%20of%20Man.pdf> accessed 25 April 2017

van der Does de Willebois E and others, *The Puppet Masters: How the Corrupt Use Legal Structures to Hide Stolen Assets and What to Do About It* (World Bank Publications 2011)

Financial Action Task Force (*Financial Action Task Force*) <www.fatf-gafi.org> accessed 27 April 2017

——, 'The Misuse of Corporate Vehicles Including Trust and Company Service Providers' (*Financial Action Task Force*, 13 October 2006) <www.fatf-gafi.org/media/fatf/documents/reports/Misuse%20of%20Corporate%20Vehicles%20including%20Trusts%20and%20Company%20Services%20Providers.pdf> accessed 30 April 2017

——, 'FATF Recommendations 2012' (*Financial Action Task Force*, 16 February 2012) <www.fatf-gafi.org/publications/fatfrecommendations/documents/fatf-recommendations.html> accessed 30 April 2017

——, 'FATF Guidance on Transparency and Beneficial Ownership' (*Financial Action Task Force*, October 2014) <www.fatf-gafi.org/media/fatf/documents/reports/Guidance-transparency-beneficial-ownership.pdf> accessed 30 April 2017

G20, 'G20 Anti-Corruption Action Plan 2017–2018: 2016 Hangzhou Summit: Hangzhou, September 5, 2016' (*University of Toronto*, 2016) <www.g20.utoronto.ca/2016/160905-anticorruption.html> accessed 30 April 2017

——, 'G20 High-Level Principles on Beneficial Ownership Transparency' (*Australian Government, Attorney General's Department*, 2014) <www.ag.gov.au/

CrimeAndCorruption/AntiCorruption/Documents/G20High-LevelPrinciples OnBeneficialOwnershipTransparency.pdf> accessed 30 April 2017

——, 'G20 Information Centre' (*University of Toronto, Munk School of Global Affairs*) <www.g20.utoronto.ca> accessed 30 April 2017

——, 'G20 Leaders' Communiqué: Hangzhou Summit, Hangzhou' (*University of Toronto*, 5 September 2016) <www.g20.utoronto.ca/2016/160905-com munique.html> accessed 30 April 2017

Hollingshead A, 'Recent Efforts to Regulate Bitcoin Fall Flat' (*Financial Transparency Coalition*, 31 July 2014) <https://financialtransparency.org/recent-efforts-to-regulate-bitcoin-fall-flat> accessed 5 January 2017

Levy D, 'Lawrence Graham Seeks to Revolutionise Offshore Trust Structures' (*Citywire*, 23 April 2010) <http://citywire.co.uk/wealth-manager/news/lawrence-graham-seeks-to-revolutionise-offshore-trust-structures/a395505/print?section=wealth-manager> accessed 5 January 2017

Organisation for Economic Co-operation and Development (OECD), 'Standard for Automatic Exchange of Financial Account Information in Tax Matters' (*OECD*, 14 July 211AD) <www.oecd.org/ctp/exchange-of-tax-information/standard-for-automatic-exchange-of-financial-account-information-for-tax-matters-97892642 16525-en.htm> accessed 30 April 2017

——, 'G20/OECD Principles of Corporate Governance' (*University of Toronto*, September 2015) <www.g20.utoronto.ca/2015/G20-OECD-Principles-of-Corporate-Governance.pdf> accessed 30 April 2017

——, 'OECD Secretary-General's Report to G20 Finance Ministers, April 2016' (*OECD*, April 2016) <www.oecd.org/tax/oecd-secretary-general-tax-report-g20-finance-ministers-april-2016.pdf> accessed 30 April 2017

——, 'OECD Secretary-General Report to G20 Finance Ministers: Chengdu People's Republic of China 23–24 July 2016' (*OECD*, 2016) <www.oecd.org/ctp/oecd-secretary-general-tax-report-g20-finance-ministers-july-2016.pdf> accessed 30 April 2017

——, 'G20/OECD Progress Report on the Implementation of the G20/OECD High- Level Principles of Corporate Governance' (*University of Toronto*, July 2016) <www.g20.utoronto.ca/2016/g20-oecd-progress-report-corporate-gover-nance.pdf> accessed 23 April 2017

Pacific Islands Legal Information Institute <www.paclii.org> accessed 1 May 2017

Palan R, Murphy R, Chavagneux C, *Tax Havens – How Globalization Really Works* (Cornell University Press, 2010)

Sharman A, 'HMRC Revises Common Reporting Standard on Human Rights' (*Civil Society News*, 23 January 2017) <www.civilsociety.co.uk/news/hmrc-revises-common-reporting-standard-guidance-over-human-rights-implications.ht ml> accessed 27 April 2017

United Kingdom Government, Companies House, 'PSC Requirements for Companies and Limited Liability Partnerships' (*gov.uk*, 27 January 2016) <www.gov.uk/government/publications/guidance-to-the-people-with-significant-control-require-ments-for-companies-and-limited-liability-partnerships> accessed 30 April 2017

United Kingdom Government, Her Majesty's Revenue and Customs, 'HMRC Internal Manual: International Exchange of Information Manual: IEIM 406000: Charities: Protection on Human Rights Grounds' (*gov.uk*, 27 April 2017) <www.gov.uk/hmrc-internal-manuals/international-exchange-of-information/ieim406000> accessed 27 April 2017

Walker Guevara M, 'ICIJ Releases Offshore Leaks Database Revealing Names Behind Secret Companies, Trusts' (*ICIJ*, 14 June 2013) <www.icij.org/offshore/icij-releases-offshore-leaks-database-revealing-names-behind-secret-companies-trusts> accessed 25 April 2017

Walker Guevara M and others, 'Who Uses the Offshore World' (*ICIJ*, 16 April 2013) <www.icij.org/offshore/who-uses-offshore-world> accessed 25 April 2017

The World Bank, 'Corrupt Money Concealed in Shell Companies and Other Opaque Legal Entities, Finds New StAR Study' (*The World Bank*, 24 October 2011) <www.worldbank.org/en/news/press-release/2011/10/24/corrupt-money-concealed-in-shell-companies-and-other-opaque-legal-entities-finds-new-star-study> accessed 30 April 2017

4   Tax avoidance and tax evasion

Introduction

Studies and analyses on tax avoidance and tax evasion are legion, and the role of tax havens has been central to much of the research currently available. This has focused, naturally enough, on the fiscal implications of tax avoidance and tax evasion, and little regard has been paid to the collateral damage done to international human rights compliance which results from the disappearance into carefully constructed fiscal black holes of enormous wealth and resources, which could in principle be used by governments to fulfil their human rights obligations.

To evaluate the threat posed in monetary terms to human rights implementation globally by the tax havens, it is essential to understand at least in outline the issues surrounding what for many of those tax havens has been their *raison d'être*. The minimisation of taxation exposure – legitimately avoided or blatantly evaded – became the engine driving the development and expansion of the tax havens. As late as the 1970s, the industry was unsophisticated and smacked of the wild frontier. 'Tax havens, like any other sphere of human activity, attract their fair share of rogues and fools. There is no substitute for the use of good common sense to avoid being made to look a fool by either rogues or other fools.'[1]

The global initiatives, particularly those aimed at tax havens, which have been pursued by such institutions as the European Union, FATF, OECD, and the G20, have generated a vast literature,[2] and a comparative analysis of them is outside the scope of this work. Some indeed have already failed and fallen by the wayside.[3]

---

1   Mark Solly, *Anatomy of a Tax Haven: The Isle of Man* (Shearwater Press, 1975) 10.
2   See eg the extensive studies published by The Tax Justice Network <www.taxjustice.net> accessed 8 May 2017.
3   For example, the European Union Savings Tax Directive which was introduced in 2005 and repealed in 2015 (Council Directive 2003/48/EC of 3 June 2003 on taxation of savings income in the form of interest payments [2003] OJ L 157/38) required the automatic exchange of information between EU member states on private savings income. This enabled interest payments made in one member state to residents of other member states to be taxed in accordance with the laws of the state of tax residence. In its stead Council

This chapter therefore focuses primarily on the twenty-year programme of the OECD, beginning with its Harmful Tax Competition project in the late 1990s, which came to nothing, and moving on to its system of blacklisting and whitelisting in the early part of this century based on transparency and information exchange models. Many of the tax havens have adopted a triumphalist stance upon being placed on the whitelist. In 2014, the OECD introduced its Common Reporting Standard[4] in response to (and as a more targeted replacement of) the earlier initiative of the United States in FATCA.[5]

The chapter assesses the OECD's initiatives and suggests that their augmentation by the inclusion of human rights norms focusing on global standards of corporate governance which apply to the reporting entities themselves (which norms currently do not feature at all) has the potential to be both beneficial and practicable.

The proposition put forward in this chapter is that because the OECD's initiatives on taxation information exchange have had limited success, and the information which is being gathered is of limited practical utility, human rights norms should also be applied. This broadens the field of view to include the substantive conduct of the entities which are subject to the Common Reporting Standard and not merely their taxation strategies. The suggested human rights norms are the Global Compact[6] and the Ruggie Principles.[7] Neither has had any great impact, but this lack of impact does not detract from the substantive quality of the norms themselves. To enable the reporting institutions under the Common Reporting Standard to undertake a common assessment and analysis, the International Organization for Standardization would produce a new ISO Standard dealing with business and human rights in general terms and the use of tax havens in particular.

'Human rights impact' immediately conjures up a picture of embattled human rights under threat of extinction. The idea of tax avoidance and tax

---

Directive 2014/107/EU (of 9 December 2014 amending Directive 2011/16/EU as regards mandatory automatic exchange of information in the field of taxation [2014] OJ L 359, 16.12.2014/1) implements the single global standard developed by the OECD for the automatic exchange of information. The OECD standard was endorsed by G20 finance ministers in September 2014. The European Council, 'Savings Taxation Directive Repealed' (*The European Council*) <www.consilium.europa.eu/en/press/press-releases/2015/11/10-savings-taxation-directive-repealed> accessed 8 May 2017.

4   OECD, *Standard for Automatic Exchange of Financial Account Information in Tax Matters* (OECD 2014) ('*Standard for Automatic Exchange*').

5   Foreign Account Tax Compliance Act <www.irs.gov/businesses/corporations/foreign-account-tax-compliance-act-fatca> accessed 8 May 2017.

6   'United Nations Global Compact' <www.globalcompact.org> accessed 8 May 2017.

7   UNGA, Human Rights Council, 'Report of the Special Representative of the Secretary General on the Issue of Human Rights and Transnational Corporations and Other Business Enterprises, John Ruggie, Guiding Principles on Business and Human Rights: Implementing the United Nations 'Protect, Respect and Remedy' Framework' (21 March 2011) Seventeenth Session, UN Doc A/HRC/17/31 ('Guiding Principles').

evasion impacting human rights is indeed fairly self-evident; but the reverse may also be true. Applying human rights norms to those entities which benefit from these abusive tax practices may be a 'barrier to a worldwide, voracious and highly divisive brand of supranational capitalism'.[8] No matter how sophisticated fiscally based techniques countering tax avoidance and tax evasion become – and they are currently far from effective – it does not follow that a purely fiscal strategy suffices. It rarely follows that just because one has the best hammer, the problem is always a nail. There is a need for a concurrent human rights-based approach.

The underlying question, however, is whether the human rights tools which are available are themselves either sufficiently developed or sufficiently known to the offshore industry that implementing them into a compliance or information exchange framework would be feasible.

Would there be the political will to hard wire the Ruggie Principles and the terms of reference of the Global Compact into the Common Reporting Standard?[9] It can, in an age of the emergence of neo-capitalism and a diminishing regard for human rights norms, only be a matter of speculation whether such political will exists, or whether, in the alternative, governments in the Western economies are shifting back towards the Friedman position of the 1970s that 'there is one and only one social responsibility of business–to use it resources and engage in activities designed to increase its profits so long as it stays within the rules of the game, which is to say, engages in open and free competition without deception or fraud.'[10] Tax evasion would not be within the rules of the game, but under Friedman's doctrine tax avoidance would be fair play.

As David Beetham wrote presciently over twenty years ago:

8   CA Gearty, 'Human Rights', *The Social Science Encyclopaedia* (3rd edn, Routledge, 2004) 468, 470–71. See also Monash University, Castan Centre for Human Rights Law and others, *Human Rights Translated: A Business Reference Guide* (Monash University, Castan Centre for Human Rights Law, International Business Leaders Forum, Office of the United Nations High Commissioner for Human Rights 2008), which illustrates through the use of case studies how human rights are relevant in a corporate context. Available at <www2.ohchr.org/english/issues/globalization/business/docs/Human_Rights_Translated_web.pdff> accessed 20 May 2017

9   There is evidence that the Ruggie principles have found favour in terms of domestic application in a number of European jurisdictions. For example, in the United Kingdom the Companies Act 2006 s 172 dealing with the duty to promote the success of the company requires a director to act in good faith (a subjective criterion) and to have regard for the likely consequences of any decision in the long term, the interests of the company's employees, suppliers, customers and creditors, the impact of the company's operations on the community and on the environment, and the desirability of the company maintaining a reputation for high standards of business conduct. <www.legislation.gov.uk/ukpga/2006/46/section/172> 8 May 2017.

10   Milton Friedman, 'The Social Responsibility of Business Is to Increase Its Profits' [1970] *The New York Times Magazine* <www.colorado.edu/studentgroups/libertarians/ issues/friedman-soc-resp-business.html> accessed 8 May 2017.

Whether new forms of revolutionary movement or social uprising will take place in the future, to provide the spur to reform, is an open question. Equally unpredictable is the point at which the more ruthless strategies of the rich to seal themselves off from the effects of destitution on their own doorstep become politically unsustainable.[11]

Definitions

Until the blurring of the distinction in the early twenty-first century, born of the desire to apply conservative principles of morality to what had been regarded as a liberal pursuit of the wealthy, tax avoidance and tax evasion were respectively the light and the shade of financial planning.

Tax avoidance was the legitimate (albeit amoral) arrangement of tax affairs, applying the law creatively and usually not in ways which the legislators foresaw (the rules of statutory interpretation being almost infinitely malleable) in order to minimise a future and as yet uncrystallised liability to taxation. Tax evasion involved the use of illegal means to escape a liability to tax which had already been incurred.

This has now evolved into a global '"income defence industry" consisting of a high-priced phalanx of lawyers, estate planners, lobbyists and anti-tax activists who exploit and defend a dizzying array of tax maneuvers ...'.[12]

11 David Beetham, 'What Future for Economic and Social Rights?' (1995) XLIII Pol Stud 41, 59.
12 Noam Scheiber and Patricia Cohen, 'For the Wealthiest, a Private Tax System That Saves Them Billions' *The New York Times* (New York, 29 December 2015) <www.nytimes.com/2015/12/30/business/economy/for-the-wealthiest-private-tax-system-saves-them-billions.html?smid=li-share&_r=> accessed 9 May 2017. By contrast, some states have taken a domestic initiative to counter such an approach. Examples:

1   United Kingdom. (a) 'Taxation is not to be treated as a game where taxpayers can indulge in any ingenious scheme in order to eliminate or reduce their tax liability.' HM Revenue and Customs (HMRC), 'HM Revenue and Customs (HMRC) General Anti-Abuse Rule (GAAR) Guidance' (*gov.uk*, 31 March 2017) <www.gov.uk/government/uploads/system/uploads/attachment_data/file/605501/gaar-parts-a-c-2017.pdf> accessed 9 May 2017, Para B.2.2. (b) Criminal Finances Bill 2016-2017 creating a new offence of failure to prevent the facilitation of tax evasion, which from the perspective of the tax havens is of concern because wholly non-UK conduct by a non-UK entity can be covered if it is directed at the evasion of UK tax – for an overview see the briefing paper by Herbert Smith Freehills, 'New UK Criminal Offences of Failure to Prevent Facilitation of Tax Evasion' (*Herbert Smith Freehills*, 5 December 2016) <www.herbertsmithfreehills.com/latest-thinking/new-uk-criminal-offences-of-failure-to-prevent-facilitation-of-tax-evasion> accessed 9 May 2017. (c) Generally on tax anti-avoidance strategy in the United Kingdom see HM Revenue & Customs and HM Treasury, 'Dealing with HMRC: Tax Avoidance' (*gov.uk*) <www.hmrc.gov.uk/avoidance/index.htm> accessed 9 May 2017;
2   In Russia a law on the taxation of controlled foreign companies came into force on 1 January 2015, requiring Russian tax resident individuals to disclose ownership of

The role of tax havens

Tax avoidance and tax evasion strategies are implemented worldwide and are not confined to the use of tax havens. In the case of legitimate tax avoidance, there is currently a global race to the bottom on corporate tax in an attempt to attract business. Oxfam estimates that in the past three decades while net profits posted by the world's richest corporations tripled in real terms, from US$2 trillion in 1980 to US$7.2 trillion in 2013, this increase is not reflected in a proportional increase in tax revenue, which Oxfam attributes partly to the tax havens. Developing countries lose US$100 billion annually as a result of corporate tax avoidance schemes.[13] By their very nature, illicit corporate tax evasion schemes are largely unquantifiable.

Self-evidently, if an individual moves to a tax haven, in the classic way in which from the mid-twentieth century onwards the wealthy have sought to alienate themselves from their original taxation domicile, the role of tax havens is simply to provide the service which their sobriquet suggests. In the case of corporations however, the position is more nuanced. The global standard for the taxation of business income is residency. The default position is that a corporation is resident for tax purposes in the jurisdiction in which it was incorporated, but this residence can shift if the management and control of the corporation is considered to be from elsewhere. If a corporation goes a step further and generates its income from an offshore subsidiary, it is particularly beneficial if that offshore location offers low or zero taxation. Either way, the fiscal allure of a tax haven is strong.

The tax havens have developed arcane, chimeric structures designed to hold and protect assets which would otherwise be accessible to taxation elsewhere, and have themselves adopted low or zero tax regimes, specifically in relation to the taxation of corporations.[14]

foreign companies and wealth planning vehicles. A summary by Withersworldwide 27 November 2014 is available at 'Russian De-Offshorisation Legislation – How the New Law on Taxation of Controlled Foreign Companies Affects You and Your Clients' (*Withersworldwide*, 27 November 2014) <www.withersworldwide.com/news-publications/russian-de-offshorisation-legislation-%E2%80%93-how-the-new-law-on-taxation-of-controlled-foreign-companies-affects-you-and-your-clients> accessed 9 May 2017.

3   In Ireland the Finance Act 2016 introduced a comprehensive programme of targeted intervention against offshore tax evasion, taking advantage of the increased information flow which the Irish government anticipates under the OECD Common Reporting Standard <www.irishstatutebook.ie/eli/2016/act/18/enacted/en/html?q=Finance+Act+2016> accessed 9 May 2017.

13   Oxfam, 'Tax Battles: The Dangerous Global Race to the Bottom on Corporate Tax' (*Oxfam Policy Paper*, 12 December 2016) <www.oxfam.org/sites/www.oxfam.org/files/bp-race-to-bottom-corporate-tax-121216-en.pdf> accessed 9 May 2017.

14   See Chapters 1 and 2 for a discussion of tax strategies and structuring offerings. For an overview of the offshore economy at the beginning of the twenty-first century, see Ronen Palan *The Offshore World: Sovereign Markets, Virtual Places and Nomad Millionaires* (Cornell University Press, 2003) ch 1.

Human rights impact

Aggressive tax planning, evasive or avoidance, undoubtedly distorts international capital flows, and this distortion may impede the implementation by a state of its human rights obligations by limiting the means available to it to do so. In the lead up to the G8 Summit of June 2013 Paul Collier wrote:

> Private financial wealth sitting in tax havens seems to be of the order of $21 trillion, of which around $9 trillion is from developing countries.[15] Some miniscule [*sic*] jurisdictions ... have become the legal home of trillions of dollars of corporate assets through offering the unbeatable attractions of zero taxation plus secrecy. Some industries are dominated by tax havens: half the world's shipping is registered in them. ... [T]here are over 700 independent tax jurisdictions, most fundamentally ill-suited to real economic activity.[16]

Regulating tax havens solely in terms of taxation – being bound by the self-definition of such jurisdictions – will prove to be ineffective, given the chameleonic nature of international tax planning and the endless supply of camouflage cloth available to those who wish to wrap their dealings. An appeal to conscience and morality is unlikely to succeed in the context of taxation,[17] but conscience and morality are the bedrock of international human rights norms. If therefore the war on tax evasion/avoidance is constantly evolving and seemingly endless – 'the battle against tax avoidance is like that against disease: the only viable approach is repeated changing of the locks'[18] – it must follow that *the wrong war is being fought*.

The low tax area structures channel global economic power centres and serve to focus that power where it can least be resisted. As Margot Salomon has demonstrated, there exist legal obligations of developed states (and, by extension, of those channelling states) to people outside their territory; and

> the socio economic rights of people in developing countries are of particular concern in light of the fact that other states are often deeply implicated in their ability to exercise their rights. ... [I]nequality is not the result of some accidental deviation from neo-liberal capitalism, but rather a deliberate product of the international political economy.[19]

15 See Chapter 1 for examples of the wealth of developing nations funnelling into tax havens.

16 Paul Collier, 'In Pursuit of the $21 Trillion' [2013] *Prospect Magazine* <www.prospect magazine.co.uk/magazine/tax-avoidance-paul-collier-david-cameron-g8> accessed 9 May 2017.

17 See the discussion of the Morton's Fork dilemma in Chapter 1 – once a tax haven, always a tax haven.

18 Collier (n 16).

19 Margot Salomon, 'Why Should It Matter That Others Have More? Poverty, Inequality and the Potential of International Human Rights Law' [2010] LSE Legal Studies Working Paper 15/2010 <https://papers.ssrn.com/sol3/papers.cfm?abstract_id=1711657> accessed 10 May 2017, 7, 10.

These are not victimless strategies or mere games of sport with national revenue authorities. They touch the poor profoundly: 'A human rights approach ... requires States to take steps to eliminate the prevalence of tax evasion, a problem that reduces the resources available for measures to realize human rights.'[20] Tax evasion or avoidance is merely a symptom of a deeper malaise, rooted in the breach of more fundamental rights: human rights.[21]

Commenting in February 2017 on state obligations in the context of business activities,[22] the Committee on Economic, Social and Cultural Rights stated that the obligation to protect entails a positive duty to establish clear human rights standards for business, and therefore business entities should be required to exercise human rights due diligence as advocated in Article 17 of the Ruggie Principles.[23] The obligation to fulfil requires mobilisation of resources by a state, including the direct taxation of business income – and this obligation is not fulfilled unless the state takes measures against tax evasion that diminish public resources towards the realisation of economic, social and cultural rights. This duty placed upon states is extraterritorial, and requires states to take cognisance not only of the activities of business enterprises within its own jurisdiction, but also on the adverse impact of such activities outside their territories. The use of offshore-related entities falls four-square within this.

The Organisation for Economic Co-operation and Development: initiatives

OECD's origins and mission

The Organisation for Economic Co-operation and Development (OECD) was established in 1961. Its mission statement is to promote policies which

20   United Nations Human Rights Council, 'Report of the Independent Expert on the Question of Human Rights and Extreme Poverty, Magdalena Sepulveda Carmona' (17 March 2011) UN Doc A/HRC/17/34.

21   The express connection between non-payment of tax and a breach of the duties which accompany human rights is not new: 'The individual shall have the duty ... [t]o work to the best of his abilities and competence, and to pay taxes imposed by law in the interest of the society.' African Charter on Human and Peoples' Rights 1981 (adopted 27 June 1981, entered into force 21 October 1986) (1982) 21 ILM 58, art 29.6. And see East Africa Tax & Governance Network, 'Taxing Rights Policies Are Human Rights Policies' (*East Africa Tax & Governance Network*, 2016) <www.taxjustice.net/wp-content/uploads/2016/11/Tax-and-Human-Rights-Report.pdf>.

22   United Nations Economic and Social Council, 'General Comment on State Obligations under the International Covenant on Economic, Social and Cultural Rights in the Context of Business Activities' [Draft prepared by Olivier De Schutter and Zdzislaw Kedzia, Rapporteurs] (17 October 2016) 60th Session (2017) UN Doc E/C.12/60/R.1, paras 18, 28 to 38, 45.

23   Guiding Principles (n 7).

will improve the social and economic well-being of peoples around the world:

> The OECD provides a forum in which governments can work together to share experiences and seek solutions to common problems. We work with governments to understand what drives economic, social and environmental change. ... We also look at issues that directly affect everyone's daily life, like how much people pay in taxes and social security.

Its stated goal is to build 'a stronger, cleaner and fairer world.'[24]

Its track record in relation to the curtailing of tax avoidance and tax evasion, as well as to the oversight and reform of practices within tax havens, has not been particularly effective or inspiring.

OECD, human rights and taxation

The weakness in the OECD's approach to the curtailing of tax avoidance and tax evasion does not spring from a lack of awareness of the obligations on enterprises to observe human rights or of the role of taxation manipulation in human rights abuse. Rather, it is the failure of the OECD to include any human rights indicators in its anti-avoidance and anti-evasion strategies. This failure is all the more surprising given the OECD's unambiguous stance on multinational enterprises.

The *OECD Guidelines for Multinational Enterprises* (2011 edition)[25] include as General Policies that enterprises should '[r]espect the internationally recognised human rights of those affected by their activities' (General Policy II.A.2) and '[r]efrain from seeking or accepting exemptions not contemplated in the statutory or regulatory framework related to human rights, environmental, health, safety, labour, taxation, financial incentives, or other issues' (General Policy II.A.5). Seeking or accepting exemptions which were not contemplated is precisely what enterprises do when including within their businesses' architecture the fiscal and structural elements made available by the tax havens.

In dealing with taxation, the Guidelines are unequivocal:

> It is important that enterprises contribute to the public finances of host countries by making timely payment of their tax liabilities. In particular,

---

24 OECD, 'The Organisation for Economic Co-Operation and Development (OECD)' (*OECD*) <www.oecd.org/about> accessed 10 May 2017. There are currently 35 Members, plus the Commission of the European Union: OECD, 'Members and Partners' (*OECD*) <www.oecd.org/about/membersandpartners> accessed 10 May 2017.

25 OECD, *OECD Guidelines for Multinational Enterprises* (OECD 2011) <www.oecd. org/daf/inv/mne/48004323.pdf> accessed 10 May 2017.

enterprises should comply with both the letter and spirit of the tax laws and regulations of the countries in which they operate. Complying with the spirit of the law means discerning and following the intention of the legislature.

(Taxation IX Introduction, para 1)

Far too often the call of the tax havens to enterprises, urging them to follow only the letter of the law (often laws which are flawed, incomplete, out-evolved or simply out of date in commercial terms), and not the spirit and intention of the legislature, is irresistible.

On the responsibilities of enterprises for their acts and omissions in human rights terms, the Guidelines leave no room for doubt. Enterprises must adhere to international human rights and in doing so must observe the human rights obligations not only of the countries in which they are incorporated, but also of those in which they operate. They should not infringe the human rights of others, or contribute to such infringement; they should seek ways to prevent or mitigate adverse human rights impacts that are directly linked to their business operations, products or services by a business relationship, even if they do not contribute to those impacts; they should be prepared to carry out human rights due diligence as appropriate to their size, the nature and context of operations and the severity of the risks of adverse human rights impacts. If in breach, they should provide remediation. (Human Rights IV, Introduction, paras 1–6). The concept of including human rights due diligence as part of a reporting process has therefore been conceded; yet it features nowhere in the strategies which the OECD has deployed over the past twenty years.

Harmful tax competition: an emerging global issue

The OECD issued its report *Harmful Tax Competition: An Emerging Global Issue*[26] in 1998, the aim of which was to discourage the spread of tax havens. The perspective was solely fiscal, the OECD seeing harmful tax competition as damaging to the global taxation system:

> The Report is intended to develop a better understanding of how tax havens and harmful preferential tax regimes, collectively referred to as harmful tax practices, affect the location of financial and other service activities, erode the tax bases of other countries, distort trade and

---

26 <www.oecd-ilibrary.org/taxation/harmful-tax-competition_9789264162945-en> accessed 20 May 2017 ('Harmful Tax Competition'). And see Ronen Palan, Richard Murphy and Christian Chavagneux, *Tax Havens: How Globalization Really Works* (Cornell University Press, 2010) 210–18; Markus Meinzer, 'Towards an International Yardstick for Identifying Tax Havens and Facilitating Reform' in Peter Dietsch and Thomas Rixen (eds), *Global Tax Governance: What Is Wrong with It and How to Fix It* (ECPR Press, 2016).

investment patterns and undermine the fairness, neutrality and broad social acceptance of tax systems generally. Such harmful tax competition diminishes global welfare and undermines taxpayer confidence in the integrity of tax systems.[27]

There is no mention of human rights.

In the report the OECD introduced three indicators of harmful regimes: (1) Does the tax regime shift activity from one country to the country providing the preferential tax regime rather than generate new activity? (2) Is the presence and level of activities in the host country commensurate with the amount of investment income? and (3) Is the preferential tax regime the primary motivation for the location of an activity? Thirty-five countries and territories were asked to sign a 'Memorandum of Understanding' no later than 31 July 2001 that each would change their regimes. The OECD proposed issuing a list of non-co-operative jurisdictions, suggesting to the OECD member states that they impose sanctions against such jurisdictions – in essence, requiring a boycott.[28]

It is immediately apparent that all three indicators correspond with the day-to-day activities of tax havens. It was the tax havens which led the successful campaign against the proposals.[29] They claimed discrimination on the grounds of not having been consulted in the preparation of the report, that the OECD was turning a blind eye to OECD members such as Luxembourg and Switzerland, and to US states such as Montana and Colorado (both with offshore banking laws), all of which had all three indicators, and that the proposed two year timescale was impracticable in any event. When the United States also weighed in against the proposals, opposing efforts to harmonise world tax systems, the project was effectively shelved. The general consensus was that the OECD had been over-ambitious in its political agenda.[30]

The black and white (and grey) of listings

The OECD's attempt in April 2009, mandated by the G20, to classify tax havens by listing them as white, black or grey suffered from the fundamental difficulty of how to define a tax haven other than in terms of its own listing

27 OECD, 'Harmful Tax Competition' (n 26) 4.
28 OECD, 'Harmful Tax Competition' (n 26) 34–37
29 Prominent among these, formed in March 2001, was the International Tax Investment Organisation, established at the suggestion of Barbados. The organisation continues in existence as the International Trade and Investment Organisation <www.itio.org> accessed 11 May 2017. 'The ITIO is judged to have been a great success in derailing the OECD campaign.' Palan, Murphy and Chavagneux (n 26) 215.
30 'By failing, however, to deliver a consistent and objective definition and identification of tax havens, the initiative was vulnerable to accusations of illegitimacy and political bias, ultimately contributing to the project's failure.' Meinzer (n 26) 259.

criteria, and so called into question both the validity and utility of the whole exercise.[31] This was, however, not immediately apparent, and reviewing the first year of its listings operation, the OECD Global Forum on Transparency and Exchange of Information for Tax Purposes (the body formed by the OECD in 2009 at the behest of the G20, charged with monitoring the implementation of the tax transparency standard for the exchange of information on request) in January 2010 quoted the then-OECD Secretary General:

> [W]hat we are witnessing is nothing short of a revolution. By addressing the challenges posed by the dark side of the tax world, the campaign for global tax transparency is in full flow. We have equipped ourselves with the institutional means to continue the campaign. With the crisis, global public opinion's expectations are high, their tolerance of non-compliance is zero and we must deliver.[32]

The spirit of 2017 was slightly less gung-ho: 'Our work on tax represents the OECD at its best: the focal point for an inclusive conversation that leads to world class standards and effective implementation, always recognising the full range of contexts and constraints faced by countries.'[33]

The strategy was simple: to obtain white list status, a jurisdiction had to enter into not fewer than twelve Taxation Information Exchange Agreements (TIEAs) using the OECD Model Tax Convention in force at that time.[34] It was soon pilloried as a whitewash.[35] There was a scramble to sign the requisite number, many tax havens signing them with each other, and a fifth of those TIEAs signed being with Greenland, Iceland and the Faroes. Given the ease with which the TIEAs could be put in place, the OECD blacklist of jurisdictions which had failed to divest themselves of the earlier OECD harmful tax competition criteria emptied almost at once. Further, the TIEAs are limited in their effect: they cannot be used in a fishing expedition – the enquiring jurisdiction must already have identified the taxpayer whose affairs it wishes to investigate further and the offshore structures involved – something which a combination of accountability

31   See Chapter 1 for a discussion on the conflicting definitions of 'tax haven'.
32   OECD, 'Promoting Transparency and Exchange of Information for Tax Purposes' (*OECD*, 19 January 2010) <www.oecd.org/newsroom/44431965.pdf> accessed 11 May 2017.
33   Angel Gurria, OECD Secretary General, quoted in OECD, 'OECD Work on Taxation 2016-2017' (*OECD*, 2016) <www.oecd.org/tax/centre-for-tax-policy-and-administration-brochure.pdf> accessed 11 May 2017.
34   This has been frequently revised in the intervening years, the current version being the OECD, *Model Tax Convention on Income and on Capital 2014* (OECD 2015) <http://dx.doi.org/10.1787/9789264239081-en> accessed 11 May 2017.
35   See Nicholas Shaxson and John Christensen, 'Time to Blacklist the Tax Haven Whitewash' *Financial Times* (London, 4 April 2011) <www.ft.com/content/0f687dee-5eea-11e0-a2d7-00144feab49a> accessed 11 May 2017.

avoidance and beneficial ownership avoidance can easily frustrate.[36] As Gabriel Zucman points out, the seemingly arbitrary threshold of twelve TIEAs means that it is easy to send one's money to a tax haven not tied by an agreement with the country in which one lives, and actually incentivises the remaining tax havens not to co-operate.[37]

Power politics was also in play. China, itself not an OECD member (but with a multi-billion dollar commitment to the IMF), opposed the listings process on the basis that its finance centres in Hong Kong and in Macao would be blacklisted. After complex diplomatic wrangling, China itself was placed on the whitelist, with a footnote that Hong Kong and Macao would implement internationally agreed tax standards.[38]

An overarching weakness, identified by Richard Woodward, is the possibility (some would argue, the likelihood) of mock compliance. A jurisdiction enacts the legislative and regulatory framework to enable an exchange of taxation information to be made, but this then lies dormant. This may be because the bulk of the twelve TIEAs which that jurisdiction has signed are with micro-states unlikely ever to require an information exchange. Should demand suddenly arise, the very proliferation of TIEAs may overwhelm the administrative capacity of smaller jurisdictions. 'Many offshore tax havens are happily collecting the necessary information, and may even be more rigorous in doing so than their onshore counterparts, but they are collecting it safe in the knowledge that it will never have to be exchanged.'[39]

Automatic information exchange: OECD Common Reporting Standard 2014

Both of the OECD's previous attempts having produced no substantive results, in 2014 it launched its Common Reporting Standard ('CRS'), predicated on automatic information exchange.[40] In the Introduction to the CRS

---

36 See Chapters 2 and 3 for a fuller discussion of these issues.
37 Gabriel Zucman, *The Hidden Wealth of Nations: The Scourge of Tax Havens* (Teresa Lavender Fagan tr, University of Chicago Press, 2015) 61.
38 Dries Lesage, 'The G20 and Tax Havens: Maintaining the Momentum?' (Governing the Global Economy: The Role of the G20 Conference, University of Toronto – Munk School of Global Affairs, 18 June 2010) <www.g20.utoronto.ca/biblio/lesage-tax-havens.pdf> accessed 11 May 2017.
39 Richard Woodward, 'A Strange Revolution: Mock Compliance and the Failure of the OECD's International Tax Transparency Regime', in Peter Dietsch and Thomas Rixen eds, *Global Tax Governance: What Is Wrong with It and How to Fix It* (ECPR Press, 2016) 114–15.
40 OECD, *Standard for Automatic Exchange* (n 4); and see OECD, 'Standard for Automatic Exchange of Financial Account Information in Tax Matters Implementation Handbook' (*OECD*) <www.oecd.org/tax/exchange-of-tax-information/implementation-handbook-standard-for-automatic-exchange-of-financial-information-in-tax-matters.pdf> accessed 11 May 2017. A detailed technical review of the Common Reporting Standard is outside the scope of this book: see Eesh Aggarwal, *Common Reporting Standard – Survivor's Guide to OECD Automatic Exchange of Information of Offshore Financial Accounts* (SOCTA Publications, 2015).

the OECD sets out its case. It is entirely fiscally driven: 'Countries have a shared interest in maintaining the integrity of their tax systems. Co-operation between tax administrations is critical in the fight against tax evasion and in protecting the integrity of tax systems. A key aspect of that co-operation is exchange of information.' From the first substantial discussions on automatic information exchange in the OECD Secretary-General's Report to the G20 Finance Ministers on the tackling of offshore tax evasion and the automatic exchange of taxation information published to coincide with the July 2013 G20 Moscow summit, there is no mention of human rights at all.[41]

Pointing to globalisation, the OECD notes that it is easier for all taxpayers to make, hold and manage investments through financial institutions outside of their country of residence. Its focus is the transfer of taxable funds offshore:

> Vast amounts of money are kept offshore and go untaxed to the extent that taxpayers fail to comply with tax obligations in their home jurisdiction. Offshore tax evasion is a serious problem for jurisdictions all over the world, OECD and non-OECD, small and large, developing and developed.
>
> (*OECD*, 19 July 2013)

The CRS does not have automatic application in those states which decide to adopt it – domestic legislation, both primary and secondary, has first to be put in place. In essence, financial institutions report information to the tax administration in the jurisdiction in which they are located. The information consists of details of financial assets they hold on behalf of taxpayers from jurisdictions with which their tax administration exchanges information. The tax administrations then exchange that information.

In order to ensure consistency in reporting, the CRS contains the due diligence rules for financial institutions[42] to follow to collect and then report the information that underpins the automatic exchange of financial information.

---

41 OECD, 'Secretary-General Report to the G20 Finance Ministers and Central Bank Governors' (*OECD*, 19 July 2013) <www.oecd.org/ctp/exchange-of-tax-information/ OECD-tax-report-G20.pdf> accessed 11 May 2017.

42 One crucially important defect in the CRS regime, and one which has a great significance for the tax havens, is its treatment of trusts. A trust will only be classified as a financial institution if carrying on business in a given jurisdiction where more than 50% of the trust's gross income is attributable to trading in money market instruments, portfolio management or the investment and management of funds, or alternatively more than 50% of the trust's income is attributable to investing, reinvesting or trading in financial assets. Absent these, the trust is classified as a Non-Financial Entity and does not need to register or report. It takes little design effort to attain NFE status. See the useful flowchart produced by STEP (The Society of Trust and Estate Practitioners) available at <www.step.org/sites/ default/files/Policy/Trusts_under_CRS_flowchart_Jurisdiction_X.pdf> accessed 13 May 2017.

The OECD has produced its model Competent Authority Agreement ('CAA') as a blueprint for the exchange of information between jurisdictions. The automatic exchange functions between jurisdictions which have either mutually entered into a CAA or which have an information exchange agreement equivalent to this already in place.

The OECD itself identifies in the Introduction to the CRS the objective advantages to automatic, standardised exchange as being 'simplification, higher effectiveness and lower costs for all stakeholders concerned.' There is an argument that avoiding a proliferation of competing information exchange models and the consequent fragmentation of data should be cost-effective.

The OECD is however once again travelling a road paved with good intentions to a less than triumphant destination. The CRS regime is immensely time-consuming, resource hungry, and complex, and this sheer complexity may be its undoing. It places a huge burden on the reporting institutions. The quality of information exchanged can be no higher than the quality of information gathered. It presupposes that both the reporting and the receiving jurisdictions have an information infrastructure capable of processing the information – and for developing countries, this required level of resourcing is likely to prove highly problematic.[43] It also presupposes a degree of uniformity in the nature of the information to be exchanged and in the obligation to do so, but a simple example illustrates the difficulty. In which jurisdiction is a company required to comply with CRS reporting standards? There is no globally accepted definition of corporate domicile – a company may be domiciled in its jurisdiction of incorporation, or alternatively where its directors are most likely to convene their meetings or where the true management and control of the company lies. Such true management and control could be exercised in a tax haven.

In the OECD Global Forum 2016 Report on Tax Transparency,[44] there is, somewhat predictably, no reference to human rights or to the impact on human rights of the fiscal evasion techniques which the Global Forum sees as its mission to prevent. It is almost as though the garnering of revenue were an end in itself. The exchange of information on request regime continues, complemented by the automatic exchange of information. First automatic exchanges are timetabled for September 2017 and September 2018. Among those jurisdictions committed to an automatic exchange are a number of tax havens: Anguilla, Barbados, Bermuda, British Virgin Islands, Cayman

---

43 See Tax Justice Network, 'TJN Responds to New OECD Report on Automatic Information Exchange' (*Tax Justice Network*, 13 February 2014) <www.taxjustice.net/ 2014/02/13/press-release-tjn-responds-new-oecd-report-automatic-information-exchange> accessed 13 May 2017.

44 OECD, 'Tax Transparency 2016: Report on Progress' (*OECD*, 2016) <www.oecd. org/tax/transparency/GF-annual-report-2016.pdf> accessed 13 May 2017 ('Tax Transparency 2016').

Islands, Curaçao, Cyprus, Gibraltar, Guernsey, Ireland, Isle of Man, Jersey, Liechtenstein, Luxembourg, Malta, Montserrat, the Netherlands, Niue, San Marino, Seychelles, Trinidad and Tobago, Turks and Caicos Islands (2017); and Andorra, Antigua and Barbuda, Aruba, the Bahamas, Belize, Cook Islands, Dominica, Grenada, Hong Kong (China), Macau (China), Marshall Islands, Mauritius, Monaco, Nauru, Panama, Saint Kitts and Nevis, Saint Lucia, Saint Vincent and the Grenadines, Samoa, Singapore, Sint Maarten, Switzerland, Vanuatu (2018). Neither the United States at a federal level nor any state within it is participating; for these jurisdictions, FACTA continues to be the preferred route.

It remains to be seen what practical use can be made of what the Global Forum refers to as 'a flood of new information [which] will start to be provided by financial institutions all over the world', beginning in 2017 and expected to accelerate in 2018. Information uninformed by principles of analysis – particularly human rights analysis – is of itself purely raw data, a tax evasion information bubble.

The Global Forum acknowledges this:

> But EOI relationships are not enough on their own. They must be utilised. It is the combination of global transparency with domestic efforts to identify and punish taxpayers who break the rules which gives international cooperation its real potency. While we are now beginning to see some successes, the number of requests made by African countries is still tiny in a global context. Also many developing countries have yet to engage with the new AEOI standard although it offers enormous potential to detect tax evasion which might otherwise go undetected, particularly in countries jurisdictions [*sic*] where tax administrations lack the necessary investigative skills to uncover it otherwise.[45]

In light of this admission, it would be prudent to remind oneself that organisations such as the OECD are staffed by committed enthusiasts whose world is taxation, but that – just as in the field of international human rights – this self-referencing enthusiasm is not necessarily shared by many, or by any, members of the communities whom their work is intended to benefit.

And when all the information systems have been established, and data packets are criss-crossing the internet, what will be the effect on the tax havens? Arguably, the OECD initiative on automatic exchange of inform-ation will from the perspective of the tax havens be no more substantive or worrisome than have the listings processes proven to be. The availability of information and the availability of remedies are not commensurate. The mere participation of the tax havens in the automatic exchange of

45   OECD, 'Tax Transparency 2016' (n 44) 32–33.

information has no bearing on their willingness to assist in the recovery of funds held within their jurisdictions.[46]

OECD initiatives: assessment and unrealised potential

Over a twenty-year period, the OECD has never factored into its strategic planning the impact of tax avoidance or tax evasion on international human rights. It has seen its mission to be the minimisation of the impact of such schemes on the revenue returns to national taxation authorities, no more, no less.

It has failed in its original campaign to eliminate harmful tax competition. The work of the Global Forum on the tax transparency standard for the exchange of information on request has for all practical purposes been thwarted by mock compliance, particularly on the part of the tax havens. Though the Common Reporting Standard is in its infancy, it is already clear that its complexity can overwhelm the resources of the weaker countries whose economies it is intended to benefit, both in terms of the ability of those countries to introduce enforceable domestic implementation legislation and to create an infrastructure capable of processing whatever information they receive; and take up by such countries is minimal. It is heavily weighted in favour of predominantly western economies whose support systems and data processing capacity hugely outstrip those of the developing world. It creates an information mountain which few can mine, and fewer refine. Access to information is no guarantee of access to justice.

The information exchange matrix to which the OECD initiatives have given rise have a use potential which the OECD, confined within its fiscal bubble, has not identified. The reporting institutions, be they governmental under the information on request scheme or ground-based private actors under the Common Reporting Standard, can be called upon to report on more than just the basic information on which entity is holding funds in and trading from whatever jurisdiction. They can additionally be required to undertake human rights due diligence on the entities which are the subjects of their reports. In the case of corporations, two major, objective international standards which embody the principles of international human rights have already been established: the United Nations Global Compact[47] and the United Nations Guiding Principles on Business and Human Rights 2011.[48]

Neither the Global Compact nor the Guiding Principles has been free from criticism, and the rest of this chapter examines the arguments on both

---

46   See Chapter 2 for a discussion of the issues surrounding legislation in a number of tax havens blocking actions which challenge fraudulent transfers and limiting or extinguishing reciprocity in matters of court judgments.
47   United Nations, 'United Nations Global Compact' (*UN Global Compact*) <www.unglobalcompact.org> accessed 13 May 2017.
48   Guiding Principles (n 7).

sides. Governments have not necessarily shown any appetite to implement either initiative, and private actors remain largely oblivious of either (though in the absence of any published empirical studies on the extent of the awareness of private business actors of these initiatives and of their willingness to engage with them, the danger of presenting criticism which in truth is based on urban myth is ever present).

Yet corporations have had to engage with anti-money laundering, anti-terrorist financing and anti-bribery regulations, and in consequence the compliance profession has mushroomed.[49] Further, should the ability to standardise the human rights due diligence assessments be a cause for concern, the answer is already at hand. The International Organization for Standardization has engaged with the United Nations Sustainable Development Goals[50] and in January 2017 established a committee on organisational governance focusing on accountability, transparency of purpose, and values to stakeholders.[51]

An integrated approach would be to combine the information exchange matrix of the OECD, the international governance standards of the ISO and add to the mix the Guiding Principles with the option of pre-clearance through membership of the Global Compact. Financial institutions, as defined in the Common Reporting Standard, which operate through the tax havens to avoid or evade taxation would then be objectively assessed from a corporate governance perspective (including their international human rights profile) and reported upon automatically. The offshore taxation avoidance or evasive activities of these financial institutions would be brought within the framework of corporate governance.[52]

It must however be emphasised that this application of the Ruggie Principles and of the human rights principles of the Global Compact to the Common Reporting Standard in the context of tax havens is unorthodox: neither the Ruggie Principles nor the Global Compact expressly refers to tax havens, and for whatever reason those drafting the Common Reporting Standard made no mention of human rights principles.

---

49 See eg 'The Society of Corporate Compliance and Ethics' (*The Society of Corporate Compliance and Ethics*) <www.corporatecompliance.org> accessed 13 May 2017 (United States); 'International Compliance Association' (*International Compliance Association*) <www.int-comp.org> accessed 13 May 2017 (United Kingdom).
50 'ISO 26000 Social Responsibility' (*International Organization for Standardization*) <www.iso.org/iso-26000-social-responsibility.html> accessed 13 May 2017.
51 Maria Lazarte, 'New Committee on Organizational Governance' (*International Organization for Standardization*, 13 January 2017) <www.iso.org/news/2017/01/Ref2158.html> accessed 13 May 2017.
52 This is to adopt an evolutionary approach to the Ruggie Principles themselves, something which from their inception has been mooted. See eg Robert C Blitt, 'Beyond Ruggie's Guiding Principles on Business and Human Rights: Charting an Embracive Approach to Corporate Human Rights Compliance' (2012) 48 Texas Int'l L J 34.

The United Nations Global Compact

The United Nations Global Compact was launched in 2000, and its current mission statement is:

> to support companies to (1) do business responsibly by aligning their strategies and operations with Ten Principles on human rights, labour, environment and anti-corruption, and (2) take strategic action to advance broader societal goals, such as the UN Sustainable Development Goals, with an emphasis on collaboration and innovation.[53]

The Global Compact is not a trade association or a regulator charged with enforcing rules on others: participation is voluntary.

As of April 2017, 9,000 businesses and over 3,000 non-business enterprises (civil society organisations, business associations, labour organisations, academic institutions and cities) are participants in the Global Compact.[54] The take-up of membership over a seventeen year period is not impressive, and in its first decade of existence overall implementation rates for the human rights principles stood at 27%.[55] The Global Compact Office has itself been aware from the outset that enthusiasm could diminish, and the Global Compact be rendered impotent as participant energy fades (and thousands of companies have been de-listed for failure to fulfil their commitment to submit progress reports).[56] The United Nations nevertheless regards the Global Compact Office as having a vital role in strengthening the capacity of the United Nations to partner strategically with the private sector, particularly in the potential to develop global partnerships between the United Nations and the private sector in addressing the challenges of development.[57] The qualitative and administrative capacity of the Global Compact Office may just as effectively be placed at the disposal of the OECD in the context of the Common Reporting Standard.

53 UN Global Compact (n 47) 'Our Mission' <www.unglobalcompact.org/what-is-gc/mission> accessed 13 May 2017.

54 UN Global Compact (n 47) 'Our Participants' <www.unglobalcompact.org/what-is-gc/participants> accessed 13 May 2017.

55 UN Global Compact, 'Annual Review of Business Policies & Actions to Advance Sustainability: 2011 Global Compact Implementation Survey' (*UN Global Compact*, June 2012) <www.unglobalcompact.org/docs/news_events/8.1/2011_Global_Compact_Implementation_Survey.pdf> accessed 13 May 2017.

56 Steve Waddell, 'The Global Compact: An Organizational Innovation to Realize UN Principles' (2011) Global Compact Governance Papers Series <http://networking action.net/wp-content/uploads/UNGC_Organizational_Innovation_Note.pdf> accessed 13 May 2017.

57 UNGA Res 66/23 (28 March 2012) UN Doc A/RES/66/223 ('Towards Global Partnerships').

Such interaction with the OECD ought in consequence, by making membership of the Global Compact a defining tax compliance indicator,[58] to reinvigorate the currently flagging Global Compact initiative. It would provide a disincentive to companies to exit the Global Compact, which they can do at any time as currently the Global Compact has no enforcement mechanisms.

The UN Global Compact's Ten Principles are derived from the Universal Declaration of Human Rights,[59] the International Labour Organization's Declaration on Fundamental Principles and Rights at Work,[60] the Rio Declaration on Environment and Development,[61] and the United Nations Convention Against Corruption.[62] Of the Ten Principles, those relating to Human Rights are: 'Principle 1 – Businesses should support and respect the protection of internationally proclaimed human rights; and Principle 2 – make sure that they are not complicit in human rights abuses.'[63]

The corporate responsibility to respect exists independently of states' human rights duties. Businesses have a responsibility to respect human rights whether they are operating in an area of weak governance or in a more stable context. This requirement is interpreted under the Global Compact to refer to conflict-affected and high risk areas,[64] but the principle applies equally to activities within tax havens. 'Weak governance' can be taken to be a synonym for lax fiscal and structuring policies, and if a tax haven offers corporations the opportunity to pay little or no taxation, to disguise their beneficial ownership, to have immunity from civil law suits, and iron-clad secrecy, in short to avoid all accountability, then such corporations cannot claim merely to be taking advantage of the menu on offer and turn a blind eye to the international human rights impact of being invisibly cloaked in this way.

---

58 A review of United Nations human rights indicators is outside the scope of this book. See United Nations, Office of the High Commissioner for Human Rights, 'Human Rights Indicators: A Guide to Measurement and Implementation' (2012) HR/PUB/12/5 <www.ohchr.org/Documents/Publications/Human_rights_indicators_en.pdf> accessed 13 May 2017.
59 (adopted 10 December 1948 UNGA Res 217 A(III)).
60 International Labour Organization, ILO Declaration on Fundamental Principles and Rights at Work (June 1988) <www.ilo.org/declaration/lang—en/index.htm> accessed 13 May 2017.
61 See United Nations, 'Future We Want – Outcome Document' (*UN Sustainable Development Knowledge Platform*, 2012) <https://sustainabledevelopment.un.org/rio20/futurewewant> accessed 13 May 2017.
62 UNGA, United Nations Convention Against Corruption (adopted 31 October 2003, entered into force 14 December 2015) UN Doc A/58/422 <www.unodc.org/unodc/en/treaties/CAC/index.html> accessed 14 May 2017.
63 UN Global Compact, 'Principle One: Human Rights' (*UN Global Compact*) <www.unglobalcompact.org/what-is-gc/mission/principles/principle-1> accessed 14 May 2017; UN Global Compact, 'Principle Two: Human Rights' (*UN Global Compact*) <Principle Two: Human Rights> accessed 14 May 2017.
64 UN Global Compact and Principles for Responsible Investment, 'Guidance on Responsible Business in Conflict-Affected and High-Risk Areas: A Resource for Companies and Investors' (*UN Global Compact*, 2010) <www.unglobalcompact.org/docs/issues_doc/Peace_and_Business/Guidance_RB.pdf> accessed 14 May 2017.

Complicity means being implicated in a human rights abuse that another company, government, individual or other group is causing. Taxation and structural offerings of tax havens which have human rights abusive consequences clearly implicate those entities which take advantage of them. It is at least what the Global Compact classifies as 'silent complicity' – when the corporation is silent or inactive in the face of systematic or continuous human rights abuse. It may be seen as 'beneficial complicity', in that the corporation benefits from human rights abuses (the offerings of its host tax haven) even though it did not positively assist or cause them.

A company which may be required as part of an automatic exchange of information procedure to demonstrate compliance with Principles 1 and 2 cannot therefore be one which is either based in, or which runs a substantial part of its business affairs through, tax havens.

Though participation to date in the Global Compact has been thin, this does not detract from the ethical rigor of the Ten Principles. Those principles can, added to the information exchange matrix, expose the root cause of abuse.

The Ruggie Principles

The United Nations Guiding Principles on Business and Human Rights 2011, more commonly known as the Ruggie Principles (named for their architect, John Ruggie), have not yet had the impact which enthusiasts at the time of their introduction anticipated.[65] John Ruggie continues to promote the Principles which bear his name and to argue that human rights in a business development context ought not to be side-lined, and that 'far from being at the 'immature' end of a transformative trajectory of business models, respect for human rights, respect for the dignity of every person, is at the very core of the people part of sustainable development.'[66]

Up to 31 December 2016 only twelve countries, ten of which are in Europe, have produced National Action Plans implementing the Ruggie Principles: the United Kingdom (2013, 2016), the Netherlands (2013),

---

65 See the dissemination and implementation strategy put forward by the United Nations on 12 August 2012 *Human rights and transnational corporations and other business enterprises* [UNGA Res 67/285 (12 August 2012) UN Doc A/67/285 Sixty-seventh Session <www.ohchr.org/EN/HRBodies/SP/Pages/GA67session.aspx> accessed 14 May 2017]. In his 14 November 2016 address to the UN Forum on Business and Human Rights, John Ruggie drew attention to the disconnect between the United Nations 2030 Social Development Goals and the Guiding Principles, noting that the Social Development Goals make only 'a passing reference to relevant standards and agreements that address corporate accountability for human rights harm, including the Guiding Principles'. John Ruggie, 'Making Globalization Work for All: Achieving the Sustainable Development Goals through Business Respect for Human Rights' (*Shift Project*, November 2016) <www.shiftproject.org/resources/viewpoints/globalization-sustainable-development-goals-business-respect-human-rights> accessed 14 May 2017.

66 Ruggie (n 65).

Denmark (2014), Finland (2014), Lithuania (2015), Sweden (2015), Norway (2015), Colombia (2015), Switzerland (2016), Germany (2016), Italy (2016) and the United States (2016). Several other European governments (including Belgium, the Czech Republic, Poland, and Spain) are drafting or have drafted National Action Plans, as are Mexico, Kenya, and Australia.[67]

However, the national adoption of, the extent of industry awareness of, and the efficacy of the Ruggie Principles to date is not in point: what is of importance in the context of objectivising analysis of the conduct of tax haven entities is the application of the Ruggie Principles to those entities with a view to blocking – or at the very least bringing into the light of day – practices which, tax avoidance or tax evasion-driven, lead to international human rights abuse.

There is a degree of ambiguity as to which human rights are embraced by the Ruggie Principles. On the one hand, '[b]ecause business enterprises have an impact on virtually the entire spectrum of internationally recognised human rights, their responsibility to respect applies to all such rights'; but these recognised human rights are 'understood, at a minimum, as those expressed in the International Bill of Human Rights[68] and the principles concerning fundamental rights set out in the International Labour Organization's Declaration on Fundamental Principles and Rights at Work.'[69] Either way, this may in practice be an attempt to impose on states an observance of rights under instruments which those states may not have signed or ratified (or, in the case of tax havens, to which such instruments have not been extended by those states having responsibility for their external relations).

The Ruggie Principles are constructed using three 'Pillars':

> [T]he State duty to protect [Pillar One] because it lies at the very core of the international human rights regime; the corporate responsibility to protect [Pillar Two] because it is the basic expectation society has of business in relation to human rights; and access to remedy [Pillar Three] because even the most concerted efforts cannot prevent all abuse.[70]

---

67 Beata Faracik, *Implementation of the UN Guiding Principles on Business and Human Rights* (European Parliament, Directorate-General for External Policies, European Union 2017) <www.europarl.europa.eu/RegData/etudes/STUD/2017/578031/EXPO_STU(2017) 578031_EN.pdf> accessed 14 May 2017, 8: 'Certainly, less declaration and more real political will is needed on the side of governments, as so far their commitments to develop National Action Plans (NAPs) implementing the Guiding Principles have been far too slow to materialise.'

68 The term generally used to refer to the International Covenant on Civil and Political Rights (adopted 16 December 1966, entered into force 23 March 1976) 999 UNTS 171 and the International Covenant on Economic, Social and Cultural Rights (adopted 16 December 1966, entered into force 3 January 1976) 993 UNTS 3.

69 These seemingly contradictory propositions are both found in the Ruggie Principles (n 7) Appendix, para 12.

70 Ruggie Principles (n 7) Introduction to the Guiding Principles, para 6.

The tax avoidance or evasive relationship between jurisdictions is one which under Pillar One impacts on a state's duty to protect, by failing to curb (or worse, in the case of the tax havens, actively facilitating) taxation abuse. The state must take retaliatory action; the tax haven must cease it abusive practices.[71] 'States are not per se responsible for human rights abuse by private actors. However, states may breach their international human rights law obligations where such abuse can be attributed to them, or where they fail to take appropriate steps to prevent, investigate, punish and redress private actors' abuse.' The responsibility is both domestic and extraterritorial.[72] 'Laws and policies that govern the creation and ongoing operation of business enterprises, such as corporate and security laws, directly shape business behaviour.'[73]

Bearing in mind that the laws of a tax haven are valid within its own jurisdiction, an entity formed in such a jurisdiction or managed and controlled from it cannot simply on the basis of complying with those domestic laws, seek immunity from its responsibility to respect human rights under Pillar Two. 'The responsibility of business enterprises to respect human rights is distinct from issues of legal liability and enforcement, which remain defined largely by national law provisions in relevant jurisdictions.'[74] The business enterprise is obliged to 'seek ways to honour the principles of internationally recognised human rights when faced with conflicting requirements'[75] (and in the context of tax havens all the more so when faced with conflicting fiscal temptations).

The concept of combining the Ruggie Principles and the human rights principles of the Global Compact with the Common Reporting Standard is not contradictory. The data to be added to the Common Reporting Standard information exchange procedure ought already to be available. Pillar Two sets out required standards of human rights due diligence:

> In order to identify, prevent, mitigate and account for how they address their adverse human rights impacts, business enterprises should carry out human rights due diligence. The process should include assessing actual and potential human rights impacts, integrating and acting upon the findings, tracking responses, and communicating how impacts are addressed [and] should cover adverse human rights impacts that the business enterprise may cause or contribute to through its own activities, or which may be directly linked to its operations, products or services by its business relationships.[76]

---

71 But see the discussion in Chapter 1 of the domestic economic difficulties facing tax havens which contemplate abandoning their tax haven status.
72 Ruggie Principles (n 7) Annex, paras 1 and 2.
73 Ruggie Principles (n 7) Annex, para 3.
74 Ruggie Principles (n 7) Annex, para 12.
75 Ruggie Principles (n 7) Annex, para 23(b).
76 Ruggie Principles (n 7) Annex, para 17.

Complementary to the approach taken in the Common Reporting Standard, the business enterprise is required to verify objectively whether adverse human rights impacts are being addressed, by tracking the effectiveness of their response 'based on appropriate qualitative and quantitative indicators.'[77]

Though the requirement under Pillar Two to undertake human rights due diligence may have been intended to cover business relationships in the sense of supply chain mechanisms or other party-to-party contractual arrangements, it can be applied directly to the relationships of enterprises whose holding or subsidiary entities are domiciled in or managed or controlled from tax havens. The adverse human rights impacts of such subsidiaries or holding companies arising out of tax avoidance or tax evasion are attributable to the business enterprise itself.

The relationship of the Ruggie Principles to the Global Compact

The Ruggie Principles and the first two of the Ten Principles of the Global Contract are complementary.

> As a global standard applicable to all business enterprises, the UN Guiding Principles provide further conceptual and operational clarity for the two human rights principles championed by the Global Compact. They reinforce the Global Compact and provide an authoritative framework for participants on the policies and processes they should implement in order to ensure that they meet their responsibility to respect human rights.[78]

This compatibility means that consolidated provisions to be included in the Common Reporting Standard are a practicable possibility. The body best suited to formulate such a standardised approach and to suggest an implementation strategy is the International Organization for Standardization.

The International Organization for Standardization

The International Organization for Standardization ('ISO')[79] was founded in 1946 and is an independent, non-governmental international organisation

---

77 Ruggie Principles (n 7) Annex, para 20.
78 United Nations, Office of the High Commissioner for Human Rights and UN Global Compact, 'The UN Guiding Principles on Business and Human Rights: Relationship to UN Global Compact Commitments' (*UN Global Compact*, July 2011) <www.unglobal compact.org/docs/issues_doc/human_rights/Resources/GPs_GC%20note.pdf> accessed 14 May 2017.
79 <www.iso.org> accessed 13 May 2017. For an introduction to the ISO standardisation system, its output and partners see International Organization for Standardization, *ISO in Brief* (5th edn, ISO 2016) <www.iso.org/publication/PUB100007.html> accessed 14 May 2017.

which today has a membership of 162 national standards bodies. In its own words, the ISO 'brings together experts to share knowledge and develop voluntary, consensus-based, market-relevant International Standards that support innovation and provide solutions to global challenges.' A fundamental goal is to facilitate free and fair global trade.[80]

In 2010, *ISO 26000 Guidance on Social Responsibility* was published.[81] The standard is intended to assist organisations in contributing to sustainable development. It takes legal compliance as a starting point, it being a given that this is key to an organisation's social responsibility programme. The standard seeks to promote a common understanding of social responsibility: 'When applying IOS 26000, organisations should consider societal, environmental, legal, cultural, political and organisational diversity as well as differences in economic conditions, while being consistent with international norms of behaviour.'[82] The seven core subjects which it addresses are organisational governance, human rights, labour practices, the environment, fair operating practices, consumer issues, and community involvement and development.

In October 2016, *ISO 37001:2016, Anti-bribery Management Systems* was published, presented as the first international anti-bribery management system standard designed to help organisations combat bribery risk in their own operations and throughout their global value chains. It is confined to issues of bribery and does not specifically address fraud, cartels and other anti-trust/competition offences, money laundering or other activities related to corrupt practices.[83]

This global standardisation initiative with regard to social responsibility, with specific reference to bribery, has been further extended by the setting up

---

80 ISO, 'About ISO' (*ISO*) <www.iso.org/about-us.html> accessed 14 May 2017. The strategy of the ISO for the years 2016 to 2020 both globally and specifically in relation to developing countries is set out in ISO, *ISO Strategy 2016–2020* (ISO 2015) <www.iso. org/files/live/sites/isoorg/files/archive/pdf/en/iso_strategy_2016-2020.pdf> accessed 14 May 2017 and ISO, *ISO Action Plan for Developing Countries 2016-2020* (ISO 2016) <www.iso.org/files/live/sites/isoorg/files/archive/pdf/en/ iso_action_plan_2016-2020_en_ld.pdf> accessed 14 May 2017. Neither engages with issues of taxation. The ISO does however regard its standards as a key factor in meeting the United Nations Sustainable Development Goals. See Maria Lazarte, 'ISO Standards Help Meet SDGs Says World Bank Group Expert' (*ISO*, 12 September 2016) <www.iso.org/news/2016/09/Ref2118.html> accessed 14 May 2017.
81 ISO, *ISO 26000:2010: Guidance on Social Responsibility* (ISO 2010). The full text is available for purchase from www.iso.org and a summary is available: ISO, *ISO 26000: Guidance on Social Responsibility: Discovering ISO 26000* (1st edn, ISO 2014) <www.iso.org/ publication/PUB100258.html> accessed 14 May 2017 ('*Discovering ISO 26000*').
82 ISO, *Discovering ISO 26000* (n 81) 7.
83 ISO, *ISO 37001:2016: Anti-Bribery Management Systems – Requirements with Guidance for Use* (ISO 2016) <www.iso.org/standard/65034.html> accessed 14 May 2017. The full text is available for purchase from www.iso.org. See Elizabeth Gasiorowski-Denis, 'ISO Publishes Powerful New Tool to Combat Bribery' (*ISO*, 14 October 2016) <www.iso.org/news/2016/10/Ref2125.html> accessed 14 May 2017.

of an ISO technical committee in November 2016, ISO/TC 309 *Governance of Organisations*. The technical committee's brief is to consolidate good practice for effective governance of organisational performance to include direction, control and accountability. The technical committee may further extend its remit to include whistleblowing, compliance and corruption. The hope is that its work will help meet the targets of United Nations Sustainable Development Goal 16[84] by increasing transparency and accountability.[85]

It would seem both logical and feasible to extend the scope of activity of the technical committee to include not only tax avoidance and tax evasion, but the facilitation of each by means of the taxation policies and structuring opportunities of the tax havens.

Conclusions: incorporating a human rights-based approach into the combatting of tax avoidance and tax evasion

Facilitating the implementation of tax avoidance and tax evasion strategies has for many tax havens been their *raison d'être*. The various OECD initiatives have either not found acceptance or have been the object of mock compliance, reflected particularly strongly in the self-congratulatory triumphalism of those tax havens which, with little effort, found themselves placed on the OECD white list. The current initiative, the Common Reporting Standard, may fall victim to its own complexity or may produce such vast quantities of raw data as to overwhelm the processing capacities of those whom it is principally intended to benefit.

What must not be overlooked is that the gathered data is simply about the payment or non-payment of tax. It is intended to reinforce taxpayer confidence in the integrity of tax systems. It entirely misses the opportunity to look behind the figures at the means by which tax avoidance schemes are made possible and the human rights abuse which flows from that. Jurisdictions may legitimately claim domestic sovereignty in matters of taxation, but they remain bound by international human rights obligations.

The information exchange matrix which has been created in response to the various OECD initiatives has a utility value nonetheless. Though 'human rights impact' often implies that human rights are being abused, the reverse may also be true, and human rights may themselves impact other situations. Adding human rights indicators to the OECD reporting process, using the existing matrix to carry that information to where it is most needed, turns the victim into the foe.

---

84   'Promote peaceful and inclusive societies for sustainable development, provide access to justice for all, and build effective, accountable and inclusive institutions at all levels'. 'Sustainable Development Goal 16' (*UN Sustainable Development Knowledge Platform*) <https://sustainabledevelopment.un.org/sdg16> accessed 14 May 2017.
85   Lazarte (n 51).

The reporting entities under the Common Reporting Standard require guidance as to which human rights indicators are to be included. These can be standardised by the ISO in the same way that the ISO has standardised approaches to corporate governance and bribery. The new ISO standard human rights abuse indicators, drawn from the Ruggie Principles, would be applied universally by the reporting entities. Any enterprise otherwise reportable under the Common Reporting Standard which became a member of the Global Compact and which complied with its ongoing Global Compact reporting requirements would be exempted from the Common Reporting Standard procedure, on the assumption that as a Global Compact member it would not be engaged in tax abusive (or human rights abusive) practices. The Global Compact Office has no enforcement powers within its voluntary system, but the sanction to be imposed on a non-compliant member – expulsion – would return that member to one to whom Common Reporting Standards would be applied.

Incorporating the Ruggie Principles into an ISO standard would give them a second bite of the cherry. The ISO has the machinery, in the form of technical committee ISO/TC 39, to produce the new standard. Adding that new ISO Standard to the reporting requirements under the Common Reporting Standard would provide a qualitative, globalised means of assessing abuse (enhancing the current quantitative assessment of fiscal abuse arising from taxes paid, avoided or evaded). Attaching attractive Common Reporting Standards exemptions to membership status of the Global Compact would reinvigorate that institution.

Bibliography

Legislation, regulations and legislative debates

Companies Act 2006 <www.legislation.gov.uk/ukpga/2006/46/section/172> accessed 8 May 2017 (UK)
Criminal Finances Bill 2016–2017 (UK)
Finance Act 2016 <www.irishstatutebook.ie/eli/2016/act/18/enacted/en/html?q-Finance+Act+2016> accessed 9 May 2017 (Ireland)
Foreign Account Tax Compliance Act <www.irs.gov/businesses/corporations/foreign-account-tax-compliance-act-fatca> accessed 8 May 2017 (US)

European directives

Council Directive 2003/48/EC of 3 June 2003 on taxation of savings income in the form of interest payments [2003] OJ L 157/38
Council Directive 2014/107/EU of 9 December 2014 amending Directive 2011/16/EU as regards mandatory automatic exchange of information in the field of taxation [2014] OJ L 359, 16.12.2014/1

International treaties and declarations

African Charter on Human and Peoples' Rights (adopted 27 June 1981, entered into force 21 October 1986) (1982) 21 ILM 58

International Covenant on Civil and Political Rights 1966 (adopted 16 December 1966, entered into force 23 March 1976) 999 UNTS 171

International Covenant on Economic, Social and Cultural Rights (adopted 16 December 1966, entered into force 3 January 1976) 993 UNTS 3

International Labour Organization, ILO Declaration on Fundamental Principles and Rights at Work (June 1988) <www.ilo.org/declaration/lang—en/index.htm> accessed 13 May 2017

United Nations Convention Against Corruption (adopted 31 October 2003, entered into force 14 December 2015) UN Doc A/58/422 <www.unodc.org/unodc/en/treaties/CAC/index.html> accessed 14 May 2017

Universal Declaration of Human Rights (adopted 10 December 1948 UNGA Res 217 A(III) (UDHR)

United Nations documents

UNGA, Human Rights Council, 'Report of the Special Representative of the Secretary General on the Issue of Human Rights and Transnational Corporations and Other Business Enterprises, John Ruggie Guiding Principles on Business and Human Rights: Implementing the United Nations 'Protect, Respect and Remedy' Framework' (21 March 2011) Seventeenth Session, UN Doc A/HRC/17/31

UNGA Res 66/23 (28 March 2012) UN Doc A/RES/66/223 ('Towards Global Partnerships')

UNGA Res 67/285 (12 August 2012) UN Doc A/67/285 Sixty-seventh Session <www.ohchr.org/EN/HRBodies/SP/Pages/GA67session.aspx> accessed 14 May 2017 ('Human Rights and Transnational Corporations and Other Business Enterprises')

United Nations Economic and Social Council, 'General Comment on State Obligations under the International Covenant on Economic, Social and Cultural Rights in the Context of Business Activities' [Draft prepared by Olivier De Schutter and Zdzislaw Kedzia, Rapporteurs] (17 October 2016) 60th Session (2017) UN Doc E/C.12/60/R.1

United Nations Human Rights Council, 'Report of the Independent Expert on the Question of Human Rights and Extreme Poverty, Magdalena Sepulveda Carmona' (17 March 2011) UN Doc A/HRC/17/34

United Nations, Office of the High Commissioner for Human Rights, 'Human Rights Indicators: A Guide to Measurement and Implementation' (2012) HR/PUB/12/5 <www.ohchr.org/Documents/Publications/Human_rights_indicators_en.pdf> accessed 13 May 2017

Secondary sources

Aggarwal E, *Common Reporting Standard – Survivor's Guide to OECD Automatic Exchange of Information of Offshore Financial Accounts* (SOCTA Publications, 2015)

Beetham D, 'What Future for Economic and Social Rights?' (1995) XLIII Pol Stud 41

Blitt RC, 'Beyond Ruggie's Guiding Principles on Business and Human Rights: Charting an Embracive Approach to Corporate Human Rights Compliance' (2012) 48 Texas Int'l L J 34

Collier P, 'In Pursuit of the $21 Trillion' [2013] *Prospect Magazine* <www.prospect-magazine.co.uk/magazine/tax-avoidance-paul-collier-david-cameron-g8> accessed 9 May 2017

East Africa Tax & Governance Network, 'Taxing Rights Policies Are Human Rights Policies' (*East Africa Tax & Governance Network*, 2016) <www.taxjustice.net/wp-content/uploads/2016/11/Tax-and-Human-Rights-Report.pdf>

The European Council, 'Savings Taxation Directive Repealed' (*The European Council*) <www.consilium.europa.eu/en/press/press-releases/2015/11/10-savings-taxation-directive-repealed> accessed 5 August 2017

Faracik B, *Implementation of the UN Guiding Principles on Business and Human Rights* (European Parliament, Directorate-General for External Policies, European Union 2017) <www.europarl.europa.eu/RegData/etudes/STUD/2017/578031/EXPO_STU(2017)578031_EN.pdf> accessed 14 May 2017

Friedman M, 'The Social Responsibility of Business Is to Increase Its Profits' [1970] *The New York Times Magazine* <www.colorado.edu/studentgroups/libertarians/issues/friedman-soc-resp-business.html> accessed 8 May 2017

Gasiorowski-Denis E, 'ISO Publishes Powerful New Tool to Combat Bribery' (*ISO*, 14 October 2016) <www.iso.org/news/2016/10/Ref2125.html> accessed 14 May 2017

Gearty CA, 'Human Rights', *The Social Science Encyclopaedia* (3rd edn, Routledge 2004) 468

Herbert Smith Freehills, 'New UK Criminal Offences of Failure to Prevent Facilitation of Tax Evasion' (*Herbert Smith Freehills*, 5 December 2016) <www.herbertsmithfreehills.com/latest-thinking/new-uk-criminal-offences-of-failure-to-prevent-facilitation-of-tax-evasion> accessed 9 May 2017

HM Revenue and Customs and HM Treasury, 'Dealing with HMRC: Tax Avoidance' (*gov.uk*) <www.hmrc.gov.uk/avoidance/index.htm> accessed 9 May 2017

HM Revenue and Customs (HMRC), 'HM Revenue and Customs (HMRC) General Anti-Abuse Rule (GAAR) Guidance' (*gov.uk*, 31 March 2017) <www.gov.uk/government/uploads/system/uploads/attachment_data/file/605501/gaar parts-a-c-2017.pdf> accessed 9 May 2017

'International Compliance Association' (*International Compliance Association*) <www.int-comp.org> accessed 13 May 2017

'International Organization for Standardization' (ISO) (*International Organization for Standardization*) <www.iso.org> accessed 13 May 2017

——, *ISO in Brief* (5th edn, ISO 2016) <www.iso.org/publication/ PUB 100007.html> accessed 14 May 2017

——, *ISO 26000:2010: Guidance on Social Responsibility* (ISO 2010)

——, *ISO 26000: Guidance on Social Responsibility: Discovering ISO 26000* (1st edn, ISO 2014) <www.iso.org/publication/PUB100258.html> accessed 14 May 2017

——, *ISO Strategy 2016–2020* (ISO 2015) <www.iso.org/files/live/sites/isoorg/files/archive/pdf/en/iso_strategy_2016-2020.pdf> accessed 14 May 2017

——, *ISO 37001:2016: Anti-Bribery Management Systems – Requirements with Guidance for Use* (ISO 2016) <www.iso.org/standard/65034.html> accessed 14 May 2017

——, *ISO Action Plan for Developing Countries 2016–2020* (ISO 2016) <www.iso.org/files/live/sites/isoorg/files/archive/pdf/en/iso_action_plan_20 16-2020_en_ld.pdf> accessed 14 May 2017

——, 'About ISO' (*ISO*) <www.iso.org/about-us.html> accessed 14 May 2017

——, 'ISO 26000 Social Responsibility' (*ISO*) <www.iso.org/iso-26000-social-responsibility.html> accessed 13 May 2017

'International Trade and Investment Organisation' <www.itio.org> accessed 11 May 2017

Lazarte M, 'ISO Standards Help Meet SDGs Says World Bank Group Expert' (*ISO*, 12 September 2016) <www.iso.org/news/2016/09/Ref2118.html> accessed 14 May 2017

——, 'New Committee on Organizational Governance' (*International Organization for Standardization*, 13 January 2017) <www.iso.org/news/2017/01/ Ref2158.html> accessed 13 May 2017

Lesage D, 'The G20 and Tax Havens: Maintaining the Momentum?' (Governing the Global Economy: The Role of the G20 Conference, University of Toronto – Munk School of Global Affairs, 18 June 2010) <www.g20.utoronto.ca/biblio/ lesage-tax-havens.pdf> accessed 11 May 2017

Meinzer M, 'Towards an International Yardstick for Identifying Tax Havens and Facilitating Reform', *Global Tax Governance: What Is Wrong with It and How to Fix It* (Peter Dietsch and Thomas Rixen (eds), ECPR Press 2016)

Monash University, Castan Centre for Human Rights Law and others, *Human Rights Translated: A Business Reference Guide* (Monash University, Castan Centre for Human Rights Law, International Business Leaders Forum, Office of the United Nations High Commissioner for Human Rights 2008)

OECD, 'Promoting Transparency and Exchange of Information for Tax Purposes' (*OECD*, 19 January 2010) <www.oecd.org/newsroom/44431965.pdf> accessed 11 May 2017

——, *OECD Guidelines for Multinational Enterprises* (OECD 2011) <www.oecd. org/daf/inv/mne/48004323.pdf> accessed 10 May 2017

——, *Harmful Tax Competition: An Emerging Global Issue* (OECD 1998)

——, 'Secretary-General Report To The G20 Finance Ministers And Central Bank Governors' (*OECD*, 19 July 2013) <www.oecd.org/ctp/exchange-of-tax-infor-mation/OECD-tax-report-G20.pdf> accessed 11 May 2017

——, *Standard for Automatic Exchange of Financial Account Information in Tax Matters* (OECD 2014)

——, *Model Tax Convention on Income and on Capital 2014* (OECD 2015) <http://dx.doi.org/10.1787/9789264239081-en> accessed 11 May 2017

——, 'OECD Work on Taxation 2016–2017' (*OECD*, 2016) <www.oecd.org/ tax/centre-for-tax-policy-and-administration-brochure.pdf> accessed 11 May 2017

——, 'Tax Transparency 2016: Report on Progress' (*OECD*, 2016) <www.oecd. org/tax/transparency/GF-annual-report-2016.pdf> accessed 13 May 2017

——, 'Members and Partners' (*OECD*) <www.oecd.org/about/membersandpart-ners> accessed 10 May 2017

——, 'Standard for Automatic Exchange of Financial Account Information in Tax

Matters Implementation Handbook' (*OECD*) <www.oecd.org/tax/exchange-of-tax-information/implementation-handbook-standard-for-automatic-exchange-of-financial-information-in-tax-matters.pdf> accessed 11 May 2017

——, 'The Organisation for Economic Co-operation and Development (OECD)' (*OECD*) <www.oecd.org/about> accessed 10 May 2017

Oxfam, 'Tax Battles: The Dangerous Global Race to the Bottom on Corporate Tax' (*Oxfam Policy Paper*, 12 December 2016) <www.oxfam.org/sites/ www.oxfam.org/files/bp-race-to-bottom-corporate-tax-121216-en.pdf> accessed 9 May 2017

Palan R, *The Offshore World: Sovereign Markets, Virtual Places and Nomad Millionaires* (Cornell University Press, 2003)

Palan R, Murphy R and Chavagneux C, *Tax Havens: How Globalization Really Works* (Cornell University Press, 2010)

Ruggie J, 'Making Globalization Work for All: Achieving the Sustainable Development Goals through Business Respect for Human Rights' (*Shift Project*, November 2016) <www.shiftproject.org/resources/viewpoints/globalization-sustainable-development-goals-business-respect-human-rights> accessed 14 May 2017

Salomon M, 'Why Should It Matter That Others Have More? Poverty, Inequality and the Potential of International Human Rights Law' [2010] LSE Legal Studies Working Paper 15/2010 <https://papers.ssrn.com/sol3/papers.cfm?abstract_id=1711657> accessed 10 May 2017

Scheiber N and Cohen P, 'For the Wealthiest, a Private Tax System That Saves Them Billions' *The New York Times* (New York, 29 December 2015) <www.nytimes.com/2015/12/30/business/economy/for-the-wealthiest-private-tax-system-saves-them-billions.html?smid=li-share&_r=> accessed 5 September 2017

Shaxson N and Christensen J, 'Time to Blacklist the Tax Haven Whitewash' *Financial Times* (London, 4 April 2011) <www.ft.com/content/0f687dee-5eea-11e0-a2d7-00144feab49a> accessed 11 May 2017

'The Society of Corporate Compliance and Ethics' (*The Society of Corporate Compliance and Ethics*) <www.corporatecompliance.org> accessed 13 May 2017

'The Society of Trust and Estate Practitioners (STEP)' (*STEP*) <www.step.org/sites/default/files/Policy/Trusts_under_CRS_flowchart_Jurisdiction_X.pdf> accessed 13 May 2017

Solly M, *Anatomy of a Tax Haven: The Isle of Man* (Shearwater Press, 1975)

'Tax Justice Network' <www.taxjustice.net> accessed 8 May 2017

——, 'TJN Responds to New OECD Report on Automatic Information Exchange' (*Tax Justice Network*, 13 February 2014) <www.taxjustice.net/2014/02/13/press-release-tjn-responds-new-oecd-report-automatic-information-exchange> accessed 13 May 2017

UN, 'Future We Want – Outcome Document' (*UN Sustainable Development Knowledge Platform*, 2012) <https://sustainabledevelopment.un.org/rio20/futurewewant> accessed 13 May 2017

——, 'Sustainable Development Goal 16' (*UN Sustainable Development Knowledge Platform*) <https://sustainabledevelopment.un.org/sdg16> accessed 14 May 2017

UN Global Compact, 'Annual Review of Business Policies & Actions to Advance Sustainability: 2011 Global Compact Implementation Survey' (*UN Global Compact*, June 2012) <www.unglobalcompact.org/docs/news_events/8.1/2011_Global_Compact_Implementation_Survey.pdf> accessed 13 May 2017

——, 'Principle One: Human Rights' (*UN Global Compact*) <www.unglobalcompact.org/what-is-gc/mission/principles/principle-1> accessed 14 May 2017

——, 'Principle Two: Human Rights' (*UN Global Compact*) <Principle Two: Human Rights> accessed 14 May 2017

——, UN Global Compact and Principles for Responsible Investment, 'Guidance on Responsible Business in Conflict-Affected and High-Risk Areas: A Resource for Companies and Investors' (*UN Global Compact*, 2010) <www.unglobalcompact.org/docs/issues_doc/Peace_and_Business/Guidance_RB.pdf> accessed 14 May 2017

——, 'United Nations Global Compact' (*UN Global Compact*) <www.unglobalcompact.org> accessed 13 May 2017

——, 'United Nations Global Compact' <www.globalcompact.org> accessed 8 May 2017

UN, Office of the High Commissioner for Human Rights and UN Global Compact, 'The UN Guiding Principles on Business and Human Rights: Relationship to UN Global Compact Commitments' (*UN Global Compact*, July 2011) <www.unglobalcompact.org/docs/issues_doc/human_rights/Resources/GPs_GC%20note.pdf> accessed 14 May 2017

Waddell S, 'The Global Compact: An Organizational Innovation to Realize UN Principles' (2011) Global Compact Governance Papers Series <http://networkingaction.net/wp-content/uploads/UNGC_Organizational_Innovation_Note.pdf> accessed 13 May 2017

Withersworldwide, 'Russian De-Offshorisation Legislation – How the New Law on Taxation of Controlled Foreign Companies Affects You and Your Clients' (*Withersworldwide*, 27 November 2014) <www.withersworldwide.com/news-publications/russian-de-offshorisation-legislation-%E2%80%93-how-the-new-law-on-taxation-of-controlled-foreign-companies-affects-you-and-your-clients> accessed 9 May 2017

Woodward R, 'A Strange Revolution: Mock Compliance and the Failure of the OECD's International Tax Transparency Regime', *Global Tax Governance: What Is Wrong with It and How to Fix It* (Peter Dietsch and Thomas Rixen eds, ECPR Press 2016)

Zucman G, *The Hidden Wealth of Nations: The Scourge of Tax Havens* (Teresa Lavender Fagan tr, University of Chicago Press, 2015)

5 The Isle of Man and the international human rights continuum

Introduction

In this chapter we examine the representative impact of the Isle of Man as a low tax area on the international human rights continuum, from a fiscal and structural perspective.[1]

To consider 'low tax areas' and 'tax havens' merely in general definitional terms may be intellectually legitimate when constructing a general fiscal overview of the genre, but a structural assessment of such areas requires specificity. The Isle of Man, a sophisticated and mature low tax area, affords the required level of detail, and the structural and fiscal examples used in this chapter are drawn from its legislation and jurisprudence.

The constitutional position of the Isle of Man is considered in detail in the Appendix to this chapter. It is clear that the Isle of Man is not the ad hoc political creation of tax-driven business enterprises,[2] but is a long-established parliamentary democracy whose government is well aware of, and therefore has no excuse for facilitating the breach of, its international responsibilities.

The existence of a wide and complex range of international taxation agreements, coupled with the Isle of Man's 'white listed' status accorded by the OECD[3] serves however to demonstrate that a low tax area such as the Isle of

---

1   This chapter is based on the author's essay 'The Representative Impact of the Isle of Man as a Low Tax Area on the International Human Rights Continuum from a Fiscal and Structural Perspective,' which appears in Jo Carby Hall (ed) *Essays on Human Rights: A Celebration of the Life of Dr Janusz Kochanowski* (Ius et Lex Foundation, Warsaw 2014).

2   A charge which may be laid at the door of the more aggressive tax havens whose international credentials are entirely dependent on rootless, ad hoc, business-friendly legislation whose permanence is on a par with tidal sand bars – see for example the OECD studies on aggressive tax planning: OECD, 'Aggressive Tax Planning' (*OECD*) <www.oecd.org/tax/aggressive> accessed 18 May 2017.

3   As a result of entering into various TIEAs and related agreements (details of which are available at Isle of Man Government, 'Tax Information Exchange Agreements' (*gov.im*) <www.gov.im/categories/tax-vat-and-your-money/income-tax-and-national-insurance/international-agreements/tax-information-exchange-agreements> accessed 18 May 2017), the Isle of Man has been included on the OECD 'White List' of 40 jurisdictions that have substantially implemented internationally agreed tax standards, published following the G20 meeting in London on 2 April 2009. The OECD Progress Report

Man is not necessarily synonymous with fiscal or regulatory illegitimacy.[4] The issue is not whether those doing business with and via the Isle of Man are engaged in anything underhand, but, rather, whether by using legitimate fiscal and structuring opportunities those engaged in such business are disrupting the international human rights continuum; a disruption facilitated – consciously or not – by even the most highly regulated low tax area.

International treaty obligations

Illegitimacy in the field of international human rights would at first sight seem also to be a false assumption. In addition to the well-publicised international fiscal arrangements to which it is a party, sight must not be lost of the fact that the Isle of Man has for decades been bound by the provisions of a number of international human rights documents, all of which – with or without local enabling legislation – are justiciable and may be pleaded before the courts:

- Convention for the Protection of Human Rights and Fundamental Freedoms (the European Convention) 1950[5] [and the Human Rights Act 2001[6]];
- International Covenant on Civil and Political Rights 1966;[7]
- International Covenant on Economic, Social and Cultural Rights 1966;[8]

issued on 2 November 2011 listed the Isle of Man as a jurisdiction that has substantially implemented the internationally agreed tax standard. The OECD Global Forum on Transparency and Exchange of Information for Tax Purposes, Isle of Man Peer Review Report is available at: OECD, *Peer Review Report of Isle of Man - Combined Phase 1 and Phase 2: Legal and Regulatory Framework and Implementation of the Standards in Practice* (OECD 2011) <www.oecd.org/tax/transparency/peerreviewreportofisleofman-combined phase1andphase2legalandregulatoryframeworkandimplementationofthe standardsinpractice.htm> accessed 18 May 2017.

4   Although over-zealous taxation planning is not unknown. 'Electronic Funds Transfers to the Isle of Man totalled $860M in a 12 month period and the [Canada Revenue Agency] has assessed the risk for all 3000 funds transfers involving approximately 800 taxpayers.' Government of Canada, 'Government of Canada Cracks Down on Tax Evasion' (*Government of Canada*, 11 April 2016) <http://news.gc.ca/web/article-en.do?nid= 1049689> and see Gordon Isfeld, 'Canada Revenue Agency Promises 'Blitz' on Isleof Man Tax Accounts' *Financial Post* (Toronto, 5 May 2016) <http://business.financial post.com/news/economy/canada-revenue-agency-promises-blitz-on-isle-of-man-tax-accounts> accessed 18 May 2017.

5   As amended by Protocols Nos 11 and 14 (adopted 4 November 1950, entered into force 3 September 1953) ETS 5 (European Convention on Human Rights) (ECHR).

6   <www.legislation.gov.im/cms/images/LEGISLATION/PRINCIPAL/2001/2001-0001/HumanRightsAct2001_1.pd> accessed 18 May 2017 (which received Royal Assent on 16 January 2001 but which entered into force much later, on 1 November 2006, after unsubstantiated reports in the popular media of political pressure in the Isle of Man legislature to suppress it).

7   (adopted 16 December 1966, entered into force 23 March 1976) 999 UNTS 171.

8   (adopted 16 December 1966, entered into force 3 January 1976) 993 UNTS 3.

- Convention on the Elimination of All Forms of Discrimination Against Women 1979;[9] and
- United Nations Convention on the Rights of the Child 1989.[10]

However, as highlighted by the Committee on Economic, Social and Cultural Rights in its most recently published observations in June 2009, the extent to which these obligations are implemented is unclear.[11]

While there are growing references in Isle of Man jurisprudence to obligations under ECHR 1950 (implemented domestically by virtue of the Human Rights Act 2001) the remaining obligations appear, falsely, to be regarded as having fallen, if only de facto, into desuetude.

As with many smaller, politically mature jurisdictions with a long history of stability, the Isle of Man internally encounters few examples of human rights abuse. There is in consequence no domestic pressure for Tynwald to enact legislation along the lines of the Human Rights Act 2001 which would import into domestic law the terms of the various international human rights instruments to which it is a party.

The relationship between domestic law and international treaty obligations under Isle of Man law is the same as that under the laws of the United Kingdom, to the decisions of whose courts reference may be made (bearing in mind that decisions only of the Privy Council are binding on the Isle of Man courts – the decisions of all other UK courts, from the Supreme Court downwards, are merely persuasive).

International treaties and conventions (ITCs) under which obligations are entered into by governments do not become part of Manx law unless Tynwald so enacts. However, there is a presumption that when enacting legislation Tynwald intends that legislation to comply with relevant ITCs,

---

9   (adopted 18 December 1979, entered into force 3 September 1981) 1249 UNTS 13.
10 (adopted 20 November 1989, entered into force 2 September 1990) 1577 UNTS 3.
11 United Nations Committee on Economic, Social and Cultural Rights, 'Consideration of Reports Submitted by States Parties under Articles 16 and 17 of the Covenant: Concluding observations: United Kingdom of Great Britain and Northern Ireland, the Crown Dependencies and the Overseas Dependent Territories' (12 June 2009) UN Doc E/C.12/GBR/CO/5, para 12:

> The Committee is concerned, even though it takes note of the State party's structure of government, with devolved administrations in Northern Ireland, Scotland and Wales, and separate government structures in the Overseas Territories and Crown Dependencies, about the lack of a national strategy to implement the Covenant. It is also concerned about the limited availability of information regarding the implementation of the Covenant in the Overseas Territories and Crown Dependencies.
>
> Bearing in mind that it is that State party which is responsible for the implementation of the Covenant in all its territories, the Committee urges the State party to ensure the equal enjoyment of the economic, social and cultural rights by all individuals and groups of individuals under its jurisdiction, and recommends that the State party adopt a national strategy for the implementation of the Covenant throughout the State party's territories.

even if the ITCs are not referred to.[12] Therefore, reference can be made to ITCs:

> If the terms of the legislation are not clear... but are reasonably capable of more than one meaning, the Treaty itself becomes relevant, for there is a prima facie presumption that Parliament does not intend to act in breach of international law. ... and if one of the meanings which can reasonably be ascribed to the legislation is consonant with the treaty obligations and another or others are not, the meaning which is consonant is to be preferred.[13]

But this principle must not be taken to extremes. The relationship between ITCs and domestic law was explored in the 'Brexit case' (at first instance) in the United Kingdom in November 2016:

> The Crown's prerogative power to conduct international relations is regarded as wide and as being outside the purview of the courts precisely because the Crown cannot, in ordinary circumstances, alter domestic law by using such power to make or unmake a treaty. By making and unmaking treaties the Crown creates legal effects on the plane of international law, but in doing so it does not and cannot change domestic law. It cannot without the intervention of Parliament confer rights on individuals or deprive individuals of rights.[14]

The issues

At their most fundamental, the low tax area issues which impact upon the international human rights continuum are:[15]

- The structures are subject to artificially low levels of domestic taxation, or are wholly exempt from income and capital taxes or customs duties.
- Concealment (a) of funds and (b) of beneficial ownership through the use of discretionary trusts, charities, companies and related structures

---

12 The Isle of Man is to be distinguished from the other Crown Dependencies in that certification of compatibility with human rights (and other constitutional) obligations is dealt with internally, authority having been delegated to the island's Lieutenant Governor, and Manx Bills no longer require review by the Privy Council (unlike their counterparts in Jersey and Guernsey). The procedure is discussed in Justice Committee, *Crown Dependencies: Developments since 2010* (HC 2013-14, 726) part 3 'Insular Legislation and Treaty Extension') <www.publications.parliament.uk/pa/cm201314/cmselect/cmjust/726/726.pdf> accessed 19 May 2017.
13 Diplock LJ in *Salomon v Commissioners of Customs and Excise* [1966] 3 All ER 871, 875. In the Isle of Man the reference to 'Parliament' is replaced by 'Tynwald'.
14 *R (Miller) v The Secretary of State for Exiting the European Union* (QB) [2016] EWHC 2768, para 32.
15 For an international review of these issues see Chapter 2.

(including off balance sheet structuring through the use of non-charitable purpose trusts.
- Banking secrecy.
- Reciprocal enforcement of foreign judgments in domestic courts is limited or dis-applied altogether (and domestic court proceedings may be held in secret).
- Limitation periods (the time within which a claim may be brought, at the expiration of which that right is extinguished) may be so short as to preclude in practice the preparation and filing of a claim.
- Foreign rules on forced heirship (a system common in civil law jurisdictions whereby heirs have a fixed entitlement to the property of the deceased, regardless of the deceased's preferences to the contrary) are dis-applied.
- Domestic remedies relating to fraudulent transfers (the transfer of property into a structure which either intentionally defeats or is deemed in law to defeat the interests of legitimate creditors and other claimants) are dis-applied.
- The structure may be aggressively asset protective, and assets held within it may not be capable of being alienated or passed by bankruptcy, insolvency or liquidation; or liable to be seized, sold, attached, or otherwise taken in execution by process of law.
- A structure may be an 'orphan' with no beneficial owner, in law or in equity.
- The requirement to place details of the structure, its existence, its finances and its activities, in the public domain (in the form of a publicly accessible register) may be minimal or entirely absent.
- Structures which under generally accepted legal principles have a limited life span (such as private trusts) may be given perpetual existence.
- Fiduciary responsibilities of those administering or managing structures – be they directors, trustees or any other responsible officer – may be dis-applied, or, if applied, those otherwise responsible may through a combination of manipulated limitation periods and indulgences be deemed not culpable, or culpable but absolved.
- The structure may take a form unknown under generally accepted legal principles, or may have the power to shape shift.

How are these issues reflected in the constitutional, legal and fiscal framework of the Isle of Man?

Taxation

Taxation in the Isle of Man is real and complex, but low. This is considered in greater detail in the Appendix. The crucial point is that the taxation system is sophisticated and that the rates and concessions, and international connections by way of Double Taxation Treaties and Taxation Information

Exchange Agreements have been well thought out. They are wholly state-endorsed.

Concealment of funds and of beneficial ownership

The concealment of beneficial ownership may be seen as the legitimate right to privacy of that owner, in the absence of the use of such concealment to frustrate fiscal or human rights obligations, but as with the concealment of funds it always carries the suggestion of illegitimacy. Initiatives have been taken, and are broadening, to deal with transparency issues.[16]

Banking secrecy

The interplay between the claimed right to banking secrecy and competing norms under international human rights law is not unique to low tax areas. The Isle of Man maintains a conservative stance. Foreign courts cannot compel a bank licensed in the Isle of Man to reveal details about its customers. Application must be made to the High Court of Justice of the Isle of Man pursuant to the Bankers' Books Evidence Act 1935.[17] Such assistance will only be considered in relation to legal proceedings brought within the Isle of Man and not to foreign proceedings. Further:

> A banker or officer of a bank shall not, in any legal proceedings to which the bank is not a party, be compelled to produce any banker's books the contents of which can be proved under this Act, or to appear as a witness to prove the matters, transactions and accounts therein recorded, unless by order of a Deemster[18] made for special cause.[19]

Reciprocal enforcement

The automatic exclusion of foreign judgments is unknown.[20] The choice of the law of a foreign jurisdiction as proper to settle, resolve, determine and adjudicate any disputes would, subject to forum rules under international private law, be upheld as a valid choice of law by the courts of the Isle of

---

16 See Chapter 3.
17 <www.legislation.gov.im/cms/images/LEGISLATION/PRINCIPAL/1935/1935-0001/BankersBooksEvidenceAct1935_1.pdf> accessed 19 May 2017.
18 'Deemster' is the ancient title, from the time of the early Viking settlers, of a judge of the Isle of Man High Court.
19 Bankers' Books Evidence Act 1935 section 6. This proposition was confirmed in *Re Blayney and Grace re National Irish Bank Limited* 2001-03 MLR 13 (CHD).
20 See Chapter 2 for examples of jurisdictions in which such automatic exclusion is, in relation to specific structures, enshrined in statute – eg Nevis, the Bahamas.

Man. A judgment of a higher court of a limited number of jurisdictions[21] would, pursuant to the provisions of the Judgments (Reciprocal Enforcement)(Isle of Man) Act 1968 and the regulations made under that Act be enforced by the Courts of the Isle of Man without re-examination of the merits of the case. The judgment must be one which is either final and conclusive as between the judgment debtor and the judgment creditor or requires the former to make an interim payment to the latter; and there is payable under it a sum of money, not being a sum payable in respect of taxes or other charges of a like nature or in respect of a fine or other penalty. Any judgment not coming within this description, or given by a court in a non-reciprocal jurisdiction would not be recognised or enforceable in the Isle of Man and any action brought in the Isle of Man would require a retrial or examination of the merits of the case.

Limitation periods

The application of reduced limitation periods to specific structures or actions is unknown. Limitation periods apply universally under the provisions of the Limitation Act 1984.[22]

Forced heirship

The inheritance regimes of foreign states will generally be upheld in accordance with the principles of private international law.

However, in the case of trusts governed by the law of the Isle of Man, the provisions of the Trusts Act 1995[23] apply. The principal objects of the Act are to clarify the law of the Isle of Man as to the ability of a trust to change the law which is its governing law and to ensure that in relation to trusts which are governed by Manx law the courts will not have regard to foreign laws in determining certain matters. Specifically, Section 5 of the Act provides:

> [N]o trust governed by the law of the Island and no disposition of property to be held upon the trusts of such a trust is void, voidable, liable to be set aside or defective in any fashion, nor is the capacity of any settlor to be questioned by reason that –
> (a) the law of any foreign jurisdiction prohibits or does not recognise the concept of a trust; or

---

21 Reciprocity exists between the Isle of Man and the United Kingdom (England and Wales; Scotland; Northern Ireland), Italy, Israel, Jersey, Guernsey, the Netherlands Antilles. The list has remained unaltered since the 1990s.

22 <https://legislation.gov.im/cms/images/LEGISLATION/PRINCIPAL/1984/1984-0018/LimitationAct1984_4.pdf> accessed 19 May 2017.

23 <https://legislation.gov.im/cms/images/LEGISLATION/PRINCIPAL/1995/1995-0018/TrustsAct1995_2.pdf> accessed 19 May 2017.

(b) the trust or disposition –
    (i) avoids or defeats any right, claim or interest conferred by a foreign law upon any person by reason of a personal relationship to the settlor or by way of heirship rights; or
    (ii) contravenes any rule of foreign law or any foreign judicial or administrative order or action intended to recognise, protect, enforce or give effect to such a right, claim or interest.

Section 6 of the Act defines 'heirship rights' to be:

> any right, claim or interest in, against or to the property of a person arising or accruing in consequence of that person's death, other than any such right, claim or interest created by will or other voluntary disposition by such person or resulting from an express limitation in the disposition of the property to such person.

'Personal relationship' is broadly defined in Section 6 to include 'every form of relationship by blood or marriage' and includes within this definition natural, adopted, legitimate or illegitimate children. Also specifically included are cohabiting couples who so conduct themselves 'as to give rise in any jurisdiction to any rights, obligations or responsibilities analogous to those of parent and child or husband and wife'. Such a definition of cohabitation would appear to include same-sex relationships.[24] Both the terms 'adoption' and 'marriage' are stated to include such states 'whether or not ... recognised by law'.

Fraudulent transfers

Domestic remedies relating to fraudulent transfers are of fundamental and long-standing importance. The Statute of Elizabeth (enactment entitled 13 Elizabeth 1 Ch 5 (1571)),[25] an Act passed in the reign of the English Queen Elizabeth I for the protection of creditors against fraudulent deeds of their debtors (repealed in the United Kingdom by the Law of Property Act 1925) does not, itself, apply to the Isle of Man. However, in 1736 Tynwald enacted legislation which can be seen as broadly equivalent to the Statute of Elizabeth, the Fraudulent Assignments Act 1736.[26] Under the Act, 'all fraudulent assignments or transfers of the debtor's goods or effects shall be void and of no effect against his just creditors, any custom or practice to the

---

24 Both same-sex and heterosexual civil partnerships and same-sex marriage are permissible under Isle of Man law.
25 Wikipedia, 'Fraudulent Conveyances Act 1571' (*Wikipedia*, ed 27 February 2017) <https://en.wikipedia.org/wiki/Fraudulent_Conveyances_Act_1571> accessed 19 May 2017.
26 <https://legislation.gov.im/cms/images/LEGISLATION/PRINCIPAL/1736/1736-0002/FraudulentAssignmentsAct1736_1.pdf> accessed 19 May 2017.

contrary notwithstanding'. The contemporary interpretation of these provisions is:

> A state of insolvency implies an inability to pay existing, or present debts. A person is not in a 'state of insolvency' merely because he may not be able to pay contingent or future debts, which may never materialise. ... I would construe the term 'present debts', however, to include known and ascertained debts which are to fall due on a date in the future. A transaction or contrivance designed to deprive known and ascertainable future creditors of timely recourse to property which would otherwise be applicable for their benefit ... would not be honest in the context of the relationship of debtor and creditor and would not therefore be bona fide.[27]

Asset protection

Asset protection legislation is unknown. The laws relating to bankruptcy[28] and the seizure of assets apply universally.

Orphan structures

Orphan structures exist pursuant to the Purpose Trusts Act 1996,[29] but not otherwise.

Public registration

There is no requirement to register trusts or the details of general partnerships. The Companies Registry[30] holds records of all incorporated bodies (including limited partnerships).[31]

27 *Re Heginbotham* 1999-01 MLR 53 per Deemster Cain.
28 Principally contained in the Bankruptcy Procedure Act 1892 <https://legislation.gov.im/cms/images/LEGISLATION/PRINCIPAL/1892/1892-0002/BankruptcyProcedureAct1892_1.pdf> accessed 19 May 2017 and the Bankruptcy Code 1892 <https://legislation.gov.im/cms/images/LEGISLATION/PRINCIPAL/1892/1892-0001/BankruptcyCode1892_2.pdf> accessed 19 May 2017. There is no separate corporate insolvency regime, the 1892 legislation applying in conjunction with The Companies (Winding Up) Rules 1934 <www.gov.im/media/1348302/the-companies-winding-up-rules-1934-without-forms.pdf> accessed 19 May 2017.
29 <https://legislation.gov.im/cms/images/LEGISLATION/PRINCIPAL/1996/1996-0009/PurposeTrustsAct1996_1.pdf> accessed 19 May 2017. See Chapter 3 for a fuller treatment of this topic.
30 (*Isle of Man Government*) <www.gov.im/ded/companies> accessed 19 May 2017.
31 Access requests may however be made under the Data Protection Act 2002 <https://legislation.gov.im/cms/images/LEGISLATION/PRINCIPAL/2002/2002-0002/DataProtectionAct2002_7.pdf> accessed 19 May 2017 and the Freedom of Information Act 2015 <https://legislation.gov.im/cms/images/LEGISLATION/PRINCIPAL/2015/2015-0008/FreedomofInformationAct2015_3.pdf> accessed 19 May 2017.

Non-disclosure of business objects

Corporations formed in the Isle of Man under the Companies Acts 1931 to 2004 and under the Companies Act 2006 benefit from the abolition of the principle of ultra vires. A company has all the rights, powers and privileges of an individual, and therefore no aspect of its business objects need be stated in its constitutional documents – with the exception of companies formed for an exclusively charitable purpose (the objects of which must expressly be limited to such identified purposes) it is not possible to set out why the company has been formed or what its activities are to be.[32] The effect of this is wholly to conceal *why* the company exists.

Perpetual existence

Until dissolved, all corporations and partnerships are of perpetual duration. Private trusts and charitable trusts are not subject to a perpetuity period.[33] Non-charitable purpose trusts under the Purpose Trusts Act 1996 are subject to a perpetuity period of 80 years.[34]

Fiduciary responsibilities

There are no statutory provisions for the abnegation of fiduciary responsibilities and therefore none relating to absolution.[35]

Shape shifting forms

No provision of Isle of Man law permits a structure fundamentally to alter its form and purpose.[36] On balance therefore, the Isle of Man is free from many

---

32 Isle of Man Government, Department of Economic Development, Companies Registry, 'Practice Note: Requirements with Respect to the Memorandum and Articles of Association of an Isle of Man Incorporated Company' (PN 19/2014, *gov.im*, 7 January 2014) <www.gov.im/media/1348340/pn19-2014.pdf> accessed 19 May 2017.

33 Section 1A, Perpetuities and Accumulations Act 1968 <https://legislation.gov.im/cms/images/LEGISLATION/PRINCIPAL/1968/1968-0008/Perpetuitiesand AccumulationsAct1968_2.pdf> accessed 19 May 2017 (introduced by Trusts (Amendment) Act 2015, s 5).

34 (n 29) s 1(1).

35 On the contrary, in the case of trusts a statutory duty of care exists under Part 1, Trustee Act 2001 <https://legislation.gov.im/cms/images/LEGISLATION/PRINCIPAL/2001/2001-0018/TrusteeAct2001_1.pdf> accessed 19 May 2017. See also Isle of Man Financial Services Authority, 'Financial Services Act 2008 Guidance on Directorships, Trusteeships and similar Responsibilities held by Directors and Key Persons of Licenceholders' (*Isle of Man Financial Services Authority*, January 2017) <www.iomfsa.im/lib/docs/iomfsa/rulebooks/directorshipsguidancemar2015.pdf> accessed 19 May 2017.

36 For an extreme example to the contrary, see the Nevis Multiform Foundation, discussed in Chapter 2.

of the taints which stain the aggressive low tax areas and tax havens. Yet by the very existence of the archetypical structuring possibilities it offers, it, in common with many such areas, may facilitate international human rights abuse.

An archetype

Figure 5.1 shows a fairly typical offshore structure.[37] How is the Archetype - entirely legitimate in the jurisdiction in which it is formed[38] – to be assessed in light of applicable international human rights norms, bearing in mind that 'a party may not invoke the provisions of its internal law as justification for its failure to perform a treaty'?[39] And what responsibility do the low tax areas have to take cognisance of the international human rights consequences of the structures such as the Archetype whose existence they facilitate?

The Maastricht Guidelines on Violations of Economic, Social and Cultural Rights, Maastricht, 22–26 January 1997[40] state:

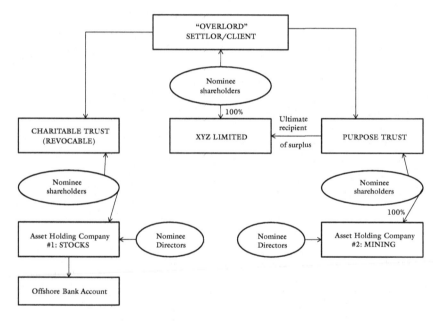

Figure 5.1 A typical offshore structure

---

37 See Chapter 2 for a fuller treatment.
38 And assumed to be wholly anti-money laundering / terrorist financing compliant.
39 Vienna Convention on the Law of Treaties 1969 (adopted 23 May 1969, entered into force 27 January 1980) 1155 UNTS 331, art 27.
40 International Commission of Jurists (ICJ), 'Maastricht Guidelines on Violations of Economic, Social and Cultural Rights' (ICJ, 26 January 1997) <www1.umn.edu/humanrts/instree/Maastrichtguidelines_.html> accessed 19 May 2017.

The obligation to protect includes the State's responsibility to ensure that private entities or individuals, including transnational corporations over which they exercise jurisdiction, do not deprive individuals of their economic, social and cultural rights. States are responsible for violations of economic, social and cultural rights that result from their failure to exercise due diligence in controlling the behaviour of such non-state actors.[41]

State neutrality is not an option:

[T]he pretense of neutrality with respect to substantive outcomes in conventional liberalism – and in conventional human rights – seems increasingly to be showing itself to be just that: a pretense, an excuse for indifference in a world of growing inequities and predictable depriva-tions that stem from, inter alia, certain economic paradigms and institutional arrangements.[42]

In its 'Statement on the Obligations of State Parties regarding the Corporate Sector and Economic, Social and Cultural Rights', issued on 12 July 2011,[43] the Committee on Economic, Social and Cultural Rights affirmed:

States parties have the primary obligation to respect, protect and fulfil the Covenant rights of all persons under their jurisdiction in the context of corporate activities undertaken by State-owned or private enter-prises.[44] ... States Parties shall ensure that companies demonstrate due diligence to make certain that they do not impede the enjoyment of the Covenant rights by those who depend on or are negatively affected by their activities.[45] ... States Parties should also take steps to prevent human rights contraventions abroad by corporations which have their main offices under their jurisdiction, without infringing the sovereignty or diminishing the obligations of the host States under the Covenant.[46]

---

41   Acts by non-state entities (para 18).
42   Alicia Ely Yamin, 'The Future in the Mirror: Incorporating Strategies for the Defense and Promotion of Economic, Social and Cultural Rights into the Mainstream Human Rights Agenda' (2005) 27 HRQ 1200, 1235.
43   United Nations Economic and Social Council, Committee on Economic, Social and Cultural Rights, 'Statement on the Obligations of State Parties regarding the Corporate Sector and Economic, Social and Cultural Rights' (12 July 2011) UN Doc E/C.12/2011/1 <http://docstore.ohchr.org/SelfServices/FilesHandler.ashx?enc=4slQ6QSmlBEDz FEovLCuW1AVC1NkPsgUedPlF1vfPMKOgNxs%2FCpnVM8K6XpeNimFvrj%2F4tQZvh H%2BXM9vEaJmHSX3FSXAcTmJ%2BWc3iPSLafnoFpGQ9KIHCX ooWHCPCpQt> accessed 19 May 2017.
44   (n 43) para 3.
45   (n 43) para 4.
46   (n 43) para 5.

How much greater is a state's obligation when it is not simply a question of a failure to control but of an abnegation of responsibility to do so coupled with the facilitation of the structures and the granting of enticing taxation breaks?

International human rights impacted

Privacy

At a time of increased, globalised surveillance, the right to privacy is uppermost in the minds of many human rights commentators. It is deeply entrenched: '[n]o one shall be subjected to arbitrary interference with his privacy';[47] '[e]veryone has the right to respect for his private and family life';[48] '[n]o one shall be subjected to arbitrary or unlawful interference with his privacy'.[49]

In the Archetype, privacy is assured through the obscuring of the nature and purpose of the business enterprise, its financial standing, the identity of its beneficial owners. At first sight, this looks like a legitimate application of the universal privacy principle. But is privacy here being used as a shield, or as a sword? Is the Archetype an example of the right to privacy, or an example of the right to privacy being used as a tool for other, not necessarily human rights compliant ends?

Looking more closely at the parameters of right to privacy, for example from a European perspective, the Archetype itself begins to appear less than legitimate: 'There shall be no interference by a public authority with the exercise of this right [to privacy] except such as is in accordance with the law and is necessary in a democratic society in the interests of ... the economic well-being of the country... or for the protection of the rights and freedoms of others.'[50] The Archetype is unlikely to affect adversely the economic well-being of the Isle of Man, generating as it does a real financial return by way of income and the taxation of that income to the local economy; but the extra-territorial effect of the structure may well be prejudicial.

Extraterritorial obligations of low tax areas: the Maastricht Principles 2011

To what extent is a low tax area free to regard its own interests as paramount and exclusive? What regard must it have for those who are affected by the operation of the structures which the low tax area facilitates?

---

47 Universal Declaration of Human Rights (adopted 10 December 1948 UNGA Res 217 A(III) (UDHR) art 12.
48 ECHR (n 5), art 8.1.
49 International Covenant on Civil and Political Rights (adopted 16 December 1966, entered into force 23 March 1976) 999 UNTS 171 (ICCPR), art 17.
50 ECHR (n 5) art 8.2.

On 28 September 2011 at a gathering convened by Maastricht University and the International Commission of Jurists, participants adopted the Maastricht Principles on Extraterritorial Obligations of States in the area of Economic, Social and Cultural Rights ('the Maastricht Principles 2011'), the definitive version of which was issued on 29 February 2012.[51]

The Maastricht Principles 2011 rank below soft law in the international human rights continuum, but are the clearest and most recent statements on the extraterritorial obligations of states. Despite the narrow title, Principle 5 is express in setting out the range of applicability of the Maastricht Principles 2011:[52] 'All human rights are universal, indivisible, interdependent, interrelated and of equal importance. The present Principles elaborate extra-territorial obligations in relation to economic, social and cultural rights, without excluding their applicability to other human rights, including civil and political rights.'

The extraterritorial obligations relevant to the low tax areas are contained in Principle 8(a): 'obligations relating to the acts and omissions of a State, within or beyond its territory, that have effects on the enjoyment of human rights outside of that State's territory.'

The facilitation of the Archetype by the Isle of Man brings it within the scope of jurisdiction set out in Principle 9:

> A State has obligations to respect, protect and fulfil economic, social and cultural rights in any of the following:
> a)   situations over which it exercises authority or effective control, whether or not such control is exercised in accordance with international law;
> b)   situations over which State acts or omissions bring about foreseeable effects on the enjoyment of economic, social and cultural rights, whether within or outside its territory;
> c)   situations in which the State, acting separately or jointly, whether through its executive, legislative or judicial branches, is in a position to exercise decisive influence or to take measures to realize economic, social and cultural rights extraterritorially, in accordance with international law.

Given that the Archetype is composed entirely of elements founded in statute and hence owes its form and nature to the legislation passed and maintained

---

51   See FIAN International, 'Maastricht Principles on Extraterritorial Obligations of States in the area of Economic, Social and Cultural Rights' (*FIAN International*, January 2013) <www.fidh.org/IMG/pdf/maastricht-eto-principles-uk_web.pdf> accessed 20 May 2017 (Maastricht Principles).

52   Echoing the provisions of the Vienna Declaration and Programme of Action 1993 (adopted by the World Conference on Human Rights in Vienna 29 June 1993) (*OHCHR*) <www.ohchr.org/EN/ProfessionalInterest/Pages/Vienna.aspx> accessed 20 May 2017, art 5.

in force by Tynwald, Tynwald has an obligation to regulate the Archetype in accordance with human rights norms, as set out in Principle 24:

> All States must take necessary measures to ensure that non-State actors which they are in a position to regulate, as set out in Principle 25, such as private individuals and organizations, and transnational corporations and other business enterprises, do not nullify or impair the enjoyment of economic, social and cultural rights. These include administrative, legislative, investigative, adjudicatory and other measures. All other States have a duty to refrain from nullifying or impairing the discharge of this obligation to protect.

Those provisions of Principle 25 which are relevant to the Archetype are found in paragraph (c):

> as regards business enterprises, where the corporation, or its parent or controlling company, has its centre of activity, is registered or domiciled, or has its main place of business or substantial business activities, in the State concerned ...

That the Archetype benefits from certain taxation advantages, including cross-border taxation arrangements, imposes on the Isle of Man an 'obligation to create an international enabling environment' in accordance with Principle 29:

> States must take deliberate, concrete and targeted steps, separately, and jointly through international cooperation, to create an international enabling environment conducive to the universal fulfilment of economic, social and cultural rights, including in matters relating to bilateral and multilateral trade, investment, taxation, finance, environmental protection, and development cooperation.

Economic liberalism or neo-colonialism?

Articles 1.2 of the International Covenant on Civil and Political Rights (ICCPR) and of the International Covenant on Economic, Social and Cultural Rights (ICESCR) are clear on the point: 'All peoples may, for their own ends, freely dispose of their natural wealth and resources....' This is not however a blue print for exploitation: 'In no case may a people be deprived of its own means of subsistence.'[53]

---

53 ICCPR (n 49); International Covenant on Economic, Social and Cultural Rights (adopted 16 December 1966, entered into force 3 January 1976) 993 UNTS 3 (ICESCR) arts 1.2, final sentence.

The Archetype may have the effect of impoverishing a people not merely by depriving the target state in which the Archetype operates of revenue which would have been due to it through local taxation but also by denying the right of adequate redress against corporations trading in its jurisdiction which have themselves no traceable beneficial ownership and which may be little more than post-box enterprises shorn of any real economic substance. The target state is thereby, albeit indirectly, rendered less able to take appropriate steps to promote the right of its citizens to an adequate standard of living, including adequate food, clothing and housing, and to the continuous improvement of living conditions.[54]

The Archetype may from the perspective of the target state, most obviously but not exclusively in Africa, be neo-colonialist: 'The free disposal of wealth and natural resources shall be exercised without prejudice to the obligation of promoting international economic co-operation based on mutual respect, equitable exchange and the principles of international law.'[55] 'States parties to the present Charter shall undertake to eliminate all forms of foreign economic exploitation particularly that practised by international monopolies so as to enable their peoples to fully benefit from the advantage derived from their natural resources.'[56]

Development

'"Developing countries" is the name that experts use to designate countries trampled by someone else's development.'[57] Given the potentially negative, even neo-colonial effect of the Archetype on the citizens of the target state, what obligations are there on the host state under whose laws the Archetype is created? To what extent are the laws rendering the Archetype legitimate themselves in breach of international human rights norms?

The Declaration on the Right to Development 1986[58] is in point: 'States have the right and the duty to formulate appropriate national development policies that aim at the constant improvement of the well-being of the entire population *and of all individuals* ... and in the fair distribution of the benefits arising therefrom.'[59] Efforts at the international level to promote and protect human rights should be accompanied by efforts to establish a new

---

54   UDHR (n 47) art 25.1; ICESCR (n 53) art 11.1.

55   African Charter on Human and Peoples' Rights (adopted 27 June 1981, entered into force 21 October 1986) CAB/LEG/67/3 rev.5, 21 ILM 58 (1982) <www.refworld.org/docid/3ae6b3630.html> accessed 20 May 2017 (African Charter) art 21.3.

56   African Charter (n 55) art 21.5.

57   Eduardo Galeano, *Upside Down: A Primer for the Looking Glass World* (Mark Fried tr, Picador, 2001) 37.

58   UNGA, Declaration on the Right to Development (adopted by the General Assembly, 4 December 1986) UN Doc A/RES/41/128 <www.un.org/documents/ga/res/41/a41r128.htm> accessed 20 May 2017.

59   Art 2.3.

international economic order.[60] In particular, 'states shall take resolute steps to eliminate the massive and flagrant violations of the human rights of the peoples and human beings affected by situations such as those resulting from ... colonialism, foreign domination and occupation ... foreign interference and threats against national sovereignty',[61] including neo-colonialism.[62]

From the perspective of the target state the neo-colonial nature of the Archetype may impede the target state in fulfilling its duty to promote development.[63]

The facilitation by host states of arrangements such as the Archetype is contrary to the principle contained in Article 2(1) of ICESCR which obliges states parties to 'take steps individually and through international assistance and co-operation, especially economic and technical' to realise the rights guaranteed: 'Developing states would certainly favour the argument that this places some level of obligation on the international community, especially on the economically powerful states to assist and co-operate with the developing states in the realisation of ESC rights.'[64]

In its General Comment 3 (1990),[65] the Committee on Economic, Social and Cultural Rights (CESCR) emphasises:

> that in accordance with Articles 55 and 56 of the Charter of the United Nations, with well-established principles of international law, and with the provisions of [ICESCR] itself, international co-operation for development and thus for the realisation of economic, social and cultural rights is an obligation of all States. It is particularly incumbent upon those States which are in a position to assist others in this regard. The Committee notes in particular the importance of the Declaration on the Right to Development [1986] ... and the need for States parties to take full account of the principles recognised therein. It emphasises that in the absence of an active programme of international assistance and cooperation on the part of all those States that are in a position to undertake one, the full realisation of economic, social and cultural rights will remain an unfulfilled aspiration in many countries.[66]

60   Preamble, art 3.3.
61   Art 5.
62   Preamble.
63   Eg African Charter, art 22.2 'States have the duty, individually or collectively, to ensure the exercise of the right to development.'
64   Bashood Baderin & Robert McCorquodale (eds) *Economic, Social and Cultural Rights in Action* (Oxford Scholarship Online, 2007) 13.
65   General Comment No 3, 'The Nature of States Parties' Obligations' (Art 2, Para 1 of the Covenant) (14 December 1990) UN Doc E/1991/23 <www.refworld.org/docid/4538838e10.html> accessed 20 May 2017 (General Comment No 3).
66   General Comment No 3 (n 65) para 14.

It is a question of power:

> The Declaration's centre of attention on norms of distributive justice for development objectives moves human rights beyond its more narrow concerns of fulfilling basic needs to the greater project of reducing material inequality, but it also seeks to confront the fact that economic inequality is so readily bound up with inequalities of power.[67]

Host states such as the Isle of Man may not appear to be jurisdictions of sufficient power or economic resource to come within this description, but crucially they channel the power of global organisations which themselves replicate the economic impact of states[68] – in effect, the low tax areas are punching above their weight; and having entered the ring are bound to compete by the rules.[69]

The low tax areas have the power both to effect change and to prevent it.

---

67   Margot Salomon, 'Why Should It Matter That Others Have More? Poverty, Inequality and the Potential of International Human Rights Law' [2010] LSE Legal Studies Working Paper 15/2010 <https://papers.ssrn.com/sol3/papers.cfm?abstract_id=1711657> accessed 10 May 2017. Sigrun I Skogly and Mark Gibney further observe:

> It is pertinent to assume that in a globalised world where individual citizens' lives are heavily influenced by operations by actors beyond one's national borders, the obligation to respect customary international human rights law in transnational operations will be considerably strengthened. It will be increasingly realised that, not only are there governments that are unwilling to ameliorate the human rights effects of foreign actors within their own borders, but also that they are unable to do so, due to political and economic inequalities, in the international community as well.

'Transnational Human Rights Obligations' (2002) 22 HRQ 781, 789.

68   The problem is not confined to low tax areas or to economic and social rights. See the 'Concluding Observations on the Sixth Periodic Report of Germany Adopted by the UN Human Rights Committee at its 106th Session 15 October – 2 November 2012' (12 November 2012) UN Doc CCPR/C/DEU/CO/6 <http://repository.un.org/bit stream/handle/11176/298828/CCPR_C_DEU_CO_6-EN.pdf?sequence=3&is Allowed=y> accessed 20 May 2017, para 16:

> The State party is encouraged to set out clearly the expectation that all business enterprises domiciled in its territory and/or its jurisdiction respect human rights standards in accordance with [ICCPR] throughout their operations. It is also encouraged to take appropriate measures to strengthen the remedies provided to protect people who have been victims of activities of such business enterprises operating abroad.

69   To what extent the low tax areas merely reflect the general business and social mores of the early twenty-first century is open to debate: 'The status of the right to development has long been unclear in international law, in part because the very concept is subversive of a global architecture that perpetuates inequalities and dependency' Alicia Ely Yamin, 'Our Place in the World: Conceptualizing Obligations beyond Borders in Human Rights-based Approaches to Health' (2010) 12 Health HRJ 1.

2030 Agenda for Sustainable Development

It is widely recognised that the implementation of Millennium Development Goals ('MDGs')[70] was not a resounding success, and the focus is now on the 2030 Agenda for Sustainable Development ('2030 Agenda').[71] The MDGs themselves were silent on the question of human rights, and one striking consequence of this (and probably the main cause of their failure) was the absence of an accountability mechanism of the type inherent in a human rights-based approach.[72]

Reviewing the MDGs in 2013, the Center for Economic and Social Rights looked to a post-2015 development agenda founded on justice. Not solely from a fiscal and taxation perspective, but focusing on 'a holistic and coherent global partnership for development founded on the principle of international human rights', it recognised the role of tax havens and commented: 'If properly designed and implemented, the post-2015 agenda can address global obstacles to open and transparent budget, tax and fiscal processes, in particular the financial secrecy regimes which encourage illicit financial flows, tax evasion and avoidance, and corruption.'[73] However, its suggested remedies to combat this were confined to the automatic exchange of taxation information and country-by-country reporting.[74] It decried state complicity in the process of preventing other countries from resourcing rights, citing support for 'cross-border tax evasion, improper regulation of abusive private financial actors, private creditors or other business enterprises, aid or trade conditionalities, and unjustifiable constraints on deficit financing'. It suggested that states be required periodically to assess the extraterritorial human rights risk of their laws, policies and practices, to include 'independent assessments of the degree to which laws or policies on trade, debt, tax, corporate accountability, fiscal, monetary, financial, environmental and investment matters effectively sustain or undermine the achievement of human rights and future sustainable development goals.'

---

70 United Nations, 'News on Millennium Development Goals' (United Nations) <www.un.org/millenniumgoals> accessed 20 May 2017.
71 UNGA, 'Transforming our World: the 2030 Agenda for Sustainable Development' (21 October 2015) Seventieth Session, UN Doc A/RES/70/1 <www.un.org/ga/search/ view_doc.asp?symbol=A/RES/70/1&Lang=E> accessed 20 May 2017.
72 See Yamin (n 69).
73 Center for Economic and Social Rights, 'A Matter of Justice – Securing Human Rights in the Post 2015 Sustainable Development Agenda (*Center for Economic and Social Rights*, 2013) <www.cesr.org/matter-justice-securing-human-rights-post-2015-sustainable-development-agenda> accessed 20 May 2017, chs 7-8.
74 For a discussion on the extent to which this approach is effective, see Chapter 4.

This anticipated level of specificity did not however materialise. The 2030 Agenda contains seventeen Sustainable Development Goals, each with a fairly vague implementation suggestion.[75]

The 2030 Agenda, unlike the MDGs, expressly engages with human rights norms:

> We envisage a world of universal respect for human rights and human dignity, the rule of law, justice, equality and non-discrimination
>
> (Para 8)

> We reaffirm the importance of the Universal Declaration of Human Rights, as well as other international instruments relating to human rights and international law. We emphasize the responsibilities of all States, in conformity with the Charter of the United Nations, to respect, protect and promote human rights and fundamental freedoms for all, without distinction of any kind as to race, colour, sex, language, religion, political or other opinion, national or social origin, property, birth, disability or other status.
>
> (Para 19)

However, the 2030 Agenda also acknowledges that 'every State has, and shall freely exercise, full permanent sovereignty over all its wealth, natural resources and economic activity' (para 18) and merely strongly urges States 'to refrain from promulgating and applying any unilateral economic, financial

---

75 Sustainable Development Goals:

> **Goal 1.** End poverty in all its forms everywhere **Goal 2.** End hunger, achieve food security and improved nutrition and promote sustainable agriculture **Goal 3.** Ensure healthy lives and promote well-being for all at all ages **Goal 4.** Ensure inclusive and equitable quality education and promote lifelong learning opportunities for all **Goal 5.** Achieve gender equality and empower all women and girls **Goal 6.** Ensure availability and sustainable management of water and sanitation for all **Goal 7** Ensure access to affordable, reliable, sustainable and modern energy for all **Goal 8.** Promote sustained, inclusive and sustainable economic growth, full and productive employment and decent work for all **Goal 9.** Build resilient infrastructure, promote inclusive and sustainable industrialization and foster innovation **Goal 10.** Reduce inequality within and among countries **Goal 11.** Make cities and human settlements inclusive, safe, resilient and sustainable **Goal 12.** Ensure sustainable consumption and production patterns **Goal 13.** Take urgent action to combat climate change and its impacts **Goal 14.** Conserve and sustainably use the oceans, seas and marine resources for sustainable development **Goal 15.** Protect, restore and promote sustainable use of terrestrial ecosystems, sustainably manage forests, combat desertification, and halt and reverse land degradation and halt biodiversity loss **Goal 16.** Promote peaceful and inclusive societies for sustainable development, provide access to justice for all and build effective, accountable and inclusive institutions at all levels **Goal 17.** Strengthen the means of implementation and revitalize the Global Partnership for Sustainable Development.

UNGA (n 71) 14.

or trade measures not in accordance with international law and the Charter of the United Nations that impede the full achievement of economic and social development, particularly in developing countries' (para 30).

In essence, the Goals are *'aspirational and global'* (para 55), and so states have a free hand as to how and to what extent to implement them, and *'each country has primary responsibility for its own economic and social development'* (para 41).

Any consideration of the role of tax havens and low tax areas in the development process is absent. Goals 16.4 to 16.6 reference the need to reduce illicit financial and arms flows, strengthen the recovery and return of stolen assets, and combat all forms of organised crime; to reduce bribery and corruption; and to develop effective, accountable, and transparent institutions. Goal 17.1 calls for support to be given to developing countries *'to improve domestic capacity for tax and other revenue collection'*. There is no mention of tax evasion or avoidance, accountability avoidance or the deliberately arranged absence of beneficial ownership.

From the perspective of the Isle of Man, and particularly of those tax havens and low tax areas far less highly regulated than the Isle of Man, the 2030 Agenda is 'business as usual'.

The Ruggie Principles[76]

In his Report as Special Representative of the UN Secretary General on the issue of human rights and transnational corporations and other business enterprises (adopted by the General Assembly of the UN on 16 June 2011) John Ruggie set out the Guiding Principles on Business and Human Rights which now bear his name.

Though written in response to the growing influence of transnational corporations, and therefore most frequently cited in that context, the 'Three Pillars' of the Ruggie Principles can be applied to low tax area structures such as the Archetype, which are fully endorsed by and legally enforceable in accordance with the laws of the relevant state, yet which betray an almost total absence of corporate responsibility or shareholder accountability:

> Each pillar is an essential component in an inter-related and dynamic system of preventative and remedial measures: the State duty to protect because it lies at the very core of the international human rights regime; the corporate responsibility to respect because it is the basic expectation society has of business in relation to human rights; and access to remedy

---

76 United Nations Human Rights Council, 'Report of the Special Representative of the Secretary General on the Issue of Human Rights and Transnational Corporations and Other Business Enterprises, John Ruggie: Guiding Principles on Business and Human Rights: Implementing the United Nations 'Protect, Respect and Remedy' Framework' (2011) UN Doc A/HRC/17/31 <www.ohchr.org/Documents/Issues/Business/A-HRC-17-31_AEV.pdf> accessed 20 May 2017 (Ruggie Principles).

because even the most concerted efforts cannot prevent all abuse.[77] ...
These Guiding Principles apply to all States and to all business enterprises, both transnational and others, regardless of their size, sector,
location, ownership and structure.[78]

Principle 1 is particularly relevant in the context of low tax areas: 'States must
protect against human rights abuse within their territory and/or jurisdiction
by third parties, including business enterprises. This requires taking appropriate steps to prevent, investigate, punish and redress such abuse through
effective policies, legislation, regulations and adjudication.'

The wording of Principle 1 is sufficiently wide to encompass not only low
tax area corporations but also low tax area trust and charitable structures. Far
from preventing structural abuse, the low tax areas thrive on the creation of
structures which themselves are unconstrained in matters of human rights. In
his commentary on Principle 1, Ruggie emphasises this point:

> Therefore, States are not per se responsible for human rights abuse by
> private actors. However, States may breach their international human
> rights law obligations where such abuse *can be attributed to them*, or
> where they fail to take appropriate steps to prevent, investigate, punish
> and redress private actors' abuse.[79]

The adoption by low tax areas such as the Isle of Man of an extensive range of
anti-money laundering and anti-terrorist financing measures[80] seeks to close the
door to criminal activity, but that is far from being the full extent of the problem. It is the nature of the structures themselves, operating within the law of the
low tax area concerned, which contravenes Principle 1. From the international
human rights perspective it is a question of what they are and what they do legitimately; not of identifying rogue entities which could be established and be
found operating in any number of jurisdictions regardless of their domestic
taxation status. In Principle 3, Ruggie tacitly acknowledges that it may simply
be a question of ignorance rather than of cupidity on the part of a state which
perpetuates these abuses: 'Laws and policies that govern the creation and ongoing operation of business enterprises, such as corporate and securities laws,
directly shape business behaviour. Yet their implications for human rights
remain poorly understood.'[81] This goes some way towards explaining, but not
excusing, the proliferation of low tax area abusive structures.[82]

---

77 Ruggie Principles (n 76) para 6.
78 Ruggie Principles (n 76) Annex, 'General principles'.
79 Ruggie Principles (n 76) Annex, para 1.
80 Details are available from the Isle of Man Financial Services Authority (*Isle of Man
    Financial Services Authority*) <www.iomfsa.im> accessed 20 May 2017.
81 Ruggie Principles (n 76) Annex para 3.
82 And bears out the concern of the Committee on Economic, Social and Cultural Rights (see
    n 11) that international human rights obligations are not being implemented in such areas.

Structures in low tax areas benefit by definition from a favourable taxation treatment. Though this in itself may not be abusive of human rights, it is the 'hook' which attracts those behind the structures to seek out solutions in such areas. This state-business nexus is reviewed in Principle 4, which although concentrating on the receipt of substantial support and services from state aid initiatives such as export credit and guarantees, must also be seen in light of the state support afforded by the availability of a low taxation regime. In his commentary on Principle 4 Ruggie stresses: 'the closer a business enterprise is to the state, or the more it relies on statutory authority or taxpayer support, the stronger the state's policy rationale becomes for ensuring that the enterprise respects human rights.' Yet the low tax areas pay no heed to, or simply remain blissfully and profitably unaware of, such matters.[83]

The low tax areas cannot ignore their responsibilities in

> the widening gap between the scope and impact of economic and financial actors, and the capacity of society to manage their adverse impacts including on human rights. ... Governments must step up to close the governance gaps that have played such a large part in both facilitating and sustaining the current economic crisis, and business must co-operate with government efforts in this regard. Implementation of the [Ruggie] Principles will be a big step in the right direction.[84]

Conclusions

The Isle of Man is clearly not among the most aggressive or secretive of the low tax areas, and is well advanced on the tax haven – international finance centre spectrum[85] towards the latter status. It cannot, however, deny that, in common with many low tax areas, a substantial part of its economy is devoted to the creation and maintenance of structures used by those who

---

83 Principle 9 deals with bilateral investment treaties, and is silent on the question of double taxation agreements, but can be seen nonetheless to be applicable to this frequently encountered low tax area device: 'States should maintain adequate domestic policy space to meet their human rights obligations when pursuing business-related policy objectives with other States or business enterprises, for instance through investment treaties or contracts.' Though the terms of a double taxation treaty may not, as can often be the case with bilateral investment treaties, constrain states from fully implementing new human rights legislation, the existence of double taxation arrangements has the potential to permit an enterprise to operate tax-efficiently, extra-territorially from the state, in a third-party state abusive of human rights; with little or no right of redress available in the host state for those abused.

84 Annual Forum on Business and Human Rights, High-Level Session Statement by Ms Navi Pillay, United Nations High Commissioner for Human Rights 4 December 2012 (no longer available online). See Chapter 4 for a fuller discussion on the interplay between the Ruggie Principles, tax evasion prevention techniques and human rights.

85 See Chapter 1 for a discussion on the multiple and often competing definitions of 'tax haven'.

have no other connection with the Isle of Man than the very structures themselves.

The tax havens and low tax areas, in facilitating what are from their domestic perspective legitimate structures and taxation advantages, are compromising the international human rights legal continuum, and providing launch facilities for human rights-abusive non-state actors.

The right to privacy has ceased to be a shield and has become a sword in the war of aggressive tax planning and in the concealment of the ownership and purpose of an evolving range of increasingly complex – yet curiously hollow and, in human rights terms, unaccountable – structures. These structures have the potential both to enable non-state actors to operate neo-colonially and to impede international development. They are wholly at odds with current thinking on the relationship of business to human rights.

That tax havens and low tax areas turn a blind eye to the extra-territorial impact of their laws and incentives exposes a shameful breach of duty on the part of those states constitutionally charged with the oversight of the good governance of such territories.

When will the abuses of international human rights inherent in the structures, and not merely the tax incentives facilitated by the low tax areas, cease? When will this become politically unsustainable? The tipping point may now, almost ten years after the crash of 2008 and the consequent realignment of global finances, have been reached. With only the first faint indications of an end to the Great Recession in sight, and money (or the lack of it) uppermost in the minds of many, international attention has shifted to the fiscal role of the tax havens and low tax areas; those tiny quasi-states which myopically make such abuse possible.

But fighting tax avoidance and tax evasion is the wrong war, one which can never constrain the ability of tax gurus constantly to reinvent the wheel.

The focus of enquiry is realigning from the victims of human rights abuse and the perpetrators of international crimes, towards the elite who benefit from it. The root cause lies in the structures which the tax havens and low tax areas facilitate, the manner of their concealment, and the power which this channels to non-state actors.

Does international human rights law provide the equality of arms necessary to win the fight? At a time when human rights observance is in retreat, the commonly held view may be that it cannot. But human rights are dynamic and reactive, and evolutionary in nature. As such, they have evolved and will continue to evolve in synchronisation with the perceived needs of society, travelling along the generational continuum. There is reason for guarded optimism.

APPENDIX

Constitutional position of the Isle of Man: United Kingdom and European Union[86]

The Isle of Man, together with the United Kingdom, the Channel Islands and the Republic of Ireland form the geographical area known as the British Isles. Although the Isle of Man acknowledges the sovereign of the United Kingdom to be its head of state, the island is politically and constitutionally not part of the United Kingdom. It is a Crown Dependency. As such, it is independent in all matters except foreign affairs and defence, which are the responsibility of the United Kingdom government. In particular, no legislation on taxation or other revenue matters of the United Kingdom Parliament applies in the Isle of Man.

The Isle of Man legislature, the Tynwald (www.tynwald.org), dates from the time of the Viking councils of the ninth century, the earliest recorded session being in the year 979 AD. The Isle of Man therefore has the longest unbroken history of parliamentary government in the world. Scandinavian rule over the island ended in 1333 with defeat by the Scots, and the island later passed under the general suzerainty of the English Crown.

The Isle of Man remained, however, outside the English (and later British) political system, and the English monarch continued to fulfil only the role originally played by the ancient Scandinavian kings. Later, the Lordship of Man was granted to a succession of ruling families by the English kings, until the British Crown itself acquired the Lordship from the Earls of Derby in 1765. The present Lord of Man is the British Queen Elizabeth II, who is represented in the island by her Lieutenant Governor. The Lieutenant Governor, who is appointed for a five-year term, now has only a limited role in executive government, the political head of which is the Chief Minister (formally appointed by the Lieutenant Governor after being elected by the Tynwald).

The Tynwald has two branches; a directly elected House of Keys with 24 members and the Legislative Council with 10 members, eight elected by the House of Keys together with the island's Bishop and Attorney-General.

The Tynwald is not a subordinate legislature and does not derive its authority from the United Kingdom Parliament. It is unlikely that there would be a conflict between an Act of Parliament and an Act of Tynwald, each legislature being closely aware of the other's activities and sensitive to the needs of its neighbour, but, were such a conflict to occur (assuming each Act to have received the Royal Assent), then in the Isle of Man the Act of Tynwald would prevail.

---

86 For a fuller account, see the author's chapter 'Isle of Man' in Timothy Lyons (ed) *European Cross-Border Estate Planning* (Sweet & Maxwell, 2017) from which this extract is taken.

With the passage of the Isle of Man Customs, Harbours and Public Purposes Act 1866 (now repealed), the Isle of Man gained the separation of its finances from those of the United Kingdom. This enabled the Tynwald to develop the island's complete financial independence. The Isle of Man has a Customs and Excise Agreement with the United Kingdom dating from 1979, and the two countries therefore constitute a common customs area.

On May 1, 2007 the following framework for developing the international identity of the Isle of Man was signed:

> Following the statement of intent agreed on 11 January 2006, the Chief Minister of the Isle of Man and the UK Secretary of State for Constitutional Affairs have agreed the following principles. They establish a framework for the development of the international identity of the Isle of Man. The framework is intended to clarify the constitutional relationship between the UK and the Isle of Man, which works well and within which methods are evolving to help achieve the mutual interests of both the UK and the Isle of Man.

1   The UK has no democratic accountability in and for the Isle of Man which is governed by its own democratically elected assembly. In the context of the UK's responsibility for the Isle of Man's international relations it is understood that:
    a   The UK will not act internationally on behalf of the Isle of Man without prior consultation.
    b   The UK recognises that the interests of the Isle of Man may differ from those of the UK, and the UK will seek to represent any differing interests when acting in an international capacity. This is particularly evident in respect of the relationship with the European Union where the UK interests can be expected to be those of an EU member state and the interests of the Isle of Man can be expected to reflect the fact that the UK's membership of the EU only extends to the Isle of Man in certain circumstances as set out in Protocol 3 of the UK's Treaty of Accession.
2   The Isle of Man has an international identity which is different from that of the UK.
3   The UK recognises that the Isle of Man is a long-standing, small democracy and supports the principle of the Isle of Man further developing its international identity.
4   The UK has a role to play in assisting the development of the Isle of Man's international identity. The role is one of support not interference.
5   The Isle of Man and the UK commit themselves to open, effective and meaningful dialogue with each other on any issue that may come to affect the constitutional relationship.

6 International identity is developed effectively through meeting international standards and obligations which are important components
of the Isle of Man's international identity.

7 The UK will clearly identify its priorities for delivery of its international obligations and agreements so that these are understood, and
can be taken into account, by the Isle of Man in developing its own
position.

8 The activities of the UK in the international arena need to have
regard to the Isle of Man's international relations, policies and
responsibilities.

9 The UK and the Isle of Man will work together to resolve or clarify
any differences which may arise between their respective interests.

10 The Isle of Man and the UK will work jointly to promote the legitimate status of the Isle of Man as a responsible, stable and mature
democracy with its own broad policy interests and which is willing
to engage positively with the international community across a wide
range of issues.

Relationship with the European Union

The Isle of Man has a special relationship with the European Union. The
Treaty of Rome provides for its application to all European territories for
whom a member state is responsible. In the case of the United Kingdom,
however, a Third Protocol was added to the United Kingdom Treaty of
Accession of 1972. This provides that the Treaty of Rome does not apply to
the Isle of Man save that the Isle of Man is included within the customs territory of the European Union and is subject to the rules on the free movement
of goods (see Article 227(5)(c) of the Treaty of Rome – this interpretation
was reaffirmed in a written reply by the President of the Commission of the
European Union in 1991 (Question 2103/91, OJC 103/33)). The Isle of
Man therefore forms part of the European Union Single European Market.
European Union taxation and competition rules do not apply to the Isle of
Man. In *Department of Health and Social Security v Barr and Montrose
Holdings Ltd* [1991] E.C.R. I-3479 the Court of Justice of the EC ruled that
all courts and tribunals of the Isle of Man were courts empowered to refer
questions to the European Court of Justice under Article 177 of the Treaty
of Rome, even though such courts do not form part of the court system of
the United Kingdom. President Mancini delivering the judgment of the
Court stated:

> ... the jurisdiction conferred on the court by art.177 of the Treaty [of
> Rome] extends to Protocol No.3. Furthermore, it would be impossible
> to ensure the uniform application of Protocol No. 3 in the Isle of Man
> if its courts and tribunals were unable to refer questions to the court
> concerning the interpretation of the Protocol, the interpretation and

validity of the Community legislation to which the Protocol refers, and the interpretation and validity of measures adopted by the Community institutions on the basis of Protocol No. 3.

The decision thus delivered by the Court of Justice of the EC was subsequently held by the Isle of Man appeal court to bind the Isle of Man court which referred the question (namely that of the Deputy High Bailiff). Although in theory the Deputy High Bailiff was entitled to make a finding of law contrary to the ruling of the European Court, which was expressed to be for guidance only, 'it is inconceivable that he will not now regard the ruling as binding' (per Hytner JA delivering the judgment of the Staff of Government Division in *Re Barr and Anglo International Holdings Ltd* 1990-92 MLR 398).

The Treaty on European Union (the 'Maastricht' Treaty) and the Agreement on the European Economic Area (1992) apply as part of the law of the Isle of Man (with effect from June 21, 1994 – European Communities (Amendment) Act 1994) but only to the limited extent set out in Protocol 3:

Protocol 3

Protocol No.3 annexed to the Act of Accession of the Kingdom of Denmark, Ireland and the United Kingdom of Great Britain and Northern Ireland to the European Economic Community and the European Atomic Energy Community 1972

Article 1

1   The Community rules on customs matters and quantitative restrictions, in particular those of the Act of Accession, shall apply to the Channel Islands and the Isle of Man under the same conditions as they apply to the United Kingdom. In particular, customs duties and charges having equivalent effect between those territories and the Community, as originally constituted and between those territories and the new Member States, shall be progressively reduced in accordance with the timetable laid down in Articles 32 and 36 of the Act of Accession. The Common Customs Tariff and the ECSC unified tariff shall be progressively applied in accordance with the timetable laid down in Articles 39 and 59 of the Act of Accession, and account being taken of Articles 109, 110 and 119 of that Act.

2   In respect of agricultural products and products processed therefrom which are the subject of a special trade regime, the levies and other import measures laid down in Community rules and applicable by the United Kingdom shall be applied to third countries.

   Such provisions of Community rules, in particular those of the Act of Accession, as are necessary to allow free movement and observance of normal conditions of competition in trade in these products shall also be applicable.

The Council, acting by a qualified majority on a proposal from the Commission, shall determine the conditions under which the provisions referred to in the preceding sub-paragraphs shall be applicable to these territories.

Article 2

The rights enjoyed by Channel Islanders or Manxmen in the United Kingdom shall not be affected by the Act of Accession. However, such persons shall not benefit from the Community provisions relating to the free movement of persons and services.

Article 3

The provision of the Euratom Treaty applicable to persons or undertakings within the meaning of Article 196 of that Treaty shall apply to those persons or undertakings when they are established in the aforementioned territories.

Article 4

The authorities of these territories shall apply the same treatment to all natural and legal persons of the Community.

Article 5

If, during the application of the arrangements defined in this Protocol, difficulties appear on either side in relations between the Community and these territories, the Commission shall without delay propose to the Council such safeguard measures as it believes necessary, specifying their terms and conditions of application.

The Council shall act by qualified majority within one month.

Article 6

In this protocol, Channel Islander or Manxman shall mean any citizen of the United Kingdom and Colonies who holds that citizenship by virtue of the fact that he, a parent or grandparent was born, adopted, naturalised or registered in the Island in question; but such a person shall not for this purpose be regarded as a Channel Islander or Manxman if he, a parent or grandparent was born, adopted, or naturalised or registered in the United Kingdom. Nor shall he be so regarded if he has at any time been ordinarily resident in the United Kingdom for five years.

The administrative arrangements necessary to identify those persons will be notified to the Commission.

Following the decision of the United Kingdom to negotiate its withdrawal from membership of the European Union, the future position of the Isle of Man in relation to the European Union once that withdrawal process has been concluded remains unclear.

The Isle of Man is a member of the Organisation for Economic Co-operation and Development (OECD), the United Kingdom Government at the request of the Isle of Man Government having declared in 1990 that the OECD Convention applies to the Isle of Man. Isle of Man financial products and financial services therefore have access to markets where membership of the OECD is a requirement. The Isle of Man became a member of the World Trade Organisation in January 1998.

These issues are considered in the Eighth Report of the House of Commons Justice Committee (of the United Kingdom Parliament) on Crown Dependencies (23 March 2010)[87] as further revised in House of Commons Justice Committee Crown Dependencies: Developments since 2010 Tenth Report of Session 2013–14 (16 January 2014).[88]

---

87 Justice Committee, *Crown Dependencies* (HC 56–I, 30 March 2010) <www.publications. parliament.uk/pa/cm200910/cmselect/cmjust/56/56i.pdf> accessed 20 May 2017.
88 (n 12).

Bibliography

Cases

Re Barr and Anglo International Holdings Ltd 1990-92 MLR 398
Department of Health and Social Security v Barr and Montrose Holdings Ltd [1991] E.C.R. I-3479
Re Blayney and Grace re National Irish Bank Limited 2001-03 MLR 13 (CHD)
Re Heginbotham 1999-01 MLR 53
R (Miller) v The Secretary of State for Exiting the European Union (QB) [2016] EWHC 2768
Salomon v Commissioners of Customs and Excise [1966] 3 All ER 871

Legislation and regulations

Bankers' Books Evidence Act 1935 <www.legislation.gov.im/cms/images/ LEGISLATION/PRINCIPAL/1935/1935-0001/BankersBooksEvidenceAct 1935_1.pdf> accessed 19 May 2017 (Isle of Man)
Bankruptcy Code 1892 <https://legislation.gov.im/cms/images/LEGISLATION/ PRINCIPAL/1892/1892-0001/BankruptcyCode1892_2.pdf> accessed 19 May 2017 (Isle of Man)
Bankruptcy Procedure Act 1892 <https://legislation.gov.im/cms/images/ LEGISLATION/PRINCIPAL/1892/1892-0002/BankruptcyProcedureAct 1892_1.pdf> accessed 19 May 2017 (Isle of Man)
Companies Act 2006 (Isle of Man) <www.gov.im/lib/docs/ded/companies/ companiesReg/2006companiesactweboct2009.pdf> accessed 21 May 2017
The Companies (Winding Up) Rules 1934 <www.gov.im/media/1348302/the-companies-winding-up-rules-1934-without-forms.pdf> accessed 19 May 2017 (Isle of Man)
Data Protection Act 2002 <https://legislation.gov.im/cms/images/LEGIS LATION/PRINCIPAL/2002/2002-0002/DataProtectionAct 2002_7.pdf> accessed 19 May 2017 (Isle of Man)
European Communities (Amendment) Act 1994) <www.legislation.gov.im/cms/ images/LEGISLATION/PRINCIPAL/1994/1994-0010/EuropeanCom munitiesAmendmentAct1994_1.pdf> accessed 20 May 2017 (Isle of Man)
Fraudulent Assignments Act 1736 <https://legislation.gov im/cms/images/ LEGISLATION/PRINCIPAL/1736/1736-0002/FraudulentAssignments Act1736_1.pdf> accessed 19 May 2017 (Isle of Man)
Freedom of Information Act 2015 <https://legislation.gov.im/cms/images/ LEGISLATION/PRINCIPAL/2015/2015-0008/FreedomofInformationAct 2015_3.pdf> accessed 19 May 2017 (Isle of Man)
Human Rights Act 2001 <www.legislation.gov.im/cms/images/LEGISLATION/ PRINCIPAL/2001/2001-0001/HumanRightsAct2001_1.pdf> accessed 18 May 2017 (UK)
Judgments (Reciprocal Enforcement) (Isle of Man) Act 1968 <www.legislation. gov.im/cms/images/LEGISLATION/PRINCIPAL/1968/1968-0006/Judg mentsReciprocalEnforcementIsleofManAct1968_1.pdf> accessed 21 May 2017
Limitation Act 1984 <https://legislation.gov.im/cms/images/LEGISLATION/ PRINCIPAL/1984/1984-0018/LimitationAct1984_4.pdf> accessed 19 May

2017 (Isle of Man)

Perpetuities and Accumulations Act 1968 <https://legislation.gov.im/cms/ images/LEGISLATION/PRINCIPAL/1968/1968-0008/Perpetuitiesand AccumulationsAct1968_2.pdf> accessed 19 May 2017 (Isle of Man)

Purpose Trusts Act 1996 <https://legislation.gov.im/cms/images/LEGIS LATION/PRINCIPAL/1996/1996-0009/PurposeTrustsAct 1996_1.pdf> accessed 19 May 2017 (Isle of Man)

Statute of Elizabeth (enactment entitled 13 Elizabeth 1 Ch 5 (1571)) (repealed in the United Kingdom by the Law of Property Act 1925)

Trustee Act 2001 <https://legislation.gov.im/cms/images/LEGISLATION/ PRINCIPAL/2001/2001-0018/TrusteeAct2001_1.pdf> accessed 19 May 2017 (Isle of Man)

Trusts Act 1995 <https://legislation.gov.im/cms/images/LEGISLATION/ PRINCIPAL/1995/1995-0018/TrustsAct1995_2.pdf> accessed 19 May 2017 (Isle of Man)

Trusts (Amendment) Act 2015 <www.legislation.gov.im/cms/legislation-2/acts-of-tynwald-as-enacted/category/20-acts-of-tynwald-as-enacted-primary-2015.html? download=230:trusts-amendment-act-2015> accessed 21 May 2017 (Isle of Man)

International Treaties and Declarations

African Charter on Human and Peoples' Rights (adopted 27 June 1981, entered into force 21 October 1986) CAB/LEG/67/3 rev.5, 21 ILM 58 (1982) <www.refworld.org/docid/3ae6b3630.html> accessed 20 May 2017

Agreement on the European Economic Area (1992) (adopted 2 May 1992, entered into force 1 January 1994) L1 03/01/1994 <http://ec.europa.eu/world/ agreements/prepareCreateTreatiesWorkspace/treatiesGeneralData.do?redirect= true&treatyId=1> accessed 20 May 2017

Convention for the Protection of Human Rights and Fundamental Freedoms, as amended by Protocols Nos 11 and 14 (adopted 4 November 1950, entered into force 3 September 1953) ETS 5 (European Convention on Human Rights)

Convention on the Elimination of All Forms of Discrimination Against Women (adopted 18 December 1979, entered into force 3 September 1981) 1249 UNTS 13

Convention on the Rights of the Child (adopted 20 November 1989, entered into force 2 September 1990) 1577 UNTS 3

International Covenant on Civil and Political Rights (adopted 16 December 1966, entered into force 23 March 1976) 999 UNTS 171

International Covenant on Economic, Social and Cultural Rights (adopted 16 December 1966, entered into force 3 January 1976) 993 UNTS 3

Treaty on European Union (Treaty of Maastricht) (adopted 7 February 1992, entered into force 1 November 1993) Official Journal of the European Communities C 325/5, 24 December 2002 <www.refworld.org/docid/3ae6b 39218.html> accessed 20 May 2017

Vienna Convention on the Law of Treaties (adopted 23 May 1969, entered into force 27 January 1980) 1155 UNTS 331

Vienna Declaration and Programme of Action (adopted by the World Conference on Human Rights in Vienna 29 June 1993) (*OHCHR*) <www.ohchr.org/EN/ ProfessionalInterest/Pages/Vienna.aspx> accessed 20 May 2017

United Nations documents

Annual Forum on Business and Human Rights, High-Level Session Statement by Ms Navi Pillay, United Nations High Commissioner for Human Rights (4 December 2012)

United Nations Economic and Social Council, Committee on Economic, Social and Cultural Rights, 'Consideration of Reports Submitted by States Parties under Articles 16 and 17 of the Covenant: Concluding observations: United Kingdom of Great Britain and Northern Ireland, the Crown Dependencies and the Overseas Dependent Territories' (12 June 2009) UN Doc E/C.12/GBR/CO/5)

——, General Comment No 3, 'The Nature of States Parties' Obligations' (Art 2, Para 1 of the Covenant) (14 December 1990) UN Doc E/1991/23 <www.refworld.org/docid/4538838e10.html> accessed 20 May 2017

——, 'Statement on the Obligations of State Parties regarding the Corporate Sector and Economic, Social and Cultural Rights' (12 July 2011) UN Doc E/C.12/2011/1 <http://docstore.ohchr.org/SelfServices/FilesHandler.ashx?enc=4slQ6QSmlBEDzFEovLCuW1AVC1NkPsgUedPlF1vfPMKOgNxs%2FCpnVM8K6XpeNimFvrj%2F4tQZvhH%2BXM9vEaJmHSX3FSXAcTmJ%2BWc3iPSLafnoFpGQ9KIHCXooWHCPCpQt> accessed 19 May 2017

United Nations General Assembly, Declaration on the Right to Development (adopted by the General Assembly, 4 December 1986) UN Doc A/RES/41/128 <www.un.org/documents/ga/res/41/a41r128.htm> accessed 20 May 2017

——, Universal Declaration of Human Rights (adopted 10 December 1948 UNGA Res 217 A(III) (UDHR)

——, 'Transforming our World: the 2030 Agenda for Sustainable Development' (21 October 2015) Seventieth Session, UN Doc A/RES/70/1

United Nations Human Rights Committee, 'Concluding Observations on the Sixth Periodic Report of Germany Adopted by the UN Human Rights Committee at its 106th Session 15 October – 2 November 2012' (12 November 2012) UN Doc CCPR/C/DEU/CO/6 <http://repository.un.org/bitstream/handle/11176/298828/CCPR_C_DEU_CO_6-EN.pdf?sequence=3&isAllowed=y> accessed 20 May 2017

United Nations Human Rights Council, 'Report of the Special Representative of the Secretary General on the Issue of Human Rights and Transnational Corporations and Other Business Enterprises, John Ruggie: Guiding Principles on Business and Human Rights: Implementing the United Nations 'Protect, Respect and Remedy' Framework' (2011) UN Doc A/HRC/17/31 <www.ohchr.org/Documents/Issues/Business/A-HRC-17-31_AEV.pdf> accessed 20 May 2017

Secondary sources

Baderin B, McCorquodale R (eds) *Economic, Social and Cultural Rights in Action* (Oxford Scholarship Online, 2007)

Beckett P, 'Isle of Man' in T Lyons (ed) *European Cross-Border Estate Planning* (Sweet & Maxwell, 2013)

——, 'The Representative Impact of the Isle of Man as a Low Tax Area on the International Human Rights Continuum from a Fiscal and Structural Perspective' in Jo Carby Hall (ed) *Essays on Human Rights: A Celebration of the Life of Dr Janusz Kochanowski* (Ius et Lex Foundation, Warsaw 2014)

Center for Economic and Social Rights, 'A Matter of Justice – Securing Human Rights in the Post 2015 Sustainable Development Agenda (*Center for Economic and Social Rights*, 2013) <www.cesr.org/matter-justice-securing-human-rights-post-2015-sustainable-development-agenda> accessed 20 May 2017.

FIAN International, 'Maastricht Principles on Extraterritorial Obligations of States in the area of Economic, Social and Cultural Rights' (*FIAN International*, January 2013) <www.fidh.org/IMG/pdf/maastricht-eto-principles-uk_web.pdf> accessed 20 May 2017 (Maastricht Principles 2011)

Galeano E, *Upside Down: A Primer for the Looking Glass World* (Mark Fried tr, Picador, 2001)

Government of Canada, 'Government of Canada Cracks Down on Tax Evasion' (*Government of Canada*, 11 April 2016) <http://news.gc.ca/web/article-en.do?nid=1049689> accessed 18 May 2017

International Commission of Jurists (ICJ), 'Maastricht Guidelines on Violations of Economic, Social and Cultural Rights' (ICJ, 26 January 1997) <www1.umn.edu/humanrts/instree/Maastrichtguidelines_.html> accessed 19 May 2017

Isfeld G, 'Canada Revenue Agency Promises 'Blitz' on Isle of Man Tax Accounts' *Financial Post* (Toronto, 5 May 2016) <http://business.financialpost.com/news/economy/canada-revenue-agency-promises-blitz-on-isle-of-man-tax-accounts> accessed 18 May 2017

Isle of Man Financial Services Authority, 'Financial Services Act 2008 Guidance on Directorships, Trusteeships and similar Responsibilities held by Directors and Key Persons of Licenceholders' (*Isle of Man Financial Services Authority*, January 2017) <www.iomfsa.im/lib/docs/iomfsa/rulebooks/directorshipsguidancemar 2015.pdf> accessed 19 May 2017

——, (*Isle of Man Financial Services Authority*) <www.iomfsa.im> accessed 20 May 2017

Isle of Man Government, 'Companies Registry' (*gov.im*) <www.gov.im/ded/companies> accessed 19 May 2017

——, 'Tax Information Exchange Agreements' (*gov.im*) <www.gov.im/ categories/tax-vat-and-your-money/income-tax-and-national-insurance/international-agreements/tax-information-exchange-agreements> accessed 18 May 2017

——, Department of Economic Development, Companies Registry, 'Practice Note: Requirements with Respect to the Memorandum and Articles of Association of an Isle of Man Incorporated Company' (PN 19/2014, *gov.im*, 7 January 2014) <www.gov.im/media/1348340/pn19-2014.pdf> accessed 19 May 2017

Justice Committee, *Crown Dependencies* (HC 56–I, 30 March 2010) <www.public ations.parliament.uk/pa/cm200910/cmselect/cmjust/56/56i.pdf> accessed 20 May 2017

——, *Crown Dependencies: Developments since 2010* (HC 2013–14, 726) <www.publications.parliament.uk/pa/cm201314/cmselect/cmjust/726/726.pdf> accessed 19 May 2017

Marks S, *Human Rights and Root Causes* 74(1) MLR 57–78, at 76 (2011)

OECD, 'Aggressive Tax Planning' (*OECD*) <www.oecd.org/tax/aggressive> accessed 18 May 2017

——, *Peer Review Report of Isle of Man - Combined Phase 1 and Phase 2: Legal and Regulatory Framework and Implementation of the Standards in Practice* (OECD 2011) <www.oecd.org/tax/transparency/peerreviewreportofisleofman-combined phase1andphase2legalandregulatoryframeworkandimplementationofthestandards

inpractice.htm> accessed 18 May 2017/ and available also at Isle of Man Government, 'Peer Review Report' (*gov.im*) <www.gov.im/treasury/incometax/sections/practitioners/peerreviewreport.xml> accessed 18 May 2017.

Salomon M, 'Why Should It Matter That Others Have More? Poverty, Inequality and the Potential of International Human Rights Law' [2010] LSE Legal Studies Working Paper 15/2010 <https://papers.ssrn.com/sol3/papers.cfm?abstract_id=1711657> accessed 10 May 2017

Skogly S I and Gibney M, 'Transnational Human Rights Obligations' (2002) 22 HRQ 781

United Nations, 'News on Millennium Development Goals' (*United Nations*) <www.un.org/millenniumgoals> accessed 20 May 2017

Wikipedia, 'Fraudulent Conveyances Act 1571' (*Wikipedia*, ed 27 February 2017) <https://en.wikipedia.org/wiki/Fraudulent_Conveyances_Act_1571> accessed 19 May 2017

Yamin A E, 'The Future in the Mirror: Incorporating Strategies for the Defense and Promotion of Economic, Social and Cultural Rights into the Mainstream Human Rights Agenda' (2005) 27 HRQ 1200

——, 'Our Place in the World: Conceptualizing Obligations beyond Borders in Human Rights-based Approaches to Health' (2010) 12 Health HRJ 1

6 Switzerland

Illicit financial flows, women's rights and gender equality

Introduction

Tax havens are characterised in the popular imagination as rogue micro-states, captured by their finance sectors and politically neutered, producing low accountability legislation, and offering bolt holes and impregnable citadels for the wealthy but unscrupulous.[1] Switzerland presents itself as a beacon of democracy[2] and is a host of the United Nations. Yet Switzerland is widely regarded as the world's leading tax haven.[3] Switzerland is now under pressure from the United Nations to reform its taxation and financial secrecy policies, which are seen as abusive of international human rights. Specifically, these policies are alleged to have encouraged illicit financial flows. This chapter focuses on one of the consequences: the deleterious effect on women's rights and gender equality worldwide. In light of what are now widely acknowledged to be the extraterritorial obligations of states in matters of economic, social and cultural rights,[4] it looks at the criticisms of

---

1   See Chapter 1 for a discussion on different approaches to defining tax havens, and Chapter 2 for examples of artificially engineered legislation of this kind, and in particular the Bahamas Enterprise Entity and the Nevis Multiform Foundation.

2   Switzerland receives a score of 96% and a maximum rating for civil and political rights in Freedom House, 'Freedom in the World 2017' (*Freedom House*) <https://freedom house.org/report/freedom-world/2017/switzerland> accessed 21 May 2017.

3   One of several competing definitions of tax havens is financial secrecy, and Switzerland ranked first in the 2015 Financial Secrecy Index of the Tax Justice Network, 'Financial Secrecy Index – 2015 Results' (*Tax Justice Network*) <www.financialsecrecyindex.com/introduction/fsi-2015-results> accessed 21 May 2017; and see the Tax Justice Network's 'Narrative Report on Switzerland' (*Tax Justice Network* 2015) which outlines Switzerland's history as 'the grandfather of the world's tax havens' <www.financialsecrecyindex.com/PDF/Switzerland.pdf> accessed 21 May 2017.

4   FIAN International, 'Maastricht Principles on Extraterritorial Obligations of States in the Area of Economic, Social and Cultural Rights' (*FIAN International*, January 2013) <www.fidh.org/IMG/pdf/maastricht-eto-principles-uk_web.pdf> accessed 20 May 2017 (Maastricht Principles).

Switzerland which have been made by the Committee on the Elimination of Discrimination Against Women (CEDAW Committee).[5]

The two elements which suffice to construct a working definition of a tax haven, from a human rights-based perspective, are firstly that legislation may or may not be regarded by the issuing state as being human rights compliant within its borders, but this domestic compliance does not extend to the effects of such legislation external to that state;[6] secondly, or in the alternative, state legislation intentionally promotes, facilitates and ensures accountability avoidance. If either of these elements is present, then the jurisdiction is one of low or zero accountability and, as such, human rights abusive. This chapter applies the findings of the CEDAW Committee to that analysis and concludes that Switzerland has a case to answer.

Illicit financial flows

Illicit financial flows are most commonly discussed in the context of their negative impact economically or on tax gathering capacities. The Communiqué of the G20 Finance Ministers and Central Bank Governors Meeting held in Chengdu, China on 24 July 2016 reported that '[w]e support the principles of the Addis Tax Initiative.[7] We recognise the significant

---

5   Office of the United Nations High Commissioner for Human Rights (OHCHR), 'Committee on the Elimination of Discrimination Against Women' (*OHCHR*) <www.ohchr.org/EN/HRBodies/CEDAW/Pages/Introduction.aspx> accessed 21 May 2017; and see CEDAW Committee, 'Concluding Observations on the Combined Fourth and Fifth Periodic Reports of Switzerland' (25 November 2016) UN Doc CEDAW/C/CHE/CO/4-5 http://tbinternet.ohchr.org/_layouts/treatybodyexternal/Download.aspx?symbolno=CEDAW/C/CHE/CO/4-5&Lang=En> accessed 21 May 2017.

6   The enacting of such legislation ought not to be justified on the basis of a jurisdiction's right to self-determination or sovereignty: 'Legislation that exclusively or primarily will have effects in other States, such as the financial regulations common to secrecy jurisdictions, is therefore not the exercise of sovereignty, but an encroachment on the sovereignty of others.' 'Norwegian Commission on Capital Flight from Developing Countries: Tax Havens and Development' (*Financial Transparency Coalition*, 18 June 2009) <https://financial transparency.org/reports/norwegian-commission-on-capital-flight-from-developing-countries-tax-havens-and-development> accessed 21 May 2017, 146, para 9.2.3. The full report is available at: Government Commission on Capital Flight from Poor Countries, 'Commission on Capital Flight from Developing Countries: Tax Havens and Development' (*Government of Norway*, 18 June 2009) <www.financialtransparency.org/wp-content/uploads/ 2015/04/norway_tax_report.pdf> accessed 21 May 2017.

7   Communiqué, G20 Finance Ministers and Central Bank Governors Meeting held in Chengdu, China, 24 July 2016 (*University of Toronto G20 Information Centre*, 24 July 2016) <www.g20.utoronto.ca/2016/160724-finance.html> accessed 21 May 2017; Addis Tax Initiative, 'About Addis Tax Initiative' (*Addis Tax Initiative*) <www.addistax initiative.net> accessed 21 May 2017. The Addis Tax Initiative was initiated by the governments of Germany, the Netherlands, the United Kingdom, and the United States of America. The initiative was launched in the course of the third Financing for Development Conference in Addis Ababa in 2015.

impact of illicit financial flows on our economies and we continue to take forward the work of the G20 on this theme.'[8] Neither the Communiqué itself nor the Addis Tax Initiative to which it refers makes any mention of the abusive effects of illicit financial flows on international human rights, though the Addis Tax Initiative is focused on development and growth, and the combatting of tax avoidance and tax evasion; and in its opening Declaration[9] stresses the need for efficient tax gathering systems in order that developing nations may have resources sufficient to enable them to achieve the post-2015 Sustainable Development Goals.[10]

In his January 2016 report to the Human Rights Council on illicit financial flows, human rights and the 2030 Agenda for Sustainable Development,[11] Independent Expert Juan Pablo Bohoslavsky states that illicit financial flows 'divert resources away from activities that are critical for poverty eradication and sustainable economic and social development' (para 2) and pinpoints cross-border tax-related transactions as forming the majority of the flows: 'Curbing tax-related illicit financial flows thus has the potential to make the largest fiscal impact and would enlarge domestic resources available for the realization of human rights' (para 5). Emphasising the deleterious effect of illicit financial flows on development and human rights, Bohoslavsky refers (in para 31) specifically to Sustainable Development Goal target 16.4: 'By 2030, significantly reduce illicit financial and arms flows, strengthen the recovery of stolen assets and combat all forms of organized crime'[12] and (in para 36), recognising that outward flows of funds so undermine a nation's administrative resources that their very capacity for tax and other revenue collection is compromised, refers to the

---

8   Communiqué (n 7) para 10.
9   Addis Tax Initiative, 'Financing for Development Conference: The Addis Tax Initiative – Declaration' (*Addis Tax Initiative*) <www.addistaxinitiative.net/documents/Addis-Tax-Initiative_Declaration_EN.pdf> accessed 21 May 2017. For a fuller discussion of the negative impact of tax avoidance and tax evasion initiatives on international human rights see Chapter 4.
10   The 2016/2017 Work Plan of the Addis Tax Initiative makes mention neither of international human rights nor of tax havens or low tax areas. Addis Tax Initiative, *Work Plan 2016/17* (Deutsche Gesellschaft für Internationale Zusammenarbeit (GIZ), 2017) <www.addistaxinitiative.net/documents/ATI_Work-Plan-2016-2017_EN.pdf> accessed 21 May 2017.
11   United Nations Human Rights Council, 'Final Study on Illicit Financial Flows, Human Rights and the 2030 Agenda for Sustainable Development of the Independent Expert on the Effects of Foreign Debt and other Related International Financial Obligations of States on the Full Enjoyment of All Human Rights, Particularly Economic, Social and Cultural Rights' (15 January 2016) Thirty-first Session, UN Doc A/HRC/31/61 <www.ohchr.org/EN/HRBodies/HRC/RegularSessions/Session31/Pages/ListReports. aspx> accessed 21 May 2017.
12   United Nations, 'Goal 16: Promote Just, Peaceful and Inclusive Societies' (*United Nations*) <www.un.org/sustainabledevelopment/peace-justice> accessed 21 May 2017.

need to strengthen domestic resource mobilisation in Sustainable Development Goal target 17.1.[13]

What constitutes 'illicit' is open to debate. At its most basic, illicit can be taken to refer to illegalities such as the transfer of funds in order to evade taxation. Yet the term also lends itself to a wider, socially orientated definition as something which is forbidden by law, rule, or custom. Bohoslavsky offers a broad and a narrow definition, the narrow encompassing funds illegally earned through crime and corruption or legitimately earned yet transferred abroad in breach of domestic laws such as those on taxation; the broad encompassing funds that, 'through legal loopholes and other artificial arrangements, circumvent the spirit of the law, including … tax avoidance schemes used by transnational corporations' (para 7).

For the purposes of this chapter, the term is used to indicate a flow of funds which serves no other purpose than to arrive and to achieve a level of inviolability in the destination jurisdiction. It is a flow which has no social or economic justification and is intended to benefit no one save the individual or entity initiating the transfer.[14] Illicit financial flows are driven by financial operations rather than real activities.[15]

The particular relevance to women's rights and gender equality of illicit financial flows is that in much of the word the unequal gender balance in society results in women forming a disproportionate number of the poor and of those holding unskilled and consequently low paid jobs. These are women who rely heavily on the state for social support in the form of education, healthcare, the means of public transport, and social support systems. It is therefore not a victimless operation.[16]

---

13 United Nations, 'Goal 17: Revitalize the Global Partnership for Sustainable Development' (*United Nations*) <www.un.org/sustainabledevelopment/globalpartnerships> accessed 21 May 2017.

14 Swissleaks revealed that US$5.26 billion of funds of Latin American residents were in HSBC bank accounts in Switzerland in 2006 and 2007 – equivalent to 26 percent of total public investment in health across the region. Quoted in Veronica Grondona, Nicole Bidegain Ponte and Corina Rodríguez Enriquez, *Illicit Financial Flows Undermining Gender Justice* (Friedrich Ebert Stiftung, December 2016) <www.dawnnet.org/feminist-resources/sites/default/files/articles/161130_ipa_genderjustice.pdf> accessed 21 May 2017, 5. The authors review the mechanics of illicit financial flows from a Latin American perspective, including money laundering and transfer pricing manipulation in human trafficking cases; contract manufacturing, toll manufacturing and purchasing services; and commodity triangulation, under-invoicing of exports, over-invoicing of exports via tax havens.

15 For a recent statistical analysis see Stefan Avdjiev, Michael Chui and Hyun Song Shin,'Non-financial Corporations from Emerging Market Economies and Capital Flows' (BIS QR, December 2014) <www.bis.org/publ/qtrpdf/r_qt1412h.htm> accessed 21 May 2017, 67–77.

16 See United Nations Human Rights Council, 'Report of the Special Rapporteur on Extreme Poverty and Human Rights, Magdalena Sepulveda Carmona' (22 May 2014) Twenty-sixth Session, UN Doc A/HRC/26/28 <www.ohchr.org/EN/HRBodies/HRC/Regular Sessions/Session26/Documents/A_HRC_26_28_ENG.doc> accessed 21 May 2017, paras 58 and 59:

In a study published in May 2013 jointly by the African Development Bank and Global Financial Integrity it was reported that during the period 1980 to 2009 the net flow of funds from Africa was up to US$1.4 trillion on a cumulative basis, and that the illicit haemorrhage of resources from Africa is quadruple its external debt and almost equivalent to Africa's current GDP. Illicit financial flows through price manipulation, tax evasion and corruption results in up to a US$50 billion a year outflow.[17] Switzerland, because of its banking secrecy laws, inadequate anti-money laundering provisions, lack of transparency regulations and criminal prosecution of whistleblowers, is a prime destination and 'turntable' (in German, *Drehscheibe*) for such funds. Switzerland has almost no double taxation treaties with poor developing nations, though dozens with developed countries.[18] Individuals and institutions in countries without double taxation agreements or taxation

58. Tax abuse includes tax evasion, fraud and other illegal practices, including the tax losses resulting from other illicit financial flows, such as bribery, corruption and money laundering. Levels of tax evasion are extremely high in many countries; globally, approximately $3 trillion of government revenue is lost to tax evasion every year. While high-income countries are the biggest losers in absolute terms, low- and middle-income countries are particularly affected by the losses, and also face particular constraints when tackling tax abuse. In 2011, developing countries lost $946.7 billion owing to illicit financial flows (a substantial portion of which relates to tax abuse), according to OECD more than seven times official development assistance for that year, and substantially more than the estimated costs of achieving the Millennium Development Goals. 59. Tax abuse is thus not a victimless practice; it limits resources that could be spent on reducing poverty and realizing human rights, and perpetuates vast income inequality. While the rich benefit from this practice, the poor feel the negative impact on their standard of living, their unequal political power and the inferior quality of health and education services for themselves and their children.

17   Dev Kar and others, 'Illicit Financial Flows and the Problem of Net Resource Transfers from Africa: 1980–2009' (African Development Bank and Global Financial Integrity, May 2013) <www.gfintegrity.org/report/report-net-resources-from-africa> accessed 21 May 2017. See also Fabian Urech, 'Milliarden aus Afrika' ('Billions from Africa') (*Neue Zürcher Zeitung*, 14 June 2013) <www.nzz.ch/milliarden-aus-afrika-1.18099274> accessed 21 May 2017 (in German), who concludes on the basis of this Joint report that the tax havens, including Switzerland, are the preferred destinations for illicit funds.

18   As at 21 March 2017, Switzerland has signed 55 Double Taxation Agreements of which 50 are in force and 10 Taxation Information Exchange Agreements of which 9 are in force. Of the nations in Africa these Double Taxation Agreements include only The Gambia (1955), Ghana (2010), Ivory Coast (1990), Malawi (1955), South Africa (2009) and Zambia (1955). A Double Taxation Agreement with Zimbabwe was initialled in 1999 but has not progressed. Swiss State Secretariat for International Financial Matters (SIF), 'Double Taxation and Administrative Assistance' (*SIF*) <www.sif.admin.ch/sif/en/home/themen/internationale-steuerpolitik/doppelbesteuerung-und-amtshilfe.html> accessed 21 May 2017. For the basis on which Switzerland will automatically exchange taxation information see the media release of the Swiss Federal Council, 'Federal Council Approves Dispatches on Legal Basis for Automatic Exchange of Information' (*Portal of the Swiss Government*, 5 June 2015) <www.admin.ch/gov/en/start/dokumentation/medienmitteilungen.msg-id-57554.html> accessed 21 May 2017.

information exchange agreements with Switzerland can without difficulty deposit funds in Swiss banks.

In addition, multinational corporations can so arrange their affairs that profits appear in specific Swiss Cantons and remain to all intent and purposes untaxed. Tax and customs authorities in developing nations, particularly in Africa, are weak, lacking funds, personnel and professional expertise to uncover and trace illicit financial flows.[19] As the piecemeal repatriation by Switzerland to Nigeria of over US$1 billion deposited in Swiss bank accounts stolen by former Nigerian President General Sani Abacha during his five year term in office from 1993 to 1998 demonstrates, however, the climate of international opinion and Switzerland's willingness (and ability) to turn a blind eye are changing. In a somewhat belated recognition of the immorality of the situation, the funds have been repatriated subject to Switzerland's condition that they be used to pay for social programmes to be monitored by the World Bank.[20]

There is, of course, the Swiss perspective, which in the interests of equity ought not to be dismissed out of hand. Switzerland sees itself somewhat differently from the analysis of it which human rights campaigners may adopt. In a report of the Swiss Federal Council approved on 12 October 2016, 'Flux Financiers Déloyaux et Illicites en Provenance des Pays en

19 Mark Herkenrath quoted in Fabian Urech, 'Ein Zentrales Entwicklungsproblem Afrikas' ('Africa's Fundamental Development Difficulty') (*Neue Zürcher Zeitung*, 14 June 2013) <www.nzz.ch/schwarzgeldabfluesse-gehoeren-zu-den-groessten-entwicklungsproblemen-afrikas-1.18099276> accessed 21 May 2017 (in German). A recent example has been the admission by HSBC that its Swiss private banking arm had a number of clients who were not fully compliant with their applicable tax obligations. 'Secret documents reveal that global banking giant HSBC [Swiss private banking arm] profited from doing business with arms dealers who channeled mortar bombs to child soldiers in Africa, bag men for Third World dictators, traffickers in blood diamonds and other international outlaws'. Gerard Ryle and others, 'Banking Giant HSBC Sheltered Murky Cash Linked to Dictators and Arms Dealers' *International Consortium of Investigative Journalists* (Washington DC, 8 February 2015) <www.icij.org/project/swiss-leaks/banking-giant-hsbc-sheltered-murky-cash-linked-dictators-and-arms-dealers> accessed 21 May 2017. Under-resourcing and inability to prioritise on the part of national revenue agencies is not confined to the poorer nations. In the case of the HSBC Swiss revelations, HMRC in the United Kingdom prosecuted only one person before winding up its inquiry in 2016. Rajeev Syal, 'HMRC Admits to Winding Up Inquiry into HSBC Tax Evasion Claims' *The Guardian* (London, 13 January 2016) <www.theguardian.com/business/2016/jan/13/hmrc-admits-to-winding-up-inquiry-into-hsbc-tax-evasion-claims> accessed 21 May 2017.

20 Conor Gaffey, 'Nigeria and Switzerland Agree Return of $321 Million in Stolen Abacha Funds' (*Newsweek*, 9 March 2016) <www.newsweek.com/nigeria-switzerland-sani-abacha-corruption-434971> accessed 21 May 2017; Morgan Winsor, 'Nigeria, Switzerland Agree on Returning $321m in Stolen Abacha Funds' *International Business Times* (9 March 2016) <www.ibtimes.com/nigeria-switzerland-agree-returning-321m-stolen-abacha-funds-2333157> accessed 21 May 2017; Morgan Winsor, 'Recovering Stolen Abacha Funds from Switzerland' *International Business Times* (28 April 2016) <www.ibtimes.com/nigeria-seeks-world-banks-help-recovering-stolen-abacha-funds-switzerland-2361114> accessed 21 May 2017.

Développement',[21] Switzerland is described as engaged in combatting the receipt of funds from developing countries, the origins of which are tax or customs evasion or avoidance, money laundering, or corruption. The prime goal of the Swiss Federal Council in this context is expressly to strengthen the integrity and reputation of the Swiss finance sector. In general terms, the report sets out the attractions of a country to which illicit funds are remitted: the rule of law, a government conscious of and fulfilling its duties and responsibilities, appropriately scoped and efficient public authorities, an attractive fiscal system, an international finance sector, and effective protection of the private domain.[22] However, as the report makes clear, Switzerland will not unilaterally assume responsibility for what it sees as a global problem: it favours a universal application of measures to combat the illicit flow of funds by virtue of the worldwide dimension of that flow. Switzerland is stated to be in the process of upgrading its anti-money laundering and corruption laws, but the report concludes unambiguously: to achieve the stated objective, there will have to be established a competent international body, because of the trans-border nature of the phenomenon.

Switzerland and the Convention on the Elimination of All Forms of Discrimination against Women 1979[23]

Switzerland signed the Convention on the Elimination of All Forms of Discrimination against Women 1979 (CEDAW) on 23 January 1987 and deposited its instrument of accession on 27 March 1997. Minor reservations made at the time of its accession have largely been withdrawn.[24] Switzerland acceded on 29 September 2008 to the Optional Protocol to CEDAW

---

21   See Swiss Federal Council, 'Le Conseil Fédéral Approuve le Rapport sur les Flux Financiers Déloyaux et Illicites en Provenance des Pays en Développement' ('Federal Council Approves Report on Illicit Financial Flows from Developing Countries') (Portal of the Swiss Government, 12 October 2016) <www.admin.ch/gov/fr/accueil/documentation/communiques.msg-id-64112.html> accessed 21 May 2017, paras 3.3.2, 7.2 and 8 (in French).

22   The unspoken question and the underlying tone of the report, is how could responsibility for triggering illicit funds flow be laid at Switzerland's door when the country is so irresistibly attractive?

23   Adopted 18 December 1979, entered into force 3 September 1981) 1249 UNTS 13 <www.un.org/womenwatch/daw/cedaw/text/econvention.htm> accessed 22 May 2017. A detailed review of CEDAW is outside the scope of this book. A short history of CEDAW prepared by UN Women is available at UN Women, 'A Short History of CEDAW Convention' (*UN Women*) <www.un.org/womenwatch/daw/cedaw/history.htm> accessed 22 May 2017.

24   United Nations Treaty Collection (UNTC), 'Chapter IV: Human Rights: 8. Convention on the Elimination of All Forms of Discrimination against Women' (*UNTC*) <https://treaties.un.org/Pages/ViewDetails.aspx?src=TREATY&mtdsg_no=IV-8& chapter=4&lang=en#EndDec> accessed 22 May 2017.

(1999)[25] (under which persons claiming to be victims of a violation of rights under CEDAW by a state party may apply directly to the CEDAW Committee).[26]

The very wide scope of CEDAW is reflected in Article 1 which contains an unlimited prohibition of discrimination 'in the political, economic, social, cultural, civil or any other field' and is encapsulated in Article 3:

> States Parties shall take in all fields, in particular in the political, social, economic and cultural fields, all appropriate measures, including legislation, to ensure the full development and advancement of women for the purpose of guaranteeing them the exercise and enjoyment of human rights and fundamental freedoms on a basis of equality with men.

CEDAW is unique among the various international human rights instruments in requiring states parties without delay[27] to modify laws and behaviour, engineering social change in the process. States are to 'modify or abolish existing laws, regulations, customs and practices which constitute discrimination against women' (art 2(f)) and 'to modify the social and cultural patterns of conduct of men and women, with a view to achieving the elimination of prejudices and customary and all other practices which are based on the idea of the inferiority or superiority of either of the sexes or on stereotyped roles for men and women' (art 5(a)).

When viewed from a distance, none of the rights referred to in CEDAW are abused in modern Switzerland – including participation in political and public life, trafficking and prostitution, education, employment, health and pregnancy, financial credit availability, equality before the law, marriage and family relations. Yet in the context of Switzerland operating as a tax haven,

---

25 (adopted 6 October 1999, entered into force 22 December 2000) 2131 UNTS 83 <www.ohchr.org/EN/ProfessionalInterest/Pages/OPCEDAW.aspx> accessed 22 May 2017.

26 United Nations, [no title] (*United Nations*) <https://treaties.un.org/Pages/showDetails.aspx?objid=08000002800030b1&clang=_en> accessed 22 May 2017.

27 Found in the opening paragraph of Article 2. Paragraph 29 of General Recommendation 28 places great emphasis on these words:

> The words 'without delay' make it clear that the obligation of States parties to pursue their policy, by all appropriate means, is of an immediate character. This language is unqualified, and does not allow for any delay or purposely chosen incremental manner in the implementation of the obligations that States assume …. It follows that a delay cannot be justified on any grounds, including political, social, cultural, religious, economic, resource or other considerations.

> CEDAW Committee, 'General Recommendation No 28 on the Core Obligations of States Parties under Article 2 of the Convention on the Elimination of All Forms of Discrimination against Women' (16 December 2010) UN Doc CEDAW/C/GC/28 <https://documents-dds-ny.un.org/doc/UNDOC/GEN/G10/472/60/PDF/G1047260.pdf?OpenElement> accessed 22 May 2017.

mere domestic compliance with its obligations under CEDAW is not the issue. The issue is one of extraterritoriality, and of the effect of Switzerland's secrecy and fiscal policies on the ability of those outside its borders to enjoy rights under CEDAW.[28]

CEDAW is approaching its fortieth anniversary and reflects the social mores of the 1970s in which it was forged. Self-evidently, there would not have been at that time an awareness of the distorting effect of tax havens on the international human rights continuum, and in none of the subsequent thirty-four general recommendations[29] is any mention made of the phenomenon. This does not necessarily imply, however, that CEDAW is incapable of addressing the problem of how gender justice is undermined by illicit financial flows facilitated by the tax havens.

In its General Recommendation No 25 (2004)[30] the CEDAW Committee stated:

> The Convention is a dynamic instrument. Since the adoption of the Convention in 1979, the Committee, as well as other actors at the national and international levels, have contributed through progressive thinking to the clarification and understanding of the substantive content of the Convention's articles and the specific nature of discrimination against women and the instruments for combatting such discrimination.
>
> (Para 3)

The Committee's dynamic, evolutionary approach was again voiced in 2010 in its General recommendation No 28, which focused on the general legal obligations under CEDAW contained in Article 2,[31] repeating in Paragraph 2

---

28 Distance however often lends enchantment: the CEDAW Committee in its Concluding Observations is critical of multiple instances of discrimination against women in Switzerland. A detailed review of the severity of discrimination against women globally is outside the scope of this book, but for a contemporary statistical analysis reference should be made to the United Nations Human Rights Council, 'Report of the Working Group on the Issue of Discrimination against Women in Law and in Practice' (8 April 2016) Thirty-second Session, UN Doc A/HRC/32/44 <www.ohchr.org/EN/Issues/Women/ WGWomen/Pages/Annualreports.aspx> accessed 22 May 2017, which addresses the issues of women's health and safety.

29 Office of the United Nations High Commissioner for Human Rights (OHCHR), 'Committee on the Elimination of Discrimination Against Women General Recommendations' (*OHCHR*) <www.ohchr.org/EN/HRBodies/CEDAW/Pages/ Recommendations.aspx> accessed 22 May 2017.

30 CEDAW Committee, 'General Recommendation No. 25: Article 4, Paragraph 1, of the Convention (Temporary Special Measures)' Thirtieth session (2004) <http://btinternet. ohchr.org/Treaties/CEDAW/Shared%20Documents/1_Global/INT_CEDAW_GEC_3 733_E.pdf> accessed 22 May 2017.

31 Article 2:

> States Parties condemn discrimination against women in all its forms, agree to pursue by all appropriate means and without delay a policy of eliminating discrimination against

its earlier statement from 2004 and augmenting this: 'The spirit of the Convention covers other rights, which are not explicitly mentioned in the Convention but which have an impact on the achievement of equality of women with men and which represent a form of discrimination against women' (para 7). One such must surely be the right to require one's state not to facilitate and perpetuate gender-based discrimination by means of illicit funds flowing to tax havens and secrecy jurisdictions such as Switzerland.

General Recommendation No 28 is also unambiguous concerning what the Committee regards as global responsibility for its domestic actions on the part of a state:

> Even though under international law, States primarily exercise territorial jurisdiction; the obligations of States parties apply without discrimination both to citizens and non-citizens, including refugees, asylum-seekers, migrant workers and stateless persons, within their territory or effective control, even if not situated within the territory. States parties are responsible for all their actions affecting human rights, regardless of whether the affected persons are in their territory.
>
> (Para 12)

In addition, the Committee regards the legal obligations within Article 2 as not being limited to the prohibition of discrimination against women caused directly or indirectly by state parties: it imposes due diligence obligations on state parties to prevent discrimination by private actors, including (of direct relevance to the Swiss financial services sector) the state regulation of banking (para 13).[32]

Switzerland's status as a tax haven is therefore, in terms of CEDAW as developed and interpreted by the CEDAW Committee, incompatible with its state obligations under CEDAW.

women and, to this end, undertake: (a) To embody the principle of the equality of men and women in their national constitutions or other appropriate legislation if not yet incorporated therein and to ensure, through law and other appropriate means, the practical realization of this principle; (b) To adopt appropriate legislative and other measures, including sanctions where appropriate, prohibiting all discrimination against women; (c) To establish legal protection of the rights of women on an equal basis with men and to ensure through competent national tribunals and other public institutions the effective protection of women against any act of discrimination; (d) To refrain from engaging in any act or practice of discrimination against women and to ensure that public authorities and institutions shall act in conformity with this obligation; (e) To take all appropriate measures to eliminate discrimination against women by any person, organization or enterprise; (f) To take all appropriate measures, including legislation, to modify or abolish existing laws, regulations, customs and practices which constitute discrimination against women; (g) To repeal all national penal provisions which constitute discrimination against women.

32 This also reflects the provisions of Article 2(e) which refers to discriminatory practices 'by any person, organization or enterprise'.

The Maastricht Principles

The Maastricht Principles on Extraterritorial Obligations in the Area of Economic, Social and Cultural Rights[33] were issued on 28 September 2011 by forty international law experts from all regions of the world. The Maastricht Principles are soft law, and as such expressly do not purport to establish new elements of human rights law, but seek to clarify the extraterritorial obligations of states on the basis of standing international law.

The Preamble to the Maastricht Principles highlights that states have repeatedly committed themselves to realising the economic, social, and cultural rights of everyone, from the time of the founding of the United Nations and the adoption of the Universal Declaration on Human Rights. Though the emphasis in the Maastricht Principles is on the extraterritorial obligations of states in relation to economic, social, and cultural rights, this is not intended to exclude their applicability to other human rights, including civil and political rights (Principle 7). Switzerland has a wide range of such international commitments.[34]

Extraterritorial obligations encompass obligations relating to the acts and omissions of a state, within or beyond its territory, that have effects on the enjoyment of human rights outside of that state's territory; and obligations of a global character found in the Charter of the United Nations and other human rights instruments to act alone or in co-operation with others to realise human rights universally (Principle 8).

The state's obligations are to respect, protect and fulfil economic, social and cultural rights in situations over which it exercises authority or effective control, over which its acts or omissions bring about foreseeable effects on the enjoyment of such rights within or outside its territory, and in which the state (through its executive, legislative or judicial branches) is in a position to exercise decisive influence or to take measures to realise such rights extraterritorially (Principle 9). Those obligations expressly include those pertaining to international trade, investment, finance and taxation (Principle 17).

State responsibility is also attributable to non-state actors acting on its instructions or under its direction, including corporations and other business enterprises empowered by the state to exercise elements of governmental authority (Principle 12). In the context of Switzerland's financial services and banking sector, all the participants in that sector being regulated by the Swiss government through the Swiss Financial Market Supervisory Authority,[35] the human rights abuses resulting from the flow of illicit funds through that sector are directly attributable to the state. The quality of the regulation of

---

33 (n 4).

34 See the Table of Instruments in the Appendix to this chapter.

35 Swiss Financial Market Supervisory Authority, 'Welcome' (*Swiss Financial Market Supervisory Authority*) <www.finma.ch/en> accessed 22 May 2017.

private individuals, and organisations, transnational corporations and other business enterprises must be commensurate with the state's human rights obligations (Principle 24), and even if a state is not in a position to regulate (or, by extension, frames regulation so as to exclude) such individuals and entities, the state must instead use its position of influence to bring pressure to bear (Principle 26).

Under the Maastricht Principles, Switzerland would be expected to:

> desist from acts and omissions that create a real risk of nullifying or impairing the enjoyment of economic, social and cultural rights extraterritorially. The responsibility of States is engaged where such nullification or impairment is a foreseeable result of their conduct. Uncertainty about potential impacts does not constitute justification for such conduct.
>
> (Principle 13)

Any defence to a charge of human rights abuse which were to be formulated on the basis that the consequences of a state's actions or of its empowerment of non-state actors were merely speculative and unsupported by empirical evidence would therefore be inadmissible. The test is one of objective foreseeability.

Switzerland's openness to illicit funds flows has the effect of draining resources from other states. Of itself, this constitutes indirect interference which is a breach of Principle 21. Switzerland ought to refrain from conduct which impairs the ability of another state to comply with its obligations; and if the other state is itself complicit in the flow,[36] then Switzerland ought not to aid, assist, direct, or control (or by implication sanction by means of lax financial regulation) that process.

From the human rights perspective of the Maastricht Principles, therefore, Switzerland's banking and investment sector coupled with a high degree of secrecy amounts to nothing less than state-sanctioned plunder and hoarding.[37]

---

36 See Chapter 1 for examples of illicit funds flow in which State executives are allegedly complicit.

37 It is important to note that other sanctions against the State or against non-State actors including corporations and financial institutions may apply, such as those relating to bribery and corruption, anti-money laundering and the countering of the financing of terrorism. In the battle to uphold human rights, no parallel enforcement regime ought to be disregarded. The Maastricht Principles are merely soft law, formulated by highly skilled but politically and economically powerless academics. Further, Switzerland, though a tax haven, has ratified a wide range of human rights instruments (see the Appendix to this chapter) which is a prerequisite for the application to a State of the Maastricht Principles (perhaps their greatest weakness and limitation). Many micro-state tax havens have no such human rights commitments.

Switzerland: state responsibility for the extraterritorial impacts of tax abuse on women's rights and gender equality

In June 2015, the CEDAW Committee published its initial consideration of the fourth and fifth combined reports submitted to it by Switzerland, which concerned itself only with the progress within Switzerland in relation to its own population in complying with the provisions of CEDAW.[38] References within it to taxation concerned only domestic revenue policy. Issues such as banking secrecy and the inward flow of foreign funds are wholly absent from the document. There was no hint of what was to come.

The CEDAW Committee made its Concluding Observations on 18 November 2016,[39] but much had changed since its initial consideration. There was a groundbreaking shift in emphasis.

The CEDAW Committee had had the benefit of reading the report of the Swiss Federal Council on illicit financial flows published the month previously[40] and in Paragraph 40 of the Concluding Observations dealing with the economic empowerment of women expressed its concern about (a) the lack of efficient and transparent regulations and mechanisms for evaluating the impact on women of budget shortfalls as a result of Switzerland's policies, particularly in developing countries; (b) the lack of impact assessment explicitly taking into account women's human rights prior to the negotiation of international trade and investment agreements; and (c) Switzerland's financial secrecy policies and rules on corporate reporting and taxation, 'which have a potentially negative impact on the ability of other states, particularly those already short of revenue, to mobilise the maximum available resources for the fulfilment of women's rights'.

Citing CEDAW's 2010 General Recommendation 28 on the Core Obligations of States Parties under CEDAW Article 2,[41] the CEDAW Committee recommended (in para 41 of the Concluding Observations) that Switzerland: (a) undertake independent, participatory and periodic impact assessments of the extraterritorial effects of its financial secrecy and corporate tax policies on women's rights and substantive equality, and ensure that such assessments are conducted in an impartial manner with public disclosure of the methodology and findings; (b) ensure that trade and investment agreements negotiated by Switzerland recognise the primacy of its obligations under CEDAW and explicitly consider their impact on women's rights; and

---

38 CEDAW Committee, 'Consideration of Reports Submitted by States Parties under Article 18 of the Convention: Combined Fourth and Fifth Periodic Reports of States Parties Due in 2014: Switzerland' (2 June 2015) UN Doc CEDAW/C/CHE/4-5 <http://tbinternet. ohchr.org/_layouts/treatybodyexternal/Download.aspx?symbolno=CEDAW%2FC%2 FCHE%2F4-5&Lang=en> accessed 22 May 2017.

39 (n 5).

40 See (n 21).

41 See (n 31).

(c) strengthen its legislation governing the conduct of corporations registered or domiciled in Switzerland in relation to their activities abroad.[42]

As the report of the Swiss Federal Council contained nothing substantive
by way of implementation strategy, confining itself to a call for the establishment of an international regulatory body, and though evidencing an
awareness of the problem failed to assess Switzerland's role as a facilitator, it
is likely that the CEDAW Committee framed its concerns partly on the basis
of a submission to which it does not expressly refer. On 22 February 2016,
the CEDAW Committee received a joint submission entitled 'State
Responsibility for the Impacts of Cross-border Tax Abuse on Women's
Rights and Gender Equality' from the Center for Economic and Social
Rights, Global Justice Clinic at NYU School of Law, Berne Declaration, and
the Tax Justice Network. This was subsequently updated on 2 November
2016 (the reference to gender equality having been removed from its title),
Berne Declaration having in the meantime been re-named Public Eye and
the submitting organisations having been joined by Alliance Sud ('Joint
Submission').[43]

---

42   See also the Recommendation to Member States in A/HRC/31/61 (see n 11) para 83:

> States should conduct human rights impact assessments of their tax policies, to ensure
> that they do not have negative impacts abroad. These should be periodic and inde-
> pendently verified, with public participation in defining the risks and potential
> extraterritorial impacts. Impact assessments should analyse not only the implications for
> revenue streams, but also the distributive and governance spillover effects of a country's
> tax regime abroad. If and when negative spillovers are found, impact assessments should
> trigger policy action including explicit recommendations for responsible parties and
> clear deadlines for remedies and redress.

> A/HRC/31/61 is however not referred to in the Concluding Observations (CEDAW/
> C/CHE/CO/4-5), and it is unclear whether the CEDAW Committee factored this into
> its deliberations.

43   Alliance Sud and others, 'Swiss Responsibility for the Extraterritorial Impacts of Tax Abuse
on Women's Rights' (*Center for Economic and Social Rights*, 2 November 2016)
<www.cesr.org/sites/default/files/downloads/switzerland_cedaw_submission_2nov2016
.pdf> accessed 22 May 2017. The following details of the submitting organisations are
taken from page 20 of the Joint Submission: Alliance Sud strives to influence Switzerland's
policies to the benefit of the poor countries and their peoples. Its goal is sustainable development, as well as a more just, peaceful and environment friendly world that offers equal
rights and opportunities to all. This calls for economic and political changes – worldwide
and in Switzerland. *Public Eye* (formerly *Berne Declaration*) is a not-for-profit, independent organisation with about 25,000 members, which has been campaigning for more
equitable relations between Switzerland and developing countries for more than forty
years. Among its most important concerns are the global safeguarding of human rights,
socially and ecologically responsible conduct of business enterprises and the promotion of
fair economic relations. The *Center for Economic and Social Rights* was established in 1993
with the mission to work for the recognition and enforcement of economic, social and
cultural rights as a powerful tool for promoting social justice and human dignity. It exposes
human rights violations through an interdisciplinary combination of legal and socio-
economic analysis. It has focused for many years on the link between fiscal policy (the
generation and allocation of resources) and the fulfilment of human rights. The *Global*

Paragraphs 40 and 41 of the Concluding Observations are brief, and appear to have been the result of a last-minute decision to address extraterritoriality in response to the Swiss somewhat hurriedly opening the debate by means of the report of the Swiss Federal Council. While the CEDAW Committee's concerns and recommendations are well presented, there is no commentary which could give an insight into how those concerns were formulated. The similarity of the proposals in the Joint Submission and the recommendations in Paragraph 41 of the Concluding Observations, however, lend legitimacy to filling that gap by reference to research materials and analysis found in the Joint Submission.

The Joint Submission contains an extensive review of current thinking on the connection between the extraterritorial impact of tax abuse and consequent breaches of human rights. It notes (para 4.6) that in 2011 the IMF, OECD, UN and the World Bank called on G20 countries

> to undertake 'spillover analyses' of any proposed changes to their tax systems that may have a significant impact on the fiscal circumstances of developing countries [which] may point to remedial measures to be incorporated into the reform and should be published for the international community to reflect upon – at a minimum, to enable developing countries to respond with parallel changes to their own systems if that would be helpful in protecting their revenue bases.[44]

In the context of abusive practices on the part of tax havens, the focus of the Joint Submission on Switzerland's contribution to what it refers to as 'this corrosive phenomenon' (para 1) is of particular relevance. The Joint Submission points to the facilitation by Switzerland of 'large-scale cross-border tax abuse which deprives other States of the public resources needed to fulfil women's rights and promote substantive equality' (para 1). It characterises such abuse as being enabled by laws and policies in some countries that afford individuals and companies undue secrecy regarding their financial transactions and offer lax rules regarding taxation and reporting; and it notes

---

Justice Clinic at NYU School of Law works to prevent, challenge, and redress rights violations in situations of global inequality. Working on cases and projects that involve cross-border human rights violations, the deleterious impacts of activities by State and non-State actors, and emerging problems that require close collaboration between actors at the local and international levels, students engage in human rights investigation, advocacy, and litigation in domestic and international settings. The *Tax Justice Network* operates as a centre of expertise for wider issues of fair taxation, in particular with respect to financial secrecy, tax havens, the taxation of multinational companies, and the importance of tax as a tool for effective development – including in supporting the delivery of the Sustainable Development Goals, and the broad human rights that underpin these.

44 IMF and others, 'Supporting the Development of More Effective Tax Systems: A Report to the G20 Development Working Group by the IMF, OECD, UN and World Bank' (*OECD*, 2011) <www.oecd.org/ctp/48993634.pdf> accessed 22 May 2017.

that in 2015 Switzerland was in first place in the Financial Secrecy Index[45] of jurisdictions ranked according to the degree of secrecy permitted by their banking, tax and corporate laws, regulations and international agreements (para 4.1).[46]

The Joint Submission further observes:

> Switzerland's long-standing protection of financial secrecy and facilitation of tax abuse … foreseeably undermines the ability of other States to mobilize the maximum available resources for the progressive realization of women's economic, social and cultural rights and the elimination of gender-based discrimination.
>
> (Para 4.2)

Over one-third of all unrecorded offshore financial wealth in the world is held in Switzerland, much of it untaxed (box 4). Switzerland has indicated that it will under any arrangements it enters into for the automatic exchange of tax information[47] include only countries 'with which there are close economic and political ties and which, if appropriate, provide their taxpayers with sufficient scope for regularization' (para 4.8). The Joint Submission interprets this as giving Switzerland liberty to deal only with countries whose resources and capacity to provide reciprocal data, and to maintain the confidentiality of that data, are on a par with its own, and that in consequence 'the administrative burden to access tax information may be simply too high for many under-resourced tax administrations in developing countries' (para 4.8). It points to 'next-to-insurmountable obstacles' facing developing countries in mobilising resources to meet their CEDAW obligations (para 4.10).[48]

The Joint Submission concludes that 'The action or inaction of the Swiss government in the coming years will have a direct impact upon the ability of developing countries to resource efforts to combat discrimination and guarantee substantive equality for women' (para 6.3).

---

45 (n 3).
46 For a detailed explanation of the methodology employed in compiling the Financial Secrecy Index see Tax Justice Network, 'Secrecy Indicators' (*Financial Secrecy Index*) <www.financialsecrecyindex.com/methodology> accessed 22 May 2017.
47 See (n 18).
48 A case study cited by the Joint Submission (in box 5) is that of India, with an unconfirmed estimate of US$2 or $3 trillion in undeclared Indian money in Swiss accounts. The Indian government has encountered severe difficulties in obtaining information from its Swiss counterpart, not least because of the criminalisation in Switzerland of whistleblowing and the need of the Indian government to rely on information received from such sources, which the Swiss government refuses to acknowledge as the basis of a legitimate enquiry. The Joint Submission notes that if a State such as India which has a strong tax authority and political support can make so little progress, then tax authorities and law enforcement agencies in weaker, poorer nations are unlikely to succeed at all.

The overarching recommendation of the Joint Submission, in near-identical terms to those of the CEDAW Committee in its Concluding Observations,[49] is that:

> Switzerland undertake independent, participatory and periodic impact assessments of the extraterritorial or 'spillover' effects of its financial secrecy and tax policies on women's rights and substantive equality. Such assessments should be conducted in an impartial manner, and both the methodology and findings should be publicly disclosed.
>
> (Para 6.4)

Conclusions

Switzerland exhibits a dichotomy. On the one hand, it is a sophisticated Western democracy with highly developed civil and political rights. On the other, it is 'the grandfather of the world's tax havens'. The potentially negative effect of state taxation policies extraterritorially on international human rights is well understood. What sets Switzerland apart as a tax haven are the very substantial illicit financial flows, both historical and present, into its banking and investment sector.

Illicit financial flows are those which have no social or economic justification. They are driven by financial operations (whose sources may be legitimate or illegitimate) rather than real activities.

Illicit financial flows impede developing nations from whose economies these funds are drained from complying effectively with their human rights obligations, and the effect on women due to the feminisation of poverty is disproportionate.

Switzerland's banking secrecy laws, inadequate anti-money laundering provisions, lack of transparency regulations and criminal prosecution of whistleblowers, the almost total absence of double taxation treaties with poorer nations, an overly bureaucratic response to requests for the exchange of taxation information, a lack of political will to turn the spotlight on itself, stand in the way of curtailing illicit financial flows. Switzerland's tax haven apparatus facilitates such flows.

In soft law terms from the human rights perspective of the Maastricht Principles, Switzerland's banking and investment sector, coupled with a high degree of secrecy, amounts to nothing less than state-sanctioned plunder and hoarding. In terms of CEDAW, Switzerland's status as a tax haven is incompatible with its obligations extraterritorially.

Switzerland is a signatory to a wide range of international human rights instruments, and this chapter has focused on just one of them, CEDAW, but

---

49   (n 5) para 41(a).

one in which groundbreaking developments have now occurred. Switzerland should follow the recommendations of the CEDAW Committee and first assess and then address the extraterritorial effects of its financial secrecy and corporate tax policies on women's rights and substantive equality. Most certainly, those extraterritorial effects impact all of Switzerland's international human rights obligations. International human rights are dynamic and evolutionary. It is just a matter of time before the next treaty body follows the CEDAW Committee into the fray.

APPENDIX

Table 6.1 International human rights instruments to which Switzerland is a party (status: 23 April 2017)

Instrument (chronological order of inception)	Swiss ratification/accession
Universal Declaration of Human Rights 1948	(none required)
General Assembly Resolution 217A 1948	(none required)
Convention for the Protection of Human Rights and Fundamental Freedoms 1950 (European Convention)	1974
Convention Relating to the Status of Refugees 1951	1955
European Social Charter 1961	Signature 1976; not ratified, not in force
International Covenant on Economic, Social and Cultural Rights 1966	1992
International Covenant on Civil and Political Rights 1966	1992
International Convention on the Elimination of All Forms of Racial Discrimination 1969	1994
Convention on the Elimination of All Forms of Discrimination against Women 1979	1997
Convention against Torture and Other Cruel, Inhuman or Degrading Treatment or Punishment 1984	1986
Declaration on the Right to Development 1986	None required
European Convention for the Prevention of Torture and Inhuman or Degrading Treatment or Punishment 1987	1989
United Nations Convention on the Rights of the Child 1989	1997
International Convention on the Protection of the Rights of All Migrant Workers and Members of Their Families 1990	No action taken
Council of Europe Convention on Action against Trafficking in Human Beings 2005	2013
Convention on the Rights of Persons with Disabilities 2006	2014
International Convention for the Protection of All Persons from Enforced Disappearance 2006	2016

Bibliography

International treaties

Convention on the Elimination of All Forms of Discrimination Against Women (adopted 18 December 1979, entered into force 3 September 1981) 1249 UNTS 13 <www.un.org/womenwatch/daw/cedaw/text/econvention.htm> accessed 22 May 2017

Optional Protocol to the Convention on the Elimination of All Forms of Discrimination Against Women (adopted 6 October 1999, entered into force 22 December 2000) 2131 UNTS 83 <www.ohchr.org/EN/ProfessionalInterest/Pages/OPCEDAW.aspx> accessed 22 May 2017

United Nations documents

Committee on the Elimination of Discrimination against Women (CEDAW Committee), 'Concluding Observations on the Combined Fourth and Fifth Periodic Reports of Switzerland' (25 November 2016) UN Doc CEDAW/C/CHE/CO/4-5 <http://tbinternet.ohchr.org/_layouts/treatybodyexternal/Download.aspx?symbolno=CEDAW/C/CHE/CO/4-5&Lang=En> accessed 21 May 2017

——, 'Consideration of Reports Submitted by States Parties under Article 18 of the Convention: Combined Fourth and Fifth Periodic Reports of States Parties Due in 2014: Switzerland' (2 June 2015) UN Doc CEDAW/C/CHE/4-5 <http://tbinternet.ohchr.org/_layouts/treatybodyexternal/Download.aspx?symbolno=CEDAW%2FC%2FCHE%2F4-5&Lang=en> accessed 22 May 2017

——, 'General Recommendation No. 25: Article 4, Paragraph 1, of the Convention (Temporary Special Measures)' Thirtieth session (2004) <http://tbinternet.ohchr.org/Treaties/CEDAW/Shared%20Documents/1_Global/INT_CEDAW_GEC_3733_E.pdf> accessed 22 May 2017

——, 'General Recommendation No 28 on the Core Obligations of States Parties under Article 2 of the Convention on the Elimination of All Forms of Discrimin-ation against Women' (16 December 2010) UN Doc CEDAW/C/GC/28 <https://documents-dds-ny.un.org/doc/UNDOC/GEN/G10/472/60/PDF/G1047260.pdf?OpenElement> accessed 22 May 2017

United Nations Human Rights Council, 'Final Study on Illicit Financial Flows, Human Rights and the 2030 Agenda for Sustainable Development of the Inde-pendent Expert on the Effects of Foreign Debt and other Related International Financial Obligations of States on the Full Enjoyment of All Human Rights, Particularly Economic, Social and Cultural Rights' (15 January 2016) Thirty-first Session, UN Doc A/HRC/31/61 <www.ohchr.org/EN/HRBodies/HRC/RegularSessions/Session31/Pages/ListReports.aspx> accessed 21 May 2017

——, 'Report of the Special Rapporteur on Extreme Poverty and Human Rights, Magdalena Sepulveda Carmona' (22 May 2014) Twenty-sixth Session, UN Doc A/HRC/26/28 <www.ohchr.org/EN/HRBodies/HRC/RegularSessions/Session26/Documents/A_HRC_26_28_ENG.doc> accessed 21 May 2017

——, 'Report of the Working Group on the Issue of Discrimination against Women in Law and in Practice' (8 April 2016) Thirty-second Session, UN Doc

A/HRC/32/44   <www.ohchr.org/EN/Issues/Women/WGWomen/Pages/Annualreports.aspx> accessed 22 May 2017

Other

Communiqué, G20 Finance Ministers and Central Bank Governors Meeting held in Chengdu, China, 24 July 2016 (*University of Toronto G20 Information Centre*, 24 July 2016) <www.g20.utoronto.ca/2016/160724-finance.html> accessed 21 May 2017

Secondary sources

Addis Tax Initiative, 'About Addis Tax Initiative' (*Addis Tax Initiative*) <www.addis-taxinitiative.net> accessed 21 May 2017
——, 'Financing for Development Conference: The Addis Tax Initiative – Declaration' (*Addis Tax Initiative*) <www.addistaxinitiative.net/documents/Addis-Tax-Initiative_Declaration_EN.pdf> accessed 21 May 2017
——, *Work Plan 2016/17* (Deutsche Gesellschaft für Internationale Zusammenarbeit (GIZ), 2017) <www.addistaxinitiative.net/documents/ATI_Work-Plan-2016-2017_EN.pdf> accessed 21 May 2017
Alliance Sud and others, 'Swiss Responsibility for the Extraterritorial Impacts of Tax Abuse on Women's Rights' (*Center for Economic and Social Rights*, 2 November 2016) <www.cesr.org/sites/default/files/downloads/switzerland_cedaw_ submission_2nov2016.pdf> accessed 22 May 2017
Avdjiev S, Chui M and Shin H S,'Non-financial Corporations from Emerging Market Economies and Capital Flows' (BIS QR, December 2014) <www.bis.org/publ/qtrpdf/r_qt1412h.htm> accessed 21 May 2017
FIAN International, 'Maastricht Principles on Extraterritorial Obligations of States in the Area of Economic, Social and Cultural Rights' (*FIAN International*, January 2013) <www.fidh.org/IMG/pdf/maastricht-eto-principles-uk_web.pdf> accessed 20 May 2017 (Maastricht Principles)
Freedom House, 'Freedom in the World 2017' (*Freedom House*) <https://freedom-house.org/report/freedom-world/2017/switzerland> accessed 21 May 2017
Gaffey C, 'Nigeria and Switzerland Agree Return of $321 Million in Stolen Abacha Funds' (*Newsweek*, 9 March 2016) <www.newsweek.com/nigeria-switzerland-sani-abacha-corruption-434971> accessed 21 May 2017
Government Commission on Capital Flight from Poor Countries, 'Commission on Capital Flight from Developing Countries: Tax Havens and Development' (*Government of Norway*, 18 June 2009) <www.financialtransparency.org/wp-content/uploads/2015/04/norway_tax_report.pdf> accessed 21 May 2017
Grondona V, Bidegain Ponte N and Rodríguez Enriquez C, *Illicit Financial Flows Undermining Gender Justice* (Friedrich Ebert Stiftung, December 2016) <www.dawnnet.org/feminist-resources/sites/default/files/articles/161130_ipa_genderjustice.pdf> accessed 21 May 2017
IMF and others, 'Supporting the Development of More Effective Tax Systems: A Report to the G20 Development Working Group by the IMF, OECD, UN and World Bank' (*OECD*, 2011) <www.oecd.org/ctp/48993634.pdf> accessed 22 May 2017

Kar D and others, 'Illicit Financial Flows and the Problem of Net Resource Transfers from Africa: 1980–2009' (*African Development Bank and Global Financial Integrity*, May 2013) <www.gfintegrity.org/report/report-net-resources-from-africa> accessed 21 May 2017.

'Norwegian Commission on Capital Flight from Developing Countries: Tax Havens and Development' (*Financial Transparency Coalition*) <https://financialtransparency.org/reports/norwegian-commission-on-capital-flight-from-developing-countries-tax-havens-and-development> accessed 21 May 2017

Office of the United Nations High Commissioner for Human Rights (OHCHR), 'Committee on the Elimination of Discrimination Against Women' (*OHCHR*) <www.ohchr.org/EN/HRBodies/CEDAW/Pages/Introduction.aspx> accessed 21 May 2017

——, 'Committee on the Elimination of Discrimination Against Women General Recommendations' (*OHCHR*) <www.ohchr.org/EN/HRBodies/CEDAW/Pages/Recommendations.aspx> accessed 22 May 2017

Ryle G and others, 'Banking Giant HSBC Sheltered Murky Cash Linked to Dictators and Arms Dealers' *International Consortium of Investigative Journalists* (Washington DC, 8 February 2015) <www.icij.org/project/swiss-leaks/banking-giant-hsbc-sheltered-murky-cash-linked-dictators-and-arms-dealers> accessed 21 May 2017

Swiss Federal Council, 'Le Conseil Fédéral Approuve le Rapport sur les Flux Financiers Déloyaux et Illicites en Provenance des Pays en Développement' ('Federal Council Approves Report on Illicit Financial Flows from Developing Countries') (Portal of the Swiss Government, 12 October 2016) <www.admin.ch/gov/fr/accueil/documentation/communiques.msg-id-64112.html> accessed 21 May 2017

——, 'Federal Council Approves Dispatches on Legal Basis for Automatic Exchange of Information' (*Portal of the Swiss Government*, 5 June 2015) <www.admin.ch/gov/en/start/dokumentation/medienmitteilungen.msg-id-57554.html> accessed 21 May 2017

Swiss Financial Market Supervisory Authority, 'Welcome' (*Swiss Financial Market Supervisory Authority*) <www.finma.ch/en> accessed 22 May 2017

Swiss State Secretariat for International Financial Matters (SIF), 'Double Taxation and Administrative Assistance' (*SIF*) <www.sif.admin.ch/sif/en/home/themen/internationale-steuerpolitik/doppelbesteuerung-und-amtshilfe.html> accessed 21 May 2017

Syal R, 'HMRC Admits to Winding Up Inquiry into HSBC Tax Evasion Claims' *The Guardian* (London, 13 January 2016) <www.theguardian.com/business/2016/jan/13/hmrc-admits-to-winding-up-inquiry-into-hsbc-tax-evasion-claims> accessed 21 May 2017

Tax Justice Network, 'Financial Secrecy Index – 2015 Results' (*Tax Justice Network*) <www.financialsecrecyindex.com/introduction/fsi-2015-results> accessed 21 May 2017

——, 'Narrative Report on Switzerland' (*Tax Justice Network*, 2015) <www.financialsecrecyindex.com/PDF/Switzerland.pdf> accessed 21 May 2017

——, 'Secrecy Indicators' (*Financial Secrecy Index*) <www.financialsecrecyindex.com/methodology> accessed 22 May 2017

——, 'Goal 16: Promote Just, Peaceful and Inclusive Societies' (*United Nations*) <www.un.org/sustainabledevelopment/peace-justice> accessed 21 May 2017

——, 'Goal 17: Revitalize the Global Partnership for Sustainable Development' (*United Nations*) <www.un.org/sustainabledevelopment/globalpartnerships> accessed 21 May 2017

United Nations Treaty Collection (UNTC), 'Chapter IV: Human Rights: 8. Convention on the Elimination of All Forms of Discrimination against Women' (*UNTC*) <https://treaties.un.org/Pages/ViewDetails.aspx?src=TREATY& mtdsg_no=IV-8&chapter=4&lang=en#EndDec> accessed 22 May 2017

UN Women, 'A Short History of CEDAW Convention' (*UN Women*) <www.un. org/womenwatch/daw/cedaw/history.htm> accessed 22 May 2017

Urech F, 'Ein Zentrales Entwicklungsproblem Afrikas' ('Africa's Fundamental Development Difficulty') (*Neue Zürcher Zeitung*, 14 June 2013) <www.nzz.ch/ schwarzgeldabfluesse-gehoeren-zu-den-groessten-entwicklungsproblemen-afrikas-1.18099276> accessed 21 May 2017 (in German)

——, 'Milliarden aus Afrika' ('Billions from Africa') (*Neue Zürcher Zeitung*, 14 June 2013) <www.nzz.ch/milliarden-aus-afrika-1.18099274> accessed 21 May 2017 (in German)

Winsor M, 'Nigeria, Switzerland Agree on Returning $321m in Stolen Abacha Funds' *International Business Times* (9 March 2016) <www.ibtimes.com/nigeria-switzerland-agree-returning-321m-stolen-abacha-funds-2333157> accessed 21 May 2017

——, 'Recovering Stolen Abacha Funds from Switzerland' *International Business Times* (28 April 2016) <www.ibtimes.com/nigeria-seeks-world-banks-help-recovering-stolen-abacha-funds-switzerland-2361114> accessed 21 May 2017

7 Concluding recommendations

The examination of how tax havens and international human rights law interact is a new field of study, and in the previous six chapters various issues have been highlighted which both lend themselves to further academic research and which demonstrate a pressing need for action to be taken. In this chapter the author presents his overarching conclusions, and outlines his research recommendations for future scholars and his policy recommendations to states, international organisations and other stakeholders.

The aim of this book, set out in the Introduction, has been to demonstrate the deleterious effect of tax havens on the international human rights continuum, and to show that the tax haven phenomenon is far more widespread than imagined. This phenomenon embraces not only the palm-fringed micro-states of popular imagination, but also jurisdictions as complex and substantial as Switzerland and the USA. The human rights abusive consequences of tax evasion and tax avoidance are well documented in a vast and growing literature on the subject, but the specific structuring mechanisms offered by the tax havens and the simple offering of secrecy and immunity, particularly in the banking and investment sector, have until now remained largely unexplored. This is not a book about international human rights law, but is instead one about the relationship between tax havens and international human rights law. It has identified what a tax haven is, what structures and strategies their governments employ, and how they facilitate the avoidance of accountability.

Those opponents who benefit from the abuse of human rights will continue to hold all the cards unless human rights defenders develop a detailed understanding of just how those opponents plan and manage their campaigns and assemble their armouries. Without that detailed understanding, and unless human rights defenders are given the ability to engage both on a jurisprudential and on a commercial level, matched strength for strength in the business arena, fully briefed before the courts, their generalised laments that tax evasion and tax avoidance are bad, or that no one is held accountable for abuse, or that states are themselves complicit, and that tax havens are the driving force, will just be cries carried away on the wind. An informed, interdisciplinary approach is essential.

Recommendation 1

In Chapters 5 and 6 the international human rights obligations of the Isle of Man and of Switzerland, measured in terms of the international human rights instruments which bind each, were weighed. The same exercise has yet to be undertaken in respect of all the tax havens. This will provide the basis for an objective assessment of the extent to which each tax haven in turn is in breach of its international human rights obligations, not merely as accomplices of other states or non-state actors for whom they are honey-traps, but in terms of their own international commitments.

Recommendation 2

Those tax havens which (either generally from the point of view of good governance or specifically with regard to international human rights obligations) are subject to the oversight of other states, such as the Crown Dependencies and Overseas Territories and individual States within the USA should no longer be reported upon by the treaty bodies as annexes to reports on those overseeing states. The tax havens must be made directly responsible for their own reporting obligations, and in the process to educate and inform their own people about their international human rights – both as affects their domestic lives and as impact extraterritorially.

Recommendation 3

A full statistical analysis is required of the range and volume of tax havens structures on offer (noting that some jurisdictions such as Liechtenstein do not make volume information publicly available, and most jurisdictions exempt trusts from public registration) and of the fund flows into and out of the tax havens. A world map of structures in the tax havens will show where avoidance mechanisms are already established and where proposals to introduce particular structures are on the legislative agenda. Particular note should be taken of proposals to introduce the chimeric structures which have no domestic necessity and which are designed specifically with avoidance in mind. Fully to achieve this, a centralised, or at least regional, effort will be necessary. Non-governmental organisations should marshal legal and other professionals and researchers in each of the tax havens to gather the material. This should then be collated by the non-governmental organisations and be analysed quantitatively and qualitatively. Only when the scale of the problem has been objectively determined can the international political will be formed to press for change.

Recommendation 4

Members of the G20 must revisit the 2014 G20 High Level Principles on Beneficial Ownership Transparency, which are not fit for purpose. Confining these principles to reviews of nominee shareholdings and shadow directors – tools of the 1970s and 1980s – and to the registration of beneficial owners shows a lack of awareness on the part of the draftspersons of the range and complexity of avoidance options available in the tax havens. The High Level Principles themselves are vague and overlapping; aspirational but lacking any implementation strategy. By existing in this inadequate form, the High Level Principles fill a political space which should be better occupied. The members of the G20 refer to them as if they are the last word on the subject, when clearly the problem of beneficial ownership avoidance has yet to be addressed.

Recommendation 5

The growing use of orphaned structures such as non-charitable purpose trusts and The Bahamas Enterprise Entity, specifically designed to facilitate accountability avoidance and aggressively marketed to promote this, should be curbed. None of these structures is born of domestic need in the jurisdiction which have adopted them, perhaps other than a desire to boost the incomes of their financial and fiduciary sectors (to which many if not all tax havens find themselves in thrall). Compounding the problem, there is a general unawareness of these structures other than within the charmed circle of the tax havens themselves and on the part of those who operate through the tax havens. In September 2016 the author gave a presentation on beneficial ownership avoidance to a group of distinguished corporate and commercial law academics at the Annual Conference of the Society of Legal Scholars (which became the basis for Chapter 3). None of those present had heard of non-charitable purpose trusts or of the concept of beneficial ownership avoidance. Just how many elephants have to be in the room before someone notices?

Recommendation 6

The United Nations Guiding Principles on Business and Human Rights 2011, more commonly known as the Ruggie Principles, have not had the impact that was hoped for. Similarly, the United Nations Global Compact has had limited take-up. Both however have a substantive utility. The Ruggie Principles should be incorporated into a new international corporate governance standard by the International Standards Organisation. This standard in turn should be made part of the OECD's Common Reporting Standard (and of The Foreign Account Tax Compliance Act in the USA). Both the CRS and FATCA have administrative reporting mechanisms which lend themselves to this inclusion. Requiring those reporting to take into account corporate governance standards informed by international human rights considerations will add substantive, utilitarian value to the gathering of fiscal information. As currently gathered, such information has no wider application than to track national revenue depletion. Compliant membership of the Global Compact should be made the basis for an exemption under both the CRS and FATCA. Both the spirit of the Ruggie Principles (subsumed into the new standard) and the Global Compact would be reinvigorated in the process.

Recommendation 7

In light of the Concluding Observations of the CEDAW Committee delivered in November 2016, Switzerland should urgently review its willingness to entertain illicit financial flows, should remove domestic penalties (such as the criminal liability of whistleblowers) and immunities (an anachronistic attachment to secrecy) which impede the investigation of international human right abuses. It should extend its network of double taxation treaties and taxation information exchange agreements, particularly with developing nations, placing an emphasis on sub-Saharan Africa. Switzerland should remove onerous administrative obstacles, particularly its requirement that reciprocity means not simply the reciprocal exchange of information but the equal application of resources by each party to such exchanges (an impossibly high bar for many developing nations to jump).

Human rights defenders, academics and professionals grow stronger through dialogue. The author's closing hope is that this book will have stimulated debate.

Index

Printed in the United States
by Baker & Taylor Publisher Services